Are You Certifiable?

That's the question that's probably on your mind. The answer is: You bet! But if you've tried and failed or you've been frustrated by the complexity of the MCSE program and the maze of study materials available, you've come to the right place. We've created our new publishing and training program, *Certification Insider Press*, to help you accomplish one important goal: to ace an MCSE exam without having to spend the rest of your life studying for it.

The book you have in your hands is part of our *Exam Cram* series. Each book is especially designed not only to help you study for an exam but also to help you understand what the exam is all about. Inside these covers you'll find hundreds of test-taking tips, insights, and strategies that simply cannot be found anyplace else. In creating our guides, we've assembled the very best team of certified trainers, MCSE professionals, and networking course developers.

Our commitment is to ensure that the *Exam Cram* guides offer proven training and active-learning techniques not found in other study guides. We provide unique study tips and techniques, memory joggers, custom quizzes, insights about trick questions, a sample test, and much more. In a nutshell, each *Exam Cram* guide is closely organized like the exam it is tied to.

To help us continue to provide the very best certification study materials, we'd like to hear from you. Write or email us (craminfo@coriolis.com) and let us know how our *Exam Cram* guides have helped you study, or tell us about new features you'd like us to add. If you send us a story about how an *Exam Cram* guide has helped you ace an exam and we use it in one of our guides, we'll send you an official *Exam Cram* shirt for your efforts.

Good luck with your certification exam, and thanks for allowing us to help you achieve your goals.

Keith Weiskamp
Publisher, Certification Insider Press

Proxy
Server 2

David Johnson, Andy Ruth,
and J. Michael Stewart

MCSE Proxy Server 2 Exam Cram
Copyright © The Coriolis Group, 1998

Limits of Liability and Disclaimer of Warranty
The author and publisher of this book have used their best efforts in preparing the book and the programs contained in it. These efforts include the development, research, and testing of the theories and programs to determine their effectiveness. The author and publisher make no warranty of any kind, expressed or implied, with regard to these programs or the documentation contained in this book.

The author and publisher shall not be liable in the event of incidental or consequential damages in connection with, or arising out of, the furnishing, performance, or use of the programs, associated instructions, and/or claims of productivity gains.

Trademarks
Trademarked names appear throughout this book. Rather than list the names and entities that own the trademarks or insert a trademark symbol with each mention of the trademarked name, the publisher states that it is using the names for editorial purposes only and to the benefit of the trademark owner, with no intention of infringing upon that trademark.

The Coriolis Group, Inc.
An International Thomson Publishing Company
14455 N. Hayden Road, Suite 220
Scottsdale, Arizona 85260

602/483-0192
FAX 602/483-0193
http://www.coriolis.com

Library of Congress Cataloging-in-Publication Data
Johnson, David
    MCSE Proxy Server 2 exam cram / by David Johnson, Andy Ruth, and
  J. Michael Stewart
      p. cm.
  Includes index.
  ISBN 1-57610-230-0
    1. Electronic data processing personnel--Certification. 2. Microsoft
software--Examinations--Study guides. 3. Microsoft Proxy server I. Ruth,
Andy II. Stewart, James Michael. III. Title.
QA76.3.T577 1998
005.7'1376--dc21   98-16420
                            CIP

Printed in the United States of America
10 9 8 7 6 5 4 3 2

Publisher
Keith Weiskamp

Acquisitions
Shari Jo Hehr

Project Editor
Jeff Kellum

Production Coordinator
Kim Eoff

Cover Design
Anthony Stock

Layout Design
April Nielsen

Marketing Specialist
Cynthia Caldwell

an International Thomson Publishing company

Albany, NY • Belmont, CA • Bonn • Boston • Cincinnati • Detroit • Johannesburg • London • Madrid
Melbourne • Mexico City • New York • Paris • Singapore • Tokyo • Toronto • Washington

About The Authors

David Johnson (a.k.a. DJ)

DJ has worked in the networking trenches as a network administrator, manager, and trainer for eight years. Working for large corporations such as Pharmaco and GTECH, he learned his way around LAN and WAN technologies in exotic locations that range from Trinidad, to the United Kingdom, to Austin, TX, to Belo Horizonte, Brazil, to Warwick, RI. Currently, DJ is General Manager of LANWrights, Inc. He has contributed to numerous NT- and MCSE-focused courses and books, on subjects that include Networking Essentials, Windows NT Server 4.0, Workstation 4.0, Windows NT Server 4.0 in the Enterprise, and TCP/IP. He hopes to complete his MCSE and ECNE in the very near future, as well as to spend more time in the classroom training while working on a series of exam preparation and MCSE study guide books. You can reach DJ at dj@lanw.com.

Andy Ruth

Andy has been involved in the computer industry since the late 1970s, when he joined the U.S. Navy and provided systems support on flight simulators. In the corporate environment, Andy has provided systems support for computers ranging from large mainframes to small PC-networked environments. He is currently Vice President of Hudlogic. Andy holds both Microsoft MCSE and MCT certifications, as well as other certifications. Andy can be reached at andy@hudlogic.com.

James Michael Stewart

Michael is an MCSE and a full-time writer, focusing on Windows NT and Internet topics. He is currently pursuing MCSE + Internet certification, with his sights set on MCT. Most recently, he has worked on several titles in the *Exam Cram* series, including *MCSE NT Server 4 Exam Cram, MCSE NT Workstation 4 Exam Cram, MCSE NT Server 4 in the Enterprise Exam Cram*, and *MCSE Windows 95 Exam Cram*. Additionally, he has co-authored the *Hip Pocket Guide to HTML 4* (1998) and the *Intranet Bible* (1997), plus made contributions to *Windows NT Networking For Dummies* (1997), *Building Windows*

NT Web Servers (1997), and *Windows NT: Step by Step* (Microsoft Press, 1995). Michael has written articles for numerous print and online publications, including *C\Net*, *InfoWorld*, *Windows NT* magazine, and *Datamation*. He is also a regular speaker at Networld+Interop, has taught at WNTIS and NT SANS, and is a former leader of an NT study group at the Central Texas LAN Association. You can reach Michael by email at michael@lanw.com, or through his Web pages at http://www.lanw.com/jmsbio.htm or http://www.impactonline.com/.

Acknowledgments

David Johnson

First, I'd like to thank the staff at Coriolis and Certification Insider Press for their work on this project. The *Exam Cram* series is going far, and it is due in no small part to the efforts of Keith Weiskamp, Shari Jo Hehr, Paula Kmetz, Ann Aken, and the rest of the staff at Coriolis. Most of all, thanks to Jeff Kellum. Jeff, you've taken on many of our projects and always made them smooth.

I'd also like to thank Barry Shilmover for his help on this manuscript. Barry, without you this really would not have been possible. Finally, I'd like to thank the staff at LANWrights. Mary and Dawn, thanks for making me sound good while not confusing the readers. Bill and Natanya, thanks for dealing with those times when your projects took a back seat because I was writing frantically. Michael, your contribution to this book is undeniable. And Ed, as always, thanks for giving me the opportunity to work with you and expand my horizons.

Andy Ruth

Thanks to the staff at Coriolis for putting in the long hours to make this project a success and LANWrights, Inc., for allowing me to have a hand in this project. Most importantly, thanks to Jaylene, my love, my life, for putting up with me while working on this project.

James Michael Stewart

Thanks to my boss, Ed Tittel, for including me in this book series. Thanks to all my co-workers, whose efforts in the trenches have enabled this series to grow to fruition. To my parents, Dave and Sue, thanks for your consistent love, evident pride, and ongoing encouragement. To Mark, even in times of sparse communication, there will never be another human to replace a friend as great as you. To John Paul "The Pope" Henry, *wink* *wink* *nudge* *nudge* say no more, say no more. To HERbert, you are the only cat I know that likes to play in the shower. And finally, as always, to Elvis—there are times when the only thing that can cheer me up is to dress in my white sequenced jump suit, sneer my upper lip, and play a bit of "Heart Break Hotel" on my trusty air guitar.

Table Of Contents

Introduction   xvii

Chapter 1   Microsoft Certification Exams   1

The Exam Situation   2

Exam Layout And Design   3

Using Microsoft's Exam Software Effectively   5

Exam-Taking Basics   5

Question-Handling Strategies   6

Mastering The Inner Game   7

Additional Resources   8

Need More Practice?   11

Chapter 2   Introduction To Microsoft
Proxy Server 2.0   13

Proxy Server: Explored And Explained   14

Overview Of Proxy Server 2.0   16

Security   16

Performance   17

Administration   17

Features And Functions Of Proxy Server 2.0   17

Proxy Services   18

New Features In Proxy Server 2.0   18

Proxy Server 2.0 Advantages   19

Software And Hardware
Requirements   20

Software Requirements   20

Hardware Requirements   21

Proxy Server Architecture   21

Web Proxy Service   21

WinSock Proxy (WSP) Service   25

SOCKS Proxy Service   28

Proxy Server On An Intranet   29

Exam Prep Questions   30

Need To Know More?   35

Chapter 3   Installing Microsoft Proxy Server 2.0   37

Hardware And Software Requirements   38

Installing Microsoft Proxy Server 2.0   38

Configuring Proxy Server Auto Dial   46

Dial-Up Security Settings   47

Removing Or Adding Proxy Components   50

Local Address Table (LAT)   51

Multiple Protocol Configuration   52

Client Configuration   53

Exam Prep Questions   55

Need To Know More?   61

Chapter 4   Proxy Server Protocols   63

The TCP/IP Protocol Suite   64

TCP/IP Structure   65

IP Addressing And Subnet Masks   66

Address Classes   68

Subnet Masks   69

TCP And UDP Ports   72

Exam Prep Questions   73

Need To Know More?   77

Chapter 5   Proxy Server Security   79

Proxy Server Security Overview   80

**Controlling Internet Access
(Coming And Going)   80**

Controlling Inbound Access   81

Controlling Outbound Access   83

Server Proxy   85

Encryption   86

Additional Proxy Server Security Measures   86

Proxy Alerts   86

Windows NT System Log And Alert Events   88

Proxy Logging   88

Logging To A Text File   91

Logging To A SQL/ODBC Database   91

Service Log Fields   92

Packet Filter Log Fields   95

Managing The Internet Publication Process   96

Reverse Proxy   96

Reverse Hosting   97

Exam Prep Questions   98

Need To Know More?   102

Chapter 6   Managing And Tuning
Proxy Server 2.0   103

Internet Service Manager Overview   104

Using ISM To Manage Proxy Server   105

Web Proxy Management   106

Proxy Publishing   110

WinSock Proxy Management   111

SOCKS Proxy Management   113

Performance Monitor Overview   114

Performance Monitor Counters   115

Monitoring And Tuning Memory 115

Monitoring And Tuning The Proxy Cache 118

Error Logging And Interpretation 121

Exam Prep Questions 124

Need To Know More? 131

Chapter 7 Internet Access Via Proxy Server 133

Proxy Server's Role On The Internet 134

Configuring And Managing Client Internet Access 135

Changing Client Configuration Parameters 135

Using Client Configuration Scripts 137

Editing The Client Configuration File 137

Creating A Client LAT File 139

Configuring Web Proxy Client Applications 139

Configuring WinSock Proxy Client Applications 139

Configuring And Managing Server Internet Access 140

Configuring Auto Dial 140

Changing The LAT 140

Configuring The Cache 142

Backing Up And Restoring Configuration 143

Tuning And Controlling Internet Access Performance 144

Internet-Specific Proxy Server Logging 145

Troubleshooting Proxy Server Internet Connections 146

Exam Prep Questions 148

Need To Know More? 151

Chapter 8   Managing Multiple Proxy Servers   153

An Overview Of Multiple Proxy Server Scenarios   154

Distributed Proxying   154

Hierarchical Proxying   156

CARP And Hashing   158

Balancing The Load Among Multiple Proxy Servers   159

Balancing Client Distribution Using DNS   159

Balancing Client Distribution Using WINS   159

Dealing With Geographical Distribution   160

Reverse Hosting With Proxy Server   160

Best Practices For Multiple Proxy Servers   161

Troubleshooting Multiple Proxy Server Situations   161

Exam Prep Questions   164

Need To Know More?   172

Chapter 9   Troubleshooting   173

The Basics Of Troubleshooting   174

Resources For Shooting Trouble: Where To Look For Help   174

Proxy Server Registry Entries (And Related Data)   176

The Windows NT Registry Editor   176

Domain Filtering Keys   178

Packet Filtering Keys   178

Proxy Server Alerting Keys   179

Proxy Server Array Keys   179

Logging Values   179
Storing Logs On A Network Share   179
Handling Web Proxy Service Problems   179
Event Messages   180
Web Proxy Service Registry Keys   181
Managing WinSock Proxy Service Problems   182
Event Messages   183
WinSock Proxy Service Registry Keys   184
Managing SOCKS Proxy Service Problems   184
Event Messages   184
SOCKS Proxy Service Registry Keys   185
Troubleshooting Proxy Server Performance   185
Exam Prep Questions   187
Need To Know More?   190

Chapter 10   Planning Your Proxy Server Implementation   191
The Site Analysis Process   192
Network Capacity Analysis   192
Needs Analysis   193
Connecting With An Internet Service Provider   195
Types Of ISPs   195
Locating An ISP   196
Test Your ISP   197
Choosing The Right Internet Connection For Your Network   200
Choosing The Right Hardware For Your Proxy Server   202
Low-Volume Network   202
Moderate-Volume Network   203
High-Volume   203
Exam Prep Questions   204
Need To Know More?   207

Chapter 11   Sample Test   209

Questions, Questions, Questions   210
Picking Proper Answers   210
Decoding Ambiguity   211
Working Within The Framework   212
  Deciding What To Memorize   212
Preparing For The Test   212
Taking The Test   213
Sample Test   214

Chapter 12   Answer Key   241

Glossary   255

Index   265

Introduction

Welcome to the *MCSE Proxy Server 2 Exam Cram*. This book aims to help you get ready to take—and pass—the Microsoft certification test "Exam 70-088: Implementing and Supporting Microsoft Proxy Server 2.0." This introduction explains Microsoft's certification programs in general and talks about how the *Exam Cram* series can help you prepare for Microsoft's certification exams.

Exam Cram books help you understand and appreciate the subjects and materials you need to pass Microsoft certification exams. *Exam Cram* books are aimed strictly at test preparation and review. They do not teach you everything you need to know about a topic (such as the ins and outs of Internet access or Proxy Server). Instead, we (the authors) examine the areas that are most likely going to be covered on the test. Our aim is to bring together as much information as possible about Microsoft certification exams.

Nevertheless, to completely prepare yourself for any Microsoft test, we recommend that you begin your studies with some classroom training, or that you pick up and read one of the many study guides available from Microsoft and third-party vendors, including the *Exam Prep* books by Certification Insider Press. We also strongly recommend that you install, configure, and explore the software or environment you'll be tested on, because nothing beats hands-on experience and familiarity when it comes to understanding the questions you're likely to encounter on a certification test. Book learning is essential, but hands-on experience is the best teacher of all!

The Microsoft Certified Professional (MCP) Program

The MCP program currently includes five separate tracks, each of which boasts its own special acronym (as a would-be certified professional, you need to have a high tolerance for alphabet soup of all kinds):

➤ **MCP (Microsoft Certified Professional)** This is the least prestigious of all the certification tracks from Microsoft. Attaining MCP status requires an individual to pass at least one core operating system exam.

Passing any of the major Microsoft operating system exams—including those for Windows 95, Windows NT Workstation, or Windows NT Server—qualifies an individual for MCPS credentials. Individuals can demonstrate proficiency with additional Microsoft products by passing additional certification exams.

➤ **MCSD (Microsoft Certified Solution Developer)** This track is aimed primarily at developers. This credential indicates that individuals who pass it are able to design and implement custom business solutions around particular Microsoft development tools, technologies, and operating systems. To obtain an MCSD, an individual must demonstrate the ability to analyze and interpret user requirements; select and integrate products, platforms, tools, and technologies; design and implement code and customize applications; and perform necessary software tests and quality assurance operations.

To become an MCSD, an individual must pass a total of four exams: two core topics plus two elective exams. The two core exams are the Microsoft Windows Operating Systems and Services Architecture I and II (WOSSA I and WOSSA II, numbered 70-150 and 70-151). Elective exams cover specific Microsoft applications and languages, including Visual Basic, C++, the Microsoft Foundation Classes, Access, SQL Server, Excel, and more.

➤ **MCT (Microsoft Certified Trainer)** Microsoft Certified Trainers are individuals who are deemed capable of delivering elements of the official Microsoft training curriculum, based on technical knowledge and instructional ability. Therefore, it is necessary for an individual seeking MCT credentials (which are granted on a course-by-course basis) to pass the related certification exam for a course and successfully complete the official Microsoft training in the subject area, as well as demonstrate an ability to teach.

This latter criterion may be satisfied by proving that one has already attained training certification from Novell, Banyan, Lotus, the Santa Cruz Operation, or Cisco, or by taking a Microsoft-sanctioned workshop on instruction. Microsoft makes it clear that MCTs are an important cog in the Microsoft training channels. Instructors must be MCTs before Microsoft will allow them to teach in any of its official training channels, including Microsoft's affiliated Authorized Technical Education Centers (ATECs), Authorized Academic Training Programs (AATPs), and the Microsoft Online Institute (MOLI).

➤ **MCSE (Microsoft Certified Systems Engineer)** Anyone who possesses a current MCSE is warranted to possess a high level of expertise with

Windows NT (either version 3.51 or 4) and other Microsoft operating systems and products. This credential is designed to prepare individuals to plan, implement, maintain, and support information systems and networks built around Microsoft Windows NT and its BackOffice family of products.

To obtain an MCSE, an individual must pass four core operating system exams, plus two elective exams. The operating system exams require individuals to demonstrate competence with desktop and server operating systems and with networking components.

At least two Windows NT related exams must be passed to obtain an MCSE: "Implementing and Supporting Windows NT Server" (version 3.51 or 4) and "Implementing and Supporting Windows NT Server in the Enterprise" (version 3.51 or 4). These tests are intended to indicate an individual's knowledge of Windows NT in smaller, simpler networks and in larger, more complex, and heterogeneous networks, respectively.

Two more tests must be passed. These tests are related to networking and desktop operating systems. At present, the networking requirement can only be satisfied by passing the Networking Essentials test. The desktop operating system test can be satisfied by passing a Windows 3.1, Windows for Workgroups 3.11, Windows NT Workstation (the version must match whichever core curriculum is pursued), or Windows 95 test.

The two remaining exams are elective exams. The elective exams can be in any number of subject or product areas, primarily BackOffice components. These include tests on SQL Server, SNA Server, Exchange Server, Systems Management Server, and the like. However, it is also possible to test out on electives by taking advanced networking topics such as "Internetworking with Microsoft TCP/IP" (but here again, the version of Windows NT involved must match the version for the core requirements taken).

Whatever mix of tests is completed toward MCSE certification, individuals must pass six tests to meet the MCSE requirements. It's not uncommon for the entire process to take a year or so, and many individuals find that they must take a test more than once to pass. Our primary goal with the *Exam Cram* series is to make it possible, given proper study and preparation, to pass all the MCSE tests on the first try.

➤ **MCSE + Internet (Microsoft Certified Systems Engineer + Internet)** This is the newest of the Microsoft certifications, and it focuses on not just the Microsoft operating systems, but also Microsoft's Internet servers and TCP/IP.

To obtain an MCSE + Internet, an individual must pass seven core exams, plus two elective exams. The core exams consist of not only the server operating systems (NT Server and Server in the Enterprise) and a desktop environment (Windows 95, Windows 98, or Windows NT Workstation), but also Networking Essentials, TCP/IP, Internet Information Server (IIS), and the Internet Explorer Administration Kit (IEAK).

The two remaining exams are elective exams. The elective exams can be in any of four product areas: SQL Server, SNA Server, Exchange Server, and Proxy Server.

Finally, certification is an ongoing activity. Once a Microsoft product becomes obsolete, MCSEs (and other MCPs) typically have a 12- to 18-month time frame in which they can become recertified on current product versions (if individuals do not get recertified within the specified time period, their certification is no longer valid). Because technology keeps changing and new products continually supplant old ones, this should come as no surprise.

The best place to keep tabs on the MCP program and its various certifications is on the Microsoft Web site. The current root URL for the MCP program, titled Microsoft Certified Professionals, is at www.microsoft.com/mcp. However, Microsoft's Web site changes frequently, so if this URL doesn't work, try using the search tool on Microsoft's site with either "MCP" or the quoted phrase "Microsoft Certified Professional Program" as the search string. This will help you find the latest and most accurate information about the company's certification programs. You can also obtain a special CD-ROM that contains a copy of the Microsoft Education and Certification Roadmap. The Roadmap covers much of the same information as the Web site, and it's updated quarterly. To obtain your copy of the CD-ROM, call Microsoft at (800) 636-7544, Monday through Friday, 6:30 A.M. through 7:30 P.M. Pacific Time.

Taking A Certification Exam

Alas, testing is not free. You'll be charged $100 for each test you take, whether you pass or fail. In the U.S. and Canada, tests are administered by Sylvan Prometric. Sylvan Prometric can be reached at (800) 755-3926, or (800) 755-EXAM, any time from 7:00 A.M. to 6:00 P.M. Central Time, Monday through Friday. If this number doesn't work, try (612) 896-7000 or (612) 820-5707.

To schedule an exam, call at least one day in advance. To cancel or reschedule an exam, you must call at least 12 hours before the scheduled test time (or you may be charged regardless). When calling Sylvan Prometric, have the following information ready for the telesales staffer who handles your call:

➤ Your name, organization, and mailing address.

➤ Your Microsoft Test ID. (For most U.S. citizens, this will be your social security number. Citizens of other nations can use their taxpayer IDs or make other arrangements with the order taker.)

➤ The number and name of the exam you wish to take. (For this book, the exam number is 70-088, and the exam name is "Implementing and Supporting Microsoft Proxy Server 2.0.")

➤ A method of payment. (The most convenient approach is to supply a valid credit card number with sufficient available credit. Otherwise, payments by check, money order, or purchase order must be received before a test can be scheduled. If the latter methods are required, ask your order taker for more details.)

When you show up to take a test, try to arrive at least 15 minutes before the scheduled time slot. You must bring and supply two forms of identification, one of which must be a photo ID.

All exams are completely closed-book. In fact, you will not be permitted to take anything with you into the testing area, but you will be furnished with a blank sheet of paper and a pen. We suggest that you immediately write down the information about the test you're taking on the sheet of paper. In *Exam Cram* books, this information is located in The Cram Sheet, which appears on the inside front of each book. You'll have some time to compose yourself, to record this information, and even to take a sample orientation exam before you must begin the real thing. We suggest you take the orientation test before taking your first exam; however, because they're all more or less identical in layout, behavior, and controls, you probably won't need to do this more than once.

When you complete a Microsoft certification exam, the software will tell you whether you've passed or failed. All tests are scored on a basis of 1,000 points, and results are broken into several topical areas. Even if you fail, we suggest you ask for—and keep—the detailed report that the test administrator prints for you. You can use the report to help you prepare for another go-round, if needed. If you need to retake an exam, you'll have to call Sylvan Prometric, schedule a new test date, and pay another $100 to take the test again.

Tracking MCP Status

As soon as you pass any Microsoft operating system exam, you'll attain MCP status. Microsoft also generates transcripts that indicate the exams you have passed and your corresponding test scores. You can order a transcript by email at any time by sending an email addressed to mcp@msprograms.com. You can also obtain a copy of your transcript by downloading the latest version of the MCT Guide from the Web site and consulting the section titled "Key Contacts" for a list of telephone numbers and related contacts.

Once you pass the necessary set of six exams, you'll be certified as an MCSE. Official certification normally takes anywhere from four to six weeks, so don't expect to get your credentials overnight. When the package arrives, it will include a Welcome Kit that contains a number of elements, including:

➤ An MCSE certificate, suitable for framing, along with an MCSE Professional Program Membership card and lapel pin.

➤ A license to use the MCP logo, thereby allowing you to use the logo in advertisements, promotions, and documents, and on letterhead, business cards, and so on. Along with the license comes an MCP logo sheet, which includes camera-ready artwork. (Note: Before using any of the artwork, individuals must sign and return a licensing agreement that indicates they'll abide by its terms and conditions.)

➤ A one-year subscription to TechNet, a collection of CD-ROMs that include software, documentation, service packs, databases, and more technical information than you can possibly ever read. In our minds, this is the best and most tangible benefit of attaining MCSE status.

➤ A subscription to *Microsoft Certified Professional Magazine*, which provides ongoing data about testing and certification activities, requirements, and changes to the program.

➤ A free Priority Comprehensive 10-pack with Microsoft Product Support, and a 25 percent discount on additional Priority Comprehensive 10-packs. This lets you place up to 10 free calls to Microsoft's technical support operation at a higher-than-normal priority level.

➤ A one-year subscription to the Microsoft Beta Evaluation program. This subscription will get you all beta products from Microsoft for the next year. (This does not include developer products. You must join the MSDN program or become an MCSD to qualify for developer beta products.)

Many people believe that the benefits of MCSE certification go well beyond the perks that Microsoft provides to newly anointed members of this elite group. We're starting to see more job listings that request or require applicants to have an MCSE, and many individuals who complete the program can qualify for increases in pay and/or responsibility. As an official recognition of hard work and broad knowledge, an MCSE is indeed a badge of honor in many IT organizations.

How To Prepare For An Exam

At a minimum, preparing for a Windows NT Server related test requires that you obtain and study the following materials:

➤ The Microsoft Windows NT Server 4 manuals (or online documentation and help files, which ship on the CD-ROM with the product and also appear on the TechNet CD-ROMs).

➤ The *Microsoft Windows NT Server Resource Kit* (for Microsoft NT Server Version 4), published by Microsoft Press, Redmond, WA, 1996. ISBN 1-57231-343-9. Even though it costs a whopping $149.95 (list price), it's worth every penny—not just for the documentation, but also for the utilities and other software included (which add considerably to the base functionality of Windows NT Server 4).

➤ The exam prep materials, practice tests, and self-assessment exams on the Microsoft Training And Certification Download page (www.microsoft.com/Train_Cert/download/downld.htm). Find the materials, download them, and use them!

In addition, you'll probably find any or all the following materials useful in your quest for Windows NT Server expertise:

➤ **Microsoft Training Kits** Although there's no training kit currently available from Microsoft Press for Proxy Server 2.0, many other topics have such kits. It's worthwhile to check to see if Microsoft has come out with anything by the time you need the information.

➤ **The *Exam Prep* Series** These comprehensive study guides, also published by Certification Insider Press, are designed to teach you everything you need to know from an exam perspective. *MCSE Proxy Server 2 Exam Prep* is the perfect learning companion to prepare you for Exam 70-088, "Implementing and Supporting Proxy Server 2.0." Look for this book in bookstores soon.

➤ **Classroom Training** ATECs, AATPs, MOLI, and unlicensed third-party training companies (such as Wave Technologies, American Research Group, Learning Tree, Data-Tech, and others) all offer classroom training on Proxy Server. These companies aim to help prepare network administrators to run Microsoft product installations and pass the MCSE tests. Although such training runs upwards of $350 per day in class, most of the individuals lucky enough to partake (including your humble authors, who've even taught such courses) find them to be quite worthwhile.

➤ **Other Publications** You'll find direct references to other publications and resources in this text, but there's no shortage of materials available about Windows NT and Proxy Server. To help you sift through some of the publications out there, we end each chapter with a "Need To Know More?" section that provides pointers to more complete and exhaustive resources covering the chapter's information. This should give you an idea of where we think you should look for further discussion.

➤ **The TechNet CD-ROM** TechNet is a monthly CD-ROM subscription available from Microsoft. TechNet includes all the Windows NT BackOffice Resource Kits and their product documentation. In addition, TechNet provides the contents of the Microsoft Knowledge Base and many kinds of software, white papers, training materials, and other good stuff. TechNet also contains all service packs, interim release patches, and supplemental driver software released since the last major version for most Microsoft programs and all Microsoft operating systems. A one-year subscription costs $299—worth every penny, even if only for the download time it saves.

➤ **The *Exam Cram* Series** The most efficient and reliable way to study for the Microsoft certification exams. These books give you information about the material you need to know to pass the tests. If you have a basic knowledge of the product already, the *Exam Cram* series gives you what you need to polish off your preparation for the exam. All *Exam Cram* books include a Cram Sheet, which provides an at-a-glance reference for materials to pay close attention to when studying for the certification exam.

By far, this set of required and recommend materials represents a nonpareil collection of sources and resources for Proxy Server topics and software. In the section that follows, we explain how this book works, and we give you some good reasons why this book counts as a member of the required and recommended materials list.

About This Book

Each topical *Exam Cram* chapter follows a regular structure, along with graphical cues about important or useful stuff. Here's the structure of a typical chapter:

➤ **Opening Hotlists** Each chapter begins with a list of the terms, tools, and techniques that you must learn and understand before you can be fully conversant with that chapter's subject matter. We follow the hotlists with one or two introductory paragraphs to set the stage for the rest of the chapter.

➤ **Topical Coverage** After the opening hotlists, each chapter covers a series of at least four topics related to the chapter's subject title. Throughout this section, we highlight material that you should pay careful attention to, using a special Study Alert layout, like this:

 This is what a Study Alert looks like. Normally, a Study Alert stresses concepts, terms, software, or activities that you should understand thoroughly. For that reason, we think any information found offset in Study Alert format is worthy of unusual attentiveness on your part. Indeed, most of the facts appearing on The Cram Sheet appear as Study Alerts within the text.

Occasionally in *Exam Cram* books, you'll see tables called "Vital Statistics." The contents of Vital Statistics tables are worthy of an extra once-over. These tables usually contain informational tidbits that might show up in a test question, but they're not quite as serious as Study Alerts.

Pay close attention to material flagged as a Study Alert. Although all of the information in this book pertains to what you need to study, we flag certain items that are really important. That's one reason why this book is less than half the size of a typical study guide devoted to Proxy Server. It's also why, as we've said before, this book alone is probably not enough to carry you through the exam process in a single try. Nevertheless, you'll find what appears in the meat of each chapter to be worth knowing, especially when preparing for a test.

In addition to the Study Alerts and Vital Statistics tables, we have provided tips that will help build a better foundation for Proxy Server knowledge. Even if the information is not on the exam, it is certainly related and will help you become a better test taker.

 This is how tips are formatted. Keep your eyes open for these, and you'll become an Proxy Server guru in no time!

➤ **Exam Prep Questions** Although we talk about test questions and topics throughout each chapter, this section presents a series of mock test questions and explanations of both correct and incorrect answers. We also try to point out especially tricky questions by using a special icon, like this:

Ordinarily, this icon flags the presence of an especially devious question, if not an outright trick question. Trick questions are calculated to be answered incorrectly if not read more than once, and carefully, at that. Although they're not ubiquitous, such questions make regular appearances on the Microsoft exams. That's why we say exam questions are as much about reading comprehension as they are about knowing your Proxy Server material inside out and backwards.

➤ **Details And Resources** Every chapter ends with a section titled "Need To Know More?" This section provides direct pointers to Microsoft and third-party resources offering more details on the chapter's subject. In addition, this section tries to rank, or at least rate, the quality and thoroughness of the topic's coverage by each resource. If you find a resource you like in this collection, use it; but don't feel compelled to use all the resources. On the other hand, we only recommend resources we use on a regular basis, so none of our recommendations will be a waste of your time or money (but purchasing them all at once probably represents an expense that many network administrators and would-be MCSEs might find hard to justify).

The bulk of the book follows this chapter structure slavishly. But, there are a few other elements that we'd like to point out: the answer key to the sample test that appears in Chapter 12 and a reasonably exhaustive glossary of Windows NT and Microsoft terminology. Additionally, you'll find an index that you can use to track down terms as they appear in the text. Finally, on the inside of this *Exam Cram* book represents a condensed and compiled collection of facts and tips that we think you should memorize before taking the test. Because you can dump this information out of your head onto a piece of paper before answering any exam questions, you can master this information by brute force—you only need to remember it long enough to write it down when you walk into the test room. You might even want to look at it in the car or in the lobby of the testing center just before you walk in to take the test.

How To Use This Book

If you're prepping for a first-time test, we've structured the topics in this book to build on one another. Therefore, some topics in later chapters make more sense after you've read earlier chapters. That's why we suggest you read this book from front to back for your initial test preparation. If you need to brush up on a topic or you have to bone up for a second try, use the index or table of contents to go straight to the topics and questions that you need to study. Beyond the tests, we think you'll find this book useful as a tightly focused reference to some of the most important aspects of Proxy Server.

Given all the book's elements and its specialized focus, we've tried to create a tool that you can use to prepare for—and pass—Microsoft certification exam 70-088, "Implementing And Supporting Microsoft Proxy Server 2.0." Please share your feedback on the book with us, especially if you have ideas about how we can improve it for future test-takers. We'll consider everything you say carefully, and we'll respond to all suggestions. You can reach us via email at dj@lanw.com (David "DJ" Johnson), andy@hudlogic.com (Andy Ruth), and michael@lanw.com (James Michael Stewart). Please remember to include the title of the book in your message; otherwise, we'll be forced to guess which book you're making a suggestion about. And we don't like to guess—we want to *know*!

For up-to-date information, online discussion forums, sample tests, content updates, and more, visit the Certification Insider Press at www.certificationinsider.com or the authors' Web site at www.lanw.com/examcram.

Thanks, and enjoy the book!

Microsoft Certification Exams

Terms you'll need to understand:

√ Radio button

√ Checkbox

√ Exhibit

√ Multiple-choice question formats

√ Careful reading

√ Process of elimination

Techniques you'll need to master:

√ Preparing to take a certification exam

√ Practicing (to make perfect)

√ Making the best use of the testing software

√ Budgeting your time

√ Saving the hardest questions until last

√ Guessing (as a last resort)

Exam taking is not something that most people anticipate eagerly, no matter how well prepared they may be. In most cases, familiarity helps ameliorate test anxiety. In plain English, this means you probably won't be as nervous when you take your fourth or fifth Microsoft certification exam as you'll be when you take your first one.

Whether it's your first exam or your tenth, understanding the details of exam taking (how much time to spend on questions, the setting you'll be in, and so on) and the exam software will help you concentrate on the material rather than on the environment. Likewise, mastering a few basic exam-taking skills should help you recognize—and perhaps even outfox—some of the tricks and gotchas you're bound to find in some of the exam questions.

This chapter explains the exam environment and software as well as describes some proven exam-taking strategies that you should be able to use to your advantage.

The Exam Situation

When you arrive at the Sylvan Prometric Testing Center where you scheduled your exam, you'll need to sign in with an exam coordinator. He or she will ask you to produce two forms of identification, one of which must be a photo ID. Once you've signed in and your time slot arrives, you'll be asked to deposit any books, bags, or other items you brought with you, and you'll be escorted into a closed room. Typically, that room will be furnished with anywhere from one to half a dozen computers, and each workstation will be separated from the others by dividers designed to keep you from seeing what's happening on someone else's computer.

You'll be furnished with a pen or pencil and a blank sheet of paper, or, in some cases, an erasable plastic sheet and an erasable felt-tip pen. You're allowed to write down any information you want on both sides of this sheet. You should memorize as much of the material that appears on The Cram Sheet (inside the front cover of this book) as you can and then write that information down on the blank sheet as soon as you are seated in front of the computer. You can refer to your notes anytime you like during the test, but you'll have to surrender the sheet when you leave the room.

Most test rooms feature a wall with a large picture window. This permits the exam coordinator to monitor the room, to prevent exam takers from talking to one another, and to observe anything out of the ordinary that might go on. The exam coordinator will have preloaded the Microsoft certification exam you've signed up for—for this book, that's Exam 70-088—and you'll be permitted to start as soon as you're seated in front of the computer.

All Microsoft certification exams allow a certain maximum amount of time in which to complete your work (this time is indicated on the exam by an on-screen counter/clock, so you can check the time remaining whenever you like). Exam 70-088 consists of 68 randomly selected questions. You're permitted to take up to 105 minutes to complete the exam.

All Microsoft certification exams are computer generated and use a multiple-choice format. Although this may sound quite simple, the questions are constructed not only to check your mastery of basic facts and figures about Proxy Server; they also require you to evaluate one or more sets of circumstances or requirements. Often, you'll be asked to give more than one answer to a question; likewise, you may be asked to select the best or most effective solution to a problem from a range of choices, all of which technically are correct. Taking the exam is quite an adventure, and it involves real thinking. This book will show you what to expect and how to deal with the problems, puzzles, and predicaments you're likely to find on the exam.

Exam Layout And Design

The following is a typical exam question. This multiple-choice question requires you to select a single correct answer. Following the question is a brief summary of each potential answer and why it was either right or wrong.

Question 1

What is the minimum RAM size for a proxy server on a moderate volume network?

○ a. 32MB

○ b. 128MB

○ c. 64MB

○ d. 1GB

A network that sees moderate network volume requires at least 64MB in the proxy server. Therefore, answer c is correct. 32MB is insufficient to run a proxy server with a fair volume of traffic. Therefore, answer a is incorrect. Of course, more RAM is always better when dealing with Microsoft and the Internet, and although 128MB or 1GB of RAM might be preferable, the question asked for the minimum. Therefore, answers b and d are incorrect.

This sample question corresponds closely to the type you'll see on the Microsoft certification exams. The only difference on the exam is that questions are not followed by the answer key. To select the correct answer, position the cursor over the radio button next to answer c and click the mouse button to select that answer.

Let's examine a question that requires choosing multiple answers. This type of question provides checkboxes rather than radio buttons for marking all appropriate selections.

Question 2

Which of the following are not valid IP addresses? [Check all correct answers]

❑ a. 199.199.200.200

❑ b. 256.1.256.2

❑ c. 1.1.1.1

❑ d. 299.199.299.1

Answers b and d are correct. An IP address must be between 0 and 255 because it's a decimal representation of 8 bits. 256 and 299 are not valid IP addresses. Although they may look odd, 199.199.200.200 and 1.1.1.1 are valid IP addresses. Therefore, answers a and c are incorrect.

For this type of question, one or more answers are required. As far as the authors can tell (and Microsoft won't comment), such questions are scored as wrong unless all the required selections are chosen. In other words, a partially correct answer does not result in partial credit when the test is scored. For Question 2, you have to check the boxes next to items b and d to obtain credit for a correct answer. Notice also that picking the right answer means knowing what IP addresses are invalid!

Although these two basic types of questions can appear in many forms, they constitute the foundation on which all the Microsoft certification exam questions rest. More complex questions may include so-called exhibits, which are usually screen shots of the Internet Services Manager or some other TCP/IP-related Windows NT utility. For some of these questions, you'll be asked to make a selection by clicking a checkbox or radio button on the screen shot itself; for others, you'll be expected to use the information displayed therein to guide your answer to the question. Familiarity with the underlying utility is your key to choosing the correct answer(s).

Other questions involving exhibits may use charts or network diagrams to help document a workplace scenario that you'll be asked to troubleshoot or configure. Careful attention to such exhibits is the key to success. Be prepared to toggle frequently between the picture and the question as you work.

Using Microsoft's Exam Software Effectively

A well-known principle when taking exams is to first read over the entire exam from start to finish while answering only those questions you feel absolutely sure of. On subsequent passes, you can dive into more complex questions more deeply, knowing how many such questions you have left.

Fortunately, Microsoft exam software makes this approach easy to implement. At the top-left corner of each question is a checkbox that permits you to mark that question for a later visit. (Note that marking questions makes review easier, but you can return to any question if you are willing to click the Forward or Back button repeatedly.) As you read each question, if you answer only those you're sure of and mark for review those that you're not sure of, you can keep working through a decreasing list of questions as you answer the trickier ones in order.

There's at least one potential benefit to reading the exam over completely before answering the trickier questions: Sometimes, you can find information in later questions that sheds more light on earlier ones. Other times, information you read on later questions may jog your memory about Proxy Server facts, figures, or behavior that also will help with earlier questions. Either way, you'll come out ahead if you defer those questions about which you're not absolutely sure.

Keep working on the questions until you're absolutely sure of all your answers or until you know you'll run out of time. If questions are still unanswered, you'll want to zip through them and guess. Not answering a question guarantees you won't receive credit for it, and a guess has at least a chance of being correct.

At the very end of your exam period, you're better off guessing than leaving questions unanswered.

Exam-Taking Basics

The most important advice about taking any exam is this: Read each question carefully. Some questions are deliberately ambiguous, some use double negatives, and others use terminology in incredibly precise ways. We have taken numerous exams—both practice and live—and in nearly every one have missed at least one question because they didn't read it closely or carefully enough.

Here are some suggestions on how to deal with the tendency to jump to an answer too quickly:

➤ Make sure you read every word in the question. If you find yourself jumping ahead impatiently, go back and start over.

➤ As you read, try to restate the question in your own terms. If you can do this, you should be able to pick the correct answer(s) much more easily.

➤ When returning to a question after your initial read-through, read every word again—otherwise, your mind can fall quickly into a rut. Sometimes revisiting a question after turning your attention elsewhere lets you see something you missed, but the strong tendency is to see what you've seen before. Try to avoid that tendency at all costs.

➤ If you return to a question more than twice, try to articulate to yourself what you don't understand about the question, why the answers don't appear to make sense, or what appears to be missing. If you chew on the subject for a while, your subconscious may provide the details that are lacking or you may notice a "trick" that will point to the right answer.

Above all, try to deal with each question by thinking through what you know about the Proxy Server utilities, characteristics, behaviors, facts, and figures involved. By reviewing what you know (and what you've written down on your information sheet), you'll often recall or understand things sufficiently to determine the answer to the question.

Question-Handling Strategies

Based on exams the authors have taken, some interesting trends have become apparent. For those questions that take only a single answer, usually two or three of the answers will be obviously incorrect, and two of the answers will be plausible—of course, only one can be correct. Unless the answer leaps out at you (if it does, reread the question to look for a trick; sometimes those are the ones you're most likely to get wrong), begin the process of answering by eliminating those answers that are most obviously wrong.

Things to look for in obviously wrong answers include spurious menu choices or utility names, nonexistent software options, and terminology you've never seen. If you've done your homework for an exam, no valid information should be completely new to you. In that case, unfamiliar or bizarre terminology probably indicates a totally bogus answer. As long as you're sure what's right, it's easy to eliminate what's wrong.

Numerous questions assume that the default behavior of a particular utility is in effect. If you know the defaults and understand what they mean, this knowledge will help you cut through many Gordian knots.

As you work your way through the exam, another counter that Microsoft thankfully provides will come in handy—the number of questions completed and questions outstanding. Budget your time by making sure that you've completed one-quarter of the questions one-quarter of the way through the exam period (or the first 17 questions in the first 25 or 26 minutes) and three-quarters of them three-quarters of the way through (51 questions in the first 77 to 78 minutes).

If you're not finished when 100 minutes have elapsed, use the last 5 minutes to guess your way through the remaining questions. Remember, guessing is potentially more valuable than not answering, because blank answers are always wrong, but a guess may turn out to be right. If you don't have a clue about any of the remaining questions, pick answers at random or choose all a's, b's, and so on. The important thing is to submit an exam for scoring that has an answer for every question.

Mastering The Inner Game

In the final analysis, knowledge breeds confidence, and confidence breeds success. If you study the materials in this book carefully and review all the exam prep questions at the end of each chapter, you should become aware of those areas where additional learning and study are required.

Next, follow up by reading some or all of the materials recommended in the "Need To Know More?" section at the end of each chapter. The idea is to become familiar enough with the concepts and situations you find in the sample questions that you can reason your way through similar situations on a real exam. If you know the material, you have every right to be confident that you can pass the exam.

Once you've worked your way through the book, take the practice exam in Chapter 11. This will provide a reality check and help you identify areas you need to study further. Make sure you follow up and review materials related to the questions you miss before scheduling a real exam. Only when you've covered all the ground and feel comfortable with the whole scope of the practice exam should you take a real one.

 If you take the practice exam and don't score at least 75 percent correct, you'll want to practice further. At a minimum, download the Personal Exam Prep (PEP) exams and the self-assessment exams from the Microsoft Certification And Training Web site's download page (its location appears in the next section). (Unfortunately, at the time of this writing, the Proxy PEP was not yet available.) If you're more ambitious, or better funded, you might want to purchase a practice exam from one of the third-party vendors that offers them.

Armed with the information in this book and with the determination to augment your knowledge, you should be able to pass the certification exam. You need to work at it, however, or you'll spend the exam fee more than once before you finally do pass. If you prepare seriously, the execution should go flawlessly. Good luck!

Additional Resources

A good source of information about Microsoft certification exams comes from Microsoft itself. Because its products and technologies—and the exams that go with them—change frequently, the best place to go for exam-related information is online.

If you haven't already visited the Microsoft Training And Certification pages, do so right now. The Training And Certification home page resides at www.microsoft.com/Train_Cert/ (see Figure 1.1).

Note: This page may not be there by the time you read this, or it may have been replaced by something new and different, because things change regularly on the Microsoft site. Should this happen, please read the sidebar titled "Coping With Change On The Web."

The menu options in the left column of the home page point to the most important sources of information in the Training And Certification pages. Here's what to check out:

➤ **Certification Choices** Use this menu entry to read about the various certification programs that Microsoft offers.

➤ **Search/Find An Exam** Pulls up a search tool that lets you list all Microsoft exams and locate all exams relevant to any Microsoft certification (MCPS, MCSE, MCT, and so on) or those exams that cover a particular product. This tool is quite useful not only to examine the options but also to obtain specific exam preparation information, because each exam has its own associated preparation guide. This is exam 70-088.

Figure 1.1   The Training And Certification home page.

➤ **Downloads** Here, you'll find a list of the files and practice exams that Microsoft makes available to the public. These include several items worth downloading, especially the Certification Update, the Personal Exam Prep (PEP) exams, various assessment exams, and a general exam study guide. Try to make time to peruse these materials before taking your first exam.

These are just the high points of what's available in the Microsoft Training And Certification pages. As you browse through them—and we strongly recommend that you do—you'll probably find other things mentioned that are every bit as interesting and compelling.

Coping With Change On The Web

Sooner or later, all the information we've shared with you about the Microsoft Training And Certification pages and all the other Web-based resources mentioned throughout the rest of this book will go stale or be replaced by newer information. In some cases, the URLs you find here may lead you to their replacements; in other cases, the URLs will go nowhere, leaving you with the dreaded "404 File not found" error message.

When that happens, don't give up. There's always a way to find what you want on the Web if you're willing to invest some time and energy. Most large or complex Web sites—and Microsoft's qualifies on both counts— offer a search engine. Looking back at Figure 1.1, you'll see that a Search button appears along the top edge of the page. As long as you can get to Microsoft's site (it should stay at www.microsoft.com for a long while yet), you can use this tool to help you find what you need.

The more focused you can make a search request, the more likely the results will include information you can use. For example, you can search for the string "training and certification" to produce a lot of data about the subject in general, but if you're looking for the preparation guide for Exam 70-088, "Implementing and Supporting Microsoft Proxy Server 2.0," you'll be more likely to get there quickly if you use a search string similar to the following:

```
"Exam 70-088" AND "preparation guide"
```

Likewise, if you want to find the Training And Certification downloads, try a search string such as this:

```
"training and certification" AND "download page"
```

Finally, don't be afraid to use general search tools such as www.search.com, www.altavista.digital.com, or www.excite.com to search for related information. Even though Microsoft offers the best information about its certification exams online, there are plenty of third-party sources of information, training, and assistance in this area that do not have to follow the Microsoft party line. The bottom line is: If you can't find something where the book says it lives, start looking around. If worse comes to worst, you can always email me! I just might have a clue.

Need More Practice?

LANWrights, Inc., the company behind this book, also offers practice tests for sale. You can order practice exam diskettes via snail mail. Because we wrote them ourselves, we don't feel comfortable telling you how great they are—but they surely are a good deal! Currently available tests include NT Server 4.0, NT Server 4.0 in the Enterprise, NT Workstation 4.0, Networking Essentials, TCP/IP, Proxy Server 2.0, IIS 4.0, and Windows 95. Please send a check or money order to the following address: LANWrights, Inc., P.O. Box 26261, Austin, TX 78755-0261.

Each diskette includes two complete practice tests. Either Netscape Navigator 3 (or higher) or Microsoft Internet Explorer 3 (or higher) is required to use the Java-based testing system on the diskettes. Single exam diskettes are $25 each. Multiple diskettes can be purchased at a discount, as follows:

➤ Two exams for $45

➤ Three exams for $65

➤ Four exams for $85

➤ Five exams for $100

➤ Six exams for $115

➤ Seven exams for $125

➤ All eight exams for $130

Prices include U.S. shipping and required taxes. (Mexico and Canada add $5; all other countries outside North America add $10 for additional shipping charges.) Please be sure to include your name, shipping address, contact phone number, and the number and titles for those practice exams you wish to order.

Introduction To Microsoft Proxy Server 2.0

Terms you'll need to understand:

√ Proxy

√ Cache

√ Site restrictions

√ Application restrictions

√ Circuit layer restrictions

Techniques you'll need to master:

√ Understanding the hardware and software requirements for Proxy Server 2.0

√ Understanding the architecture of the Microsoft Proxy Server

By definition, *proxy* is the authority to act for another. In this chapter, we cover the role of proxy servers—Microsoft Proxy Server 2.0, in particular—in a network. In addition, we briefly discuss the history of proxy servers and describe the features, requirements, and architecture of Microsoft Proxy Server.

Proxy Server: Explored And Explained

The concept of a *proxy server* has grown from the need for corporate networks to connect to the Internet safely. Internet connections were originally provided on a dial-up basis for individual users. This method of connection is costly, time consuming, and difficult to manage. To make connection easier, some businesses installed large connections directly to their networks. However, this posed a very large security risk because traffic from the Internet was often allowed unobstructed access to the network and whatever data was available. It was this need that brought on the birth of firewalls.

A *firewall* is a piece of equipment that is used to secure an Internet connection. It is configured to allow certain outgoing traffic through, and generally not granting incoming access to the network. This type of equipment created the secure environment demanded by most companies. As this security was added, and larger companies and Internet Service Providers (ISPs) connected to the Internet, they came to realize that bandwidth limitations prevented large numbers of users from effectively connecting to the Internet. To address this problem, firewalls were given the ability to cache content.

Caching is the process of temporarily maintaining a local copy of a resource to speed up requests. By keeping a copy of the requested resource in cache, each time a local client makes a request for the resource, it is fulfilled immediately, rather than being passed through to the Internet. This decreases the response time for a request. It shouldn't be too much of a stretch to see how a product that stores a duplicate copy of a remote resource locally can also be used to restrict access.

There are several ways to prevent resources from being accessed—these include exclusions based on an IP address, domain, or Uniform Resource Locator (URL), application or information service exclusions, and user or group exclusions. When a caching (or proxy) server is used to prevent resource access, this is called *site filtering* or *user access control*. This feature gives administrators some ability to focus general Internet usage toward more productive resource locations.

The next step in the evolution of network communication products is the proxy server. A proxy server takes the capabilities of a firewall and combines them with the functions of a content caching server. The result is a hybrid tool that can cache often-used content, protect a network from unauthorized access or use (whether originating from inside or outside the network), and hide the identity of internal clients by requesting resources on their behalf. A proxy server acts as a secure Internet gateway for network clients.

A proxy server that's installed properly is completely transparent to both the user and the resource host. The only time a user interacts with the proxy server directly is when a restricted resource is requested. Then, the proxy server issues a restriction warning instead of returning the desired item.

A proxy server is deployed on a multihomed server. A *multihomed server* is a computer with two or more network interfaces connected to different networks. A proxy server will often have one connection to the Internet and one or more connections to a network (see Figure 2.1). With such a configuration, the private network can be restricted by preventing IP routing across the proxy server. Thus, only the most secure server—the one hosting the proxy server— is accessible from the Internet.

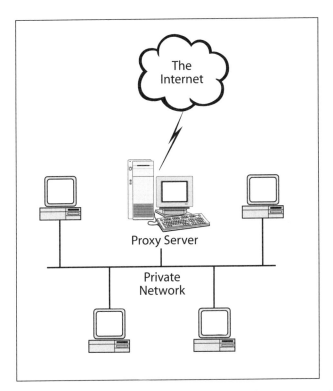

Figure 2.1   A proxy server mediating between a private network and the Internet.

Overview Of Proxy Server 2.0

In Microsoft's valiant efforts to be the quintessential resource for all things Internet, it has produced Proxy Server 2.0. Proxy Server 2.0 is the latest incarnation of the proxy product—originally released in November of 1996. Although it wasn't the first proxy server for the Microsoft Windows platform, it quickly gained on its competitors, such as Netscape's Proxy Server.

The original 1.0 version of Microsoft Proxy Server offered content caching, site restriction, and some application and circuit layer restrictions. However, it did not offer all of the security benefits of a true firewall. In addition, many large organizations found it necessary to deploy groups of proxy servers to handle the traffic load and still provide adequate performance. Proxy Server 2.0, which was released less than a year after Proxy Server 1.0, was designed to pick up where the first version left off. It includes true firewall capabilities and improved, scalable caching features.

Proxy Server 2.0 is capable of supporting networks of any size, from the perspectives of simultaneous users, amount of content, performance, and cost. Therefore, both small and large organizations can reap the benefits of Proxy Server. In fact, the average performance improvement using Proxy Server, when compared to other or traditional methods, is 50 percent. In other words, deploying Proxy Server on your network to replace current Internet connection technologies can improve the overall performance of your system rather than hinder it.

Security

When placed between a local area network (LAN) and the Internet, Proxy Server acts as a firewall security-enhanced gateway (discussed in greater detail in Chapter 5). Through dynamic packet filtering, Proxy Server maintains a protected environment in which unwanted traffic is filtered. With the addition of application layer security and circuit layer security, Proxy Server offers as much protection as any standalone firewall product on the market. Alerting and logging capabilities further expand the security benefits of this product. These capabilities provide administrators with warnings and a paper trail to track down possible perimeter breaches.

When combined with the Microsoft Routing And Remote Access Service Update for Windows NT Server, Proxy Server 2.0 provides complete virtual private network (VPN) services. This includes secure wide area network (WAN) connections, inexpensive communication costs, and reliable network links. Proxy Server can help you exploit the Internet as your own vehicle for network communications.

Additional security features include virus scanning, JavaScript and ActiveX filtering, as well as site restriction enhancements. Because of its design, Proxy Server 2.0 can easily be integrated with products from third-party manufacturers. Proxy Server's extensibility and standards compliance make it an excellent platform for other vendors as well as internal programmers to modify and enhance.

Performance

Proxy Server 2.0 introduces new scalability and performance features to enhance the speed and depth of content caching. Array-based caching and hierarchical- or chain-based caching enable multiple installations of Proxy Server to act together interactively instead of separately. Caching can be tuned to the particular needs or resource access habits of your users. The distributed caching system, employed by Proxy Server, focuses on high turnover material or often accessed resources and is a vast improvement over time-based caching. Microsoft developed a new protocol standard to manage and control this new distributed caching technique: the Cache Array Routing Protocol (CARP).

With an overall network bandwidth usage reduction of 50 percent, Proxy Server's caching capabilities reduce user wait time, eliminate network congestion, and improve administration control over resources. The key capabilities of caching that provide such a performance improvement are the automated intelligent filtering and storage of data. These include proactive caching, where frequently accessed sites are updated locally on a regular basis, based on usage history.

Administration

Microsoft has focused on maintaining tight integration among its products, especially in the realm of server software. Proxy Server 2.0 is integrated tightly into Windows NT Server 4 For Domains. With the exception of the Proxy Server configuration tool itself, most tasks are managed or viewed through existing NT Server utilities—including Performance Monitor, User Manager For Domains, Event Log, and IIS Manager. In addition to the standard executable dialog box administrative tools, Proxy Server 2.0 can be administered via the Web by using an HTML-based administration tool or from a command prompt with command-line syntax and parameters.

Features And Functions Of Proxy Server 2.0

Microsoft Proxy Server 2.0 is a rich and full-featured product, so much so that it has three distinct facets. First, it's a gateway service that enables multiple users to access the Internet over a single connection. Second, it's a content-caching system, where resources that are accessed frequently are stored locally to improve performance. Finally, it includes a secure firewall system to restrict internal users from accessing some external resources and to prevent unauthorized access from external points.

Proxy Services

To provide the widest range of support for standardized information services, Proxy Server uses three proxy services:

➤ **Web Proxy** This supports those protocols and communication mechanisms typically associated with Web documents, access, and interaction. This includes support for Hypertext Transfer Protocol (HTTP), File Transfer Protocol (FTP), Gopher, and Transmission Control Protocol/Internet Protocol (TCP/IP).

➤ **WinSock Proxy** This supports client applications designed around the Windows Sockets API. This includes utilities and services such as Telnet and RealAudio. Plus, this proxy subsystem is able to deliver content over TCP/IP or Internetwork Packet Exchange/Sequenced Packet Exchange (IPX/SPX). In other words, with WinSock Proxy, a LAN can operate with IPX/SPX and still be able to access WinSock Internet applications.

➤ **SOCKS Proxy** This is a cross-platform network service that creates a secured communications link between a client and server. SOCKS Proxy supports SOCKS 4.3a and offers non-Windows or non-WinSock applications access to Internet services. SOCKS Proxy can be used for HTTP, FTP, Gopher, and Telnet. However, it cannot be used with services that require the User Datagram Protocol (UDP), such as RealAudio, VDOLive, or Microsoft NetShow.

New Features In Proxy Server 2.0

Proxy Server 2.0 is able to boast significant operational improvements due to the many new features and modifications added to the software since version 1.0. (Each of these new features will be discussed in detail throughout this book.) Proxy Server 2.0 includes the following new features:

➤ Firewall security:

  ➤ Dynamic packet filtering

  ➤ Reverse proxy

- ➤ Reverse hosting
- ➤ Server proxying
- ➤ Realtime alerts and logging
- ➤ VPN support
- ➤ Performance/cost-savings:
  - ➤ Array-based content caching
  - ➤ Hierarchical caching
  - ➤ CARP support
  - ➤ FTP caching
  - ➤ At least 40 percent better performance
  - ➤ HTTP 1.1 support
  - ➤ SOCKS support
- ➤ Management:
  - ➤ HTML-based administration (available via Web download shortly after the Proxy 2.0 general release)
  - ➤ Command line and scripting
  - ➤ Array administration
  - ➤ Configuration backup and restoration

Proxy Server 2.0 Advantages

Microsoft's Proxy Server 2.0 is a solid, reliable, high-performance product. It is unique in its field as both a secure firewall and a high-volume scalable distributed caching proxy server. As a leader in the realm of NT, Proxy Server 2.0 is an obvious choice among the handful of competitors. In Table 2.1—which was

Table 2.1 A proxy server competitive comparison.			
Feature	**MS Proxy Server 2.0**	**Netscape Server 2.5**	**Novell Border Manager**
Automatic active caching	Yes	Manual	Manual
Cache array load balance	Automatic	No	No
Firewall security	Yes	No	Yes

(continued)

Table 2.1 A proxy server competitive comparison *(continued)*.

Feature	MS Proxy Server 2.0	Netscape Server 2.5	Novell Border Manager
Static packet filtering	Yes	No	Yes
Dynamic packet filtering	Yes	No	No
Realtime alerts	Yes	No	No
Logging (text and ODBC)	Yes	No (text only)	No (text only)
Windows NT Server integration	Best	Minimal	No
GUI-based administration	Yes	No	Yes
Browser-based administration	Yes	Yes	No
Scriptable command administration	Yes	No	No
Auto dial	Yes	No	No
Built-in IPX-to-IP gateway	Yes	No	Yes

obtained from a chart in the January 1998 edition of TechNet article titled "MS Proxy Server 2.0 Data Sheet"—the features of Microsoft Proxy Server 2.0 are compared to those of Netscape Proxy Server 2.5 and Novell Border Manager.

Software And Hardware Requirements

Microsoft Proxy Server 2.0 installs onto Windows NT Server 4. Therefore, most of the hardware and software requirements are met automatically if they are already satisfied for NT Server. However, the following sections provide a detailed list of the requirements for Proxy Server. It's very important to know these requirements.

Software Requirements

Proxy Server 2.0 requires the following software to be installed on the hosting server computer:

➤ Microsoft Windows NT Server 4

➤ Microsoft Internet Information Server (IIS) 3.0 or greater

➤ Windows NT Server 4 Service Pack 3.0 or greater (included with Microsoft Proxy Server 2.0)

Hardware Requirements

The hardware requirements for Proxy Server are basically the same as those for Windows NT Server 4; however, they should be modified to meet the expected workload.

For up to 300 clients:

➤ Intel 486 minimum/Pentium 133MHz recommended

➤ 24MB RAM minimum/32MB RAM recommended

➤ 10MB minimum/from 250MB to 2GB disk space for caching

For 301 to 2,000 clients:

➤ Intel Pentium 133MHz

➤ 64MB of memory RAM

➤ From 2GB to 4GB disk space for caching

For 2,001 or more clients:

➤ Intel Pentium 166MHz or greater

➤ 64MB of memory RAM minimum

➤ From 2GB to 4GB disk space for caching

Proxy Server Architecture

As discussed previously, Microsoft Proxy Server includes three services that are used to provide proxy Internet access. To fulfill the service requirements for networks, Proxy Server takes on the role of both client and server for PCs communicating with the Internet. It acts as a client by forwarding requests from other clients on the network as its own. In contrast, it acts as a server to internal clients by fulfilling their requests. In the following sections, we look at each of the services in detail.

Web Proxy Service

The Web Proxy service provides Internet access for CERN-compliant Web browsers. Among its many features, the Web Proxy service provides the capability for multiple computers to use a single IP address (called secure IP address aggregation), extensive caching, data encryption using Secure Sockets Layer

(SSL), client request logging, and user-level security for each application protocol and encrypted logon for browsers that support the Windows NT Challenge/Response authentication system.

The Web Proxy service acts as both a client, by making requests to servers on the Internet, and as a server, by fulfilling requests made by internal clients. By using the enhanced security of Windows NT and the functions of IIS, however, the Web Proxy service is much more than a relay between client and server. It's the Web Proxy service that requires IIS and utilizes its functionality to provide Web access.

CERN

CERN refers to the Conseil Européen pour le Recherche Nuléaire (or the European Laboratory for Particle Physics) in Switzerland. What, you may ask, does this laboratory have to do with the Web and Web browsers? Most Internet applications, including the World Wide Web, are based on HTTP. The first code libraries to support this type of client/server communication using HTTP were developed at CERN. As CERN expanded its use of these libraries and added support for application-aware proxy, the Internet took notice and adopted the CERN-proxy protocol as the industry standard. As mentioned earlier, the Microsoft Proxy Server Web Proxy service is fully compliant with this protocol.

Because the Web Proxy service is fully compliant with CERN-proxy, it's able to service the requests of many different types of browsers. Not only will it successfully process Microsoft Internet Explorer requests from a Windows 95 machine, it will also handle requests from Netscape on Unix systems as well as CERN-compliant browsers on Macintosh computers.

ISAPI Filter And ISAPI Application

The Web Proxy service is comprised of two applications: the Internet Server Application Programming Interface (ISAPI) filter interface and the ISAPI application interface. The Proxy Server ISAPI filter and application—located in W3PROXY.DLL—both perform specific functions in the realm of proxy services. Other ISAPI filters or applications can be created and called given certain circumstances.

The ISAPI filter provides an extension to the IIS Web server that is used whenever it receives an HTTP request. Because this filter is called every time a request is made to the server, it can be used to monitor or log requests, to modify a request if necessary, to provide for authentication, or to redirect a request to another server.

After the Proxy Server ISAPI filter has been loaded, it examines each request made to the server to determine whether the request is a CERN-proxy or standard HTTP request. If it's a proxy request, the ISAPI filter adds instructions to route the response to the ISAPI application. If, however, the request is a standard HTTP request—meaning it does not contain protocol or domain name information—the filter makes no changes and passes the request to the Web server for normal processing.

Each time a request is received from the ISAPI filter, the Proxy Server ISAPI application does the following:

1. Validates the request by authenticating the client.

2. Checks the domain filter to verify that the request is allowed.

3. Checks the cache for the resource.

   ➤ If the resource is found in cache, it verifies that the resource is current and sends the reply to the client.

   ➤ If the resource is not in cache, it retrieves the resource from the Internet, sends it to the client, and updates the cache.

If the ISAPI application determines that the request is valid and it's not in the cache, or the cached copy needs to be updated, the application parses the URL to extract the protocol and the domain name for the resource. If it is an HTTP request, the application calls the necessary Windows Sockets API to process the request. At this point, the ISAPI application resolves the domain name from the DNS cache and connects to the remote site. Once a connection has been made, the application is able to send the request, receive the response, and forward the response to the client. At the same time, the Proxy Server ISAPI application saves a copy of the resource in the cache.

One other benefit of using the IIS Web server to support the ISAPI application is the Web server's use of HTTP keep-alive packets. These packets allow TCP connections to remain intact after the server has responded to a request. This provides for greater performance if the client requests another resource from the same server within the time limit for connections. If this were not the case, each request to a site would go through the same steps of domain name resolution and TCP connection establishment.

Caching

As mentioned earlier, caching is the process of temporarily maintaining a local copy of a resource to speed up requests. Because Proxy Server keeps a copy of the requested resource in cache, each time a local client makes a request for the resource, it is fulfilled immediately, rather than being passed to the Web server and through to the Internet. The Microsoft Proxy Server Web Proxy service uses two types of caching—passive and active—to achieve this increase in performance.

Passive caching is the basic mode of caching used by Proxy Server. The Web Proxy service receives requests from internal clients and then services those requests. To save time, the Web Proxy first checks to see if the resource is in the cache; if not, the request is forwarded to the Web. The steps involved in caching are outlined in the flow chart in Figure 2.2.

In passive caching, an object is retrieved from the Internet and placed in cache, and assigned a time to live (TTL). For the duration of the TTL, all requests for the object are serviced from cache, rather than sending the request to the Web. After the TTL has expired, the next request made for the object is forwarded to the Web for service. Proxy Server then stores the object in cache again and assigns it a new TTL, as if it were a new object.

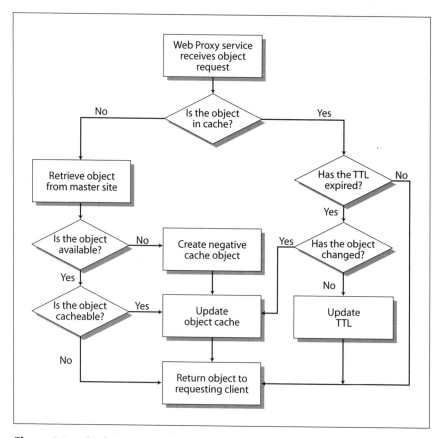

Figure 2.2   Caching is used by Proxy Server to speed Web access.

When a new request is made and the data is in the cache, Proxy Server determines whether the object is still usable—based on TTL and whether the object has changed. If it is valid, it's sent directly to the client. If not, Proxy Server updates the object in cache and returns the object to the client. If the disk space set aside for the Proxy Server cache is full, it removes older objects from cache using a formula that factors in the age, popularity, and size of the object.

Most Web browsers have a mechanism for bypassing the cache and retrieving an object directly from the Internet. In Internet Explorer, this is done by pressing F5; in Netscape Navigator, by clicking the Reload button on the toolbar while pressing the Shift key at the same time (Shift+Reload). By doing this, you instruct the Proxy Server to retrieve the object without checking the cache.

Active caching works in conjunction with passive caching to optimize performance by increasing the likelihood that a frequently requested object will be serviced from cache. Active caching automatically generates requests for objects based on the popularity of the object, the TTL of the object, and the load the server is experiencing. Servers with higher loads will perform active caching less frequently than servers with lower loads.

WinSock Proxy (WSP) Service

The WinSock Proxy (WSP) service provides many of the same features as the Web Proxy service, including secure IP aggregation, challenge/response authentication, client request logging, and SSL tunneling encryption. In addition, it provides support for Windows Sockets version 1.1, filtering by a number of different variables, blocking external user access to the internal network, and compatibility with Windows-based computers.

What exactly is WinSock? The Windows Sockets system is a mechanism for interprocess communication—whether between processes on the same computer or processes running on different computers across a LAN or WAN. This system defines a standard set of APIs that are used to communicate with one or more applications. The APIs support a client initiating a connection, a server accepting a connection, sending and receiving data over the connection, and terminating the connection when it is no longer needed.

The Windows Sockets APIs support a number of different protocol stacks. Windows Sockets is actually a part of Berkeley Sockets (Unix), with extensions for the Microsoft TCP/IP implementations Win16 and Win32. In addition, Windows Sockets includes support for other transport protocols, such as NetBEUI and IPX/SPX. It is through this mechanism that Proxy Server can support an IPX/SPX-only network and still provide Internet connectivity. It's important to note, however, that although WinSock supports NetBEUI, the WinSock Proxy service (and, by extension, Proxy Server) does not. In addition, the WinSock Proxy service supports Windows Sockets version 1.1, but not version 2.0.

Windows Sockets supports two types of communication based on the transport protocols of the TCP/IP suite—TCP and User Datagram Protocol (UDP). Point-to-point, connection-oriented communications (referred to as *stream oriented* by Microsoft) are handled by the TCP protocol, whereas point-to-point (or *multipoint*), connectionless communications (called *datagram oriented*) are handled by UDP. Each of these protocols will be covered in greater detail in Chapter 3. Most protocols used on the Internet, including HTTP, Gopher, and FTP, use connection-oriented, client/server communication. The client initiates a connection to the server to process a request while the server sits patiently, waiting for clients to initiate connections and then accepting them and fulfilling their requests.

Windows Sockets operates over communication channels called *sockets*. A socket is actually made up of two pieces of information—an address and a port. Ports are discussed further in Chapter 4. But for now, it's important to understand that a socket is created by combining an IP address and a TCP or UDP port. For example, the socket information for a connection between two computers using FTP contains the local IP address and port pair, as well as the remote IP address and port pair, as shown in Figure 2.3.

WinSock Proxy Client
The WinSock Proxy service allows Windows Sockets applications to function as if they were directly connected to the Internet, rather than going through a gateway. This is an important distinction between Web Proxy and WinSock

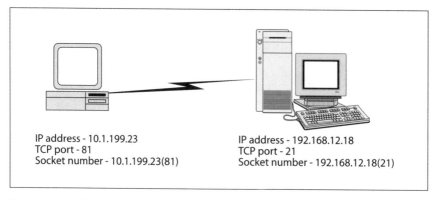

IP address - 10.1.199.23
TCP port - 81
Socket number - 10.1.199.23(81)

IP address - 192.168.12.18
TCP port - 21
Socket number - 192.168.12.18(21)

Figure 2.3   Sockets are created by combining the IP address and port number being used.

Proxy. CERN-compliant Web browsers are configured to use the Proxy Server and are aware of its existence. WinSock applications, on the other hand, still operate as though nothing were in between them and the Internet.

Each WinSock Proxy client computer is loaded with the DLL that corresponds to the version of Windows TCP/IP it is running—either WINSOCK.DLL (for Win16) or WSOCK32.DLL (for Win32). The Web Proxy client DLLs replace the ones that are installed when TCP/IP is loaded on the system. The old DLLs are retained under a different name.

When a Windows Sockets application makes a request to the Internet, the WinSock Proxy client DLL intercepts the call and establishes a communication path between the internal application and the Internet application through the Proxy Server. When a call is made that requires the old DLLs, the WinSock Proxy client DLL is given the name of the corresponding (renamed) DLL and forwards the request through it (that is, the Windows Sockets application links to the WinSock Proxy client DLL, and the WinSock Proxy client DLL links to the renamed Windows Socket DLL). In its role as interceptor, the WinSock Proxy client DLL can perform one of three things:

➤ Completely process the client's request itself

➤ Pass the request on to the renamed Windows Socket DLL

➤ Pass control information to the WinSock Proxy service running on the Proxy Server computer

Unlike the Web Proxy service, the WinSock Proxy service operates as a standalone application on a Windows NT Server 4. In addition to providing the transparent services just described, it also acts as a gateway for IPX/SPX networks that require Internet access.

WinSock Control Channel

To manage the connection between the client and the server, WinSock Proxy uses a Control Channel, which allows Windows Sockets messages to be handled remotely. This Control Channel, which uses UDP (a connectionless protocol), is established when the WinSock Proxy client DLL is loaded. Because UDP is connectionless, it is faster than other protocols that could be used, such as TCP. However, because UDP is connectionless, it is also less reliable than other protocols. The WinSock Proxy client uses acknowledgment messages to add reliability.

The Control Channel is used for four main functions. The first of these is to provide routing information between the WinSock Proxy server and client. When the client establishes a Control Channel, the server provides a list of local IP addresses in the form of a local address table (LAT). The Control Channel is also used to make TCP connections from the WinSock Proxy client to the WinSock Proxy server. This channel is only used to establish a virtual connection between the client and the remote application. Once data begins to be sent, the Control Channel is not used. Maintaining UDP connections between WinSock clients and WinSock servers is also the responsibility of the Control Channel. This channel is used to establish connections between the WinSock Proxy client and WinSock Proxy server each time a new remote peer sends data. Once the session is established, it is no longer used. Finally, the Control Channel handles the redirection of Windows Sockets database requests, such as DNS resolution, by passing the request and response via the Control Channel.

 You should know that the Control Channel for Proxy Server 2.0 uses UDP port 1745 on the WinSock Proxy client and WinSock Proxy server computers.

SOCKS Proxy Service

The SOCKS Proxy service supports SOCKS version 4.3a and also supports most SOCKS 4.0 client applications. The SOCKS protocol, by nature, functions as a proxy. It enables hosts on one side of a SOCKS server to gain full access to hosts on the other side of the server, without requiring direct IP accessibility. This is done through two operations—connect and bind.

A SOCKS client sends a connect request to the SOCKS server when a connection to an application server (on the other side of the SOCKS server) is required. The connection request is made up of the following information:

➤ The SOCKS version number

➤ The SOCKS command code

➤ The destination IP address

➤ The destination TCP port number

➤ The user ID

➤ A null field

When the server receives the request packet, it processes it and sends the client a response packet that contains the status of the request—granted, rejected, or failed.

If the request is granted, the client is immediately able to begin sending and receiving data through the SOCKS server. If the request is rejected or has failed, the reply code contained in the response packet may give some indication of the possible cause; then the SOCKS server immediately closes the connection.

The SOCKS bind operation is used to provide access control based on the TCP header information, such as the source and destination IP addresses and port numbers.

Proxy Server On An Intranet

Although Proxy Server is designed to provide a secure connection between the Internet and your local network, there may be rare occasions in which Proxy Server is used on an internal network only. This type of configuration, shown in Figure 2.4, groups intranet servers (IIS, Exchange, and so on) on their own network, separated from the network by the Proxy Server. This provides secure access to intranet servers for local users and gives network administrators greater control over the information on the intranet servers by using the security and filtering mechanisms of Proxy Server.

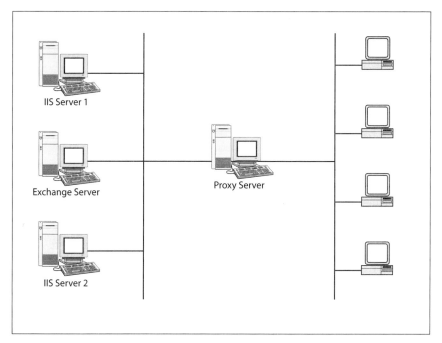

Figure 2.4   Proxy Server can be used to isolate intranet traffic from the network.

Exam Prep Questions

Question 1

Datagram-oriented communication is used by which of the following protocols?

○ a. FTP

○ b. UDP

○ c. TCP

○ d. HTTP

The correct answer to this question is b. UDP uses datagram-oriented communication. TCP, on the other hand, uses connection- or stream-oriented communication. Therefore, answer c is incorrect. HTTP and FTP utilize TCP for transport, but use neither datagram-oriented nor stream-oriented communication. Therefore, answers a and d are incorrect.

Question 2

A proxy server is a hybrid product that has the ability to perform which of the following functions? [Check all correct answers]

❑ a. Enable realtime video collaboration

❑ b. Hide the identity of internal clients by requesting resources on their behalf

❑ c. Protect a network from unauthorized access

❑ d. Cache frequently requested content

Answers b, c, and d are correct. A proxy server provides the ability to hide the identity of internal clients, protect a network from unauthorized access, and cache frequently requested content. It cannot, however, be used to enable realtime video collaboration. Therefore, answer a is incorrect.

Question 3

> Which of the following Proxy Server services provides access for IPX/SPX clients?
>
> ○ a. SOCKS
>
> ○ b. Web
>
> ○ c. WinSock
>
> ○ d. No Proxy Server service supports IPX/SPX clients

The correct answer to this question is c. The WinSock Proxy service acts as a gateway to provide access for IPX/SPX clients. None of the other answers is correct.

Question 4

> What role did CERN play in the development of the Internet?
>
> ○ a. Implemented the first TCP ports
>
> ○ b. Devised the numbering system used for IP addressing
>
> ○ c. Developed an HTTP proxy system
>
> ○ d. Provided cross-platform compatibility for TCP/IP

The correct answer to this question is c. CERN was involved in developing the basis of HTTP and an HTTP proxy system. Each of the other answers are and/or were performed by divisions of the IETF (Internet Engineering Task Force) or ARPA (Advanced Research Project Agency).

Question 5

> Which of the following features or improvements are found in Proxy Server 2.0 that were not present in the 1.0 version? [Check all correct answers]
>
> ❏ a. Distributed caching scalability
>
> ❏ b. True firewall capabilities
>
> ❏ c. Comprehensive circuit layer security
>
> ❏ d. HTTP 1.0 support

The correct answers to this question are a, b, and c. Proxy Server 2.0 includes all of these features, which were not part of Proxy Server 1.0. HTTP 1.0 was supported in version 1.0 of Proxy Server. Therefore, answer d is incorrect.

Question 6

Which of the following is used by the WinSock Proxy service to manage connections?

○ a. Management Channel

○ b. Control Channel

○ c. Connection Channel

○ d. Access Channel

The correct answer to this question is b, the Control Channel. Although the other answers may sound good, they are fictitious and have no connection to the Proxy Server architecture.

Question 7

Proxy Server enables the construction of secure VPNs when combined with which Windows NT Server 4 update?

○ a. Service Pack 3

○ b. IIS 4.0

○ c. BackOffice SDK

○ d. Routing And Remote Access Service

The correct answer to this question is d. VPNs are supported in conjunction with the Routing And Remote Access Service update for Windows NT Server 4. None of the other answers is correct.

Question 8

> Which of the following accurately describes the components re-
> quired to create a socket number?
>
> ○ a. IP address and TCP or UDP port number
>
> ○ b. IP address and computer name
>
> ○ c. MAC address and TCP or UDP port number
>
> ○ d. MAC address and computer name

The correct answer to this question is a. The station's IP address and the port number are required to create a socket number. None of the other answers is correct.

Question 9

> Which of the following protocols was designed by Microsoft to
> manage Web caching with multiple Proxy Servers?
>
> ○ a. HTTP
>
> ○ b. TCP
>
> ○ c. CARP
>
> ○ d. RRAS

The correct answer to this question is c. CARP was designed by Microsoft to manage caching for Proxy Servers. Contrary to popular opinion in Redmond, HTTP and TCP were not designed by Microsoft. Therefore, answers a and b are incorrect. RRAS was designed by Microsoft, but it is used for VPNs and Internet connectivity, not caching.

Question 10

> Which of the following ISAPI functions ensures that multiple re-
> quests to a single server do not each go through the full resolution
> and connection process?
>
> ○ a. Request redirection
>
> ○ b. Keep-alive packets
>
> ○ c. Caching
>
> ○ d. TTLs

The correct answer to this question is b. Keep-alive packets maintain a connection between the client and server so that subsequent requests do not have to go through the full resolution and connection process. Request redirection is an ISAPI function that determines the type of request. Therefore, answer a is incorrect. Caching merely holds information in memory. Therefore, answer c is incorrect. TTLs determine the amount of time that a cached object is retained. Therefore, answer d is incorrect.

Need To Know More?

 Wolfe, David: *Designing and Implementing Microsoft Proxy Server.* Sams Publishing, Indianapolis, IN, 1996. ISBN 1-57521-213-7. Chapter 1 provides an overview of Proxy Server, and Chapter 2 covers Proxy Server, IIS, and Windows NT.

 Microsoft TechNet. January, 1998. The technical notes for Proxy Server provide insight into its design and architecture.

 For more information on the SOCKS protocol and its various implementations, visit the Internet Engineering Task Force (IETF) Web site for the Authenticated Firewall Traversal (AFT) working group at http://www.ietf.org/html.charters/aft-charter.html.

 NEC is very involved with the SOCKS protocol, and information is available at its Web site at http://www.socks.nec.com/.

Installing Microsoft Proxy Server 2.0

Terms you'll need to understand:

√ LAT (local address table)

√ IPX-to-IP gateway

√ Multihomed server

√ Reverse hosting

√ Reverse proxy

√ Server proxying

√ Site filtering

√ SOCKS Proxy

√ WinSock Proxy

Techniques you'll need to master:

√ Identifying the hardware and software requirements for installing Microsoft Proxy Server 2.0

√ Installing Microsoft Proxy Server 2.0

√ Configuring Proxy Server clients

In this chapter, we examine the hardware and software requirements needed to install Microsoft Proxy Server 2.0. The discussion includes how to install Microsoft Proxy Server 2.0 and its documentation. We also discuss how to configure the local access table (LAT) to obtain the highest level of security, as well as how to configure multiple protocol support. Configuration of proxy clients is also explained.

Hardware And Software Requirements

Because Microsoft Proxy Server 2.0 installs onto Windows NT Server 4, most of the hardware and software requirements are met automatically—that is, if they are already satisfied for NT Server. For a refresher on the hardware and software requirements of Proxy Server 2.0, see Chapter 2.

Installing Microsoft Proxy Server 2.0

Before you install Microsoft Proxy Server 2.0, you need to make sure everything is ready for installation. Here are some of the things you should look for:

➤ On the server disk drive, you need to have at least 100MB of free disk space. The disk must be formatted with the NTFS file system to support the cache system.

➤ You need to have administrative privileges. The account you use to log in must be a member of the Administrators group.

➤ The network interface card (NIC) for the internal network needs to be installed and configured correctly with the protocol that's used on that network. The protocol can be either TCP/IP or NWLink.

➤ The interface being used to connect to the Internet (NIC, modem, or ISDN adapter) needs to be configured with the TCP/IP protocol. Note that when configuring the TCP/IP protocol, you'll be prompted to provide an IP address and subnet mask. This information should be obtained from your Internet Service Provider (ISP) if you're using an ISP to gain access to the Internet.

➤ The computer must be running NT Server 4 as a domain controller or member server, and Service Pack 3 must be applied.

➤ Internet Information Server (IIS) 3.0 (or newer) must be installed.

To install Microsoft Proxy Server 2.0, insert the Proxy Server CD-ROM. The AUTORUN.INF file starts the Microsoft Proxy Server 2.0 Setup. If the autorun feature is not configured on your system, do the following:

1. Run SETUP.BAT from the MSProxy directory. The Microsoft Proxy Server 2.0 Setup displays a screen similar to the one shown in Figure 3.1.

2. Click Continue. The Microsoft Proxy Server 2.0 Setup screen appears and prompts you for the CD key.

3. Enter the 10-digit key found on the sticker on the back of the CD-ROM case. Click OK. The Product Identification box appears.

4. Click OK. The system searches for installed components and then the Microsoft Proxy Server 2.0 Setup screen opens and displays the default destination folder in which Proxy Server will be installed.

5. If desired, change the folder that Proxy Server will be installed in by clicking the Change Folder button and providing the new destination path. After modifying the path, click the large button next to Installation Options.

6. The Microsoft Proxy Server 2.0—Installation Options dialog box appears (see Figure 3.2). By default, all components are selected. Accept

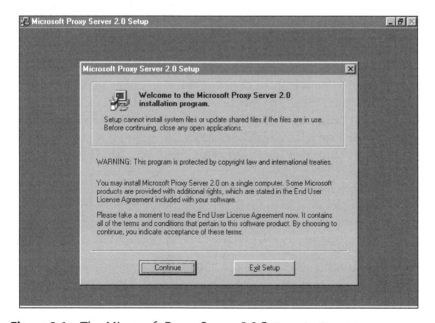

Figure 3.1   The Microsoft Proxy Server 2.0 Setup start screen.

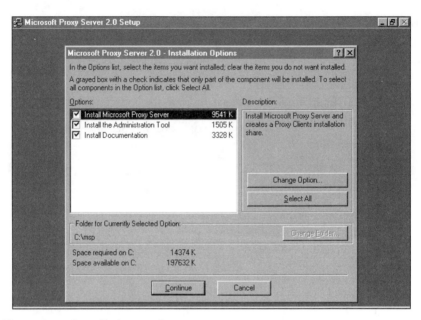

Figure 3.2 Installation options.

the default settings by clicking Continue. This will install Microsoft
Proxy Server 2.0, the administrative tool, and the online documentation.
If you want, you can choose your installation options.

Here's a list of the three installation options that can be selected, along
with a brief description of what functionality each component provides:

➤ **Install Microsoft Proxy Server—9541K** This option (shown in
Figure 3.3) installs and configures Microsoft Proxy Server 2.0, of
which there are four separate components that can be selected:
Install Server, Install NT Intel/W95 Client Share, Install NT Alpha
Client Share, and Install Win 3.x Client Share. To view and select
the specific components, click the Change Option button. By
default, client configuration software is installed for Intel-based
computers that are running Windows NT, Windows 95, Windows
for Workgroups, and Windows 3.1. Client configuration software
for Alpha-based computers running Windows NT is also installed.

➤ **Install Administration Tool—1505K** This installs the administrative tools during the installation of Microsoft Proxy Server 2.0.

➤ **Install Documentation—3328K** This installs the documentation
for Proxy Server 2.0. At the start of Setup, you can choose to install
the documentation only.

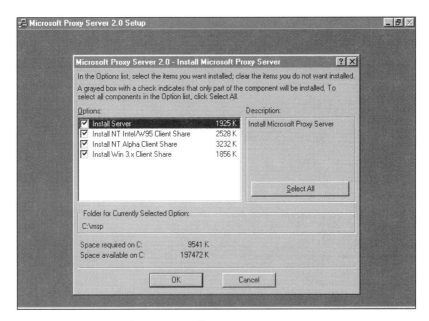

Figure 3.3   Client software installation.

Note: Total disk space required to install all components is 14,374K.

7. After selecting components to install, click the Continue button.

   ➤ If there isn't enough disk space available to install the selected options, an error message appears indicating that you need to free some disk space before continuing.

   ➤ If the SAP (Service Advertising Protocol) agent is not installed, an error message appears prompting you to install the SAP agent and the installation process ends. SAP is used by servers to advertise their services and addresses on a network.

8. Setup stops the WWW service, and the Microsoft Proxy Server Cache Drives dialog box appears (see Figure 3.4). By default, caching is enabled, and the local drives are listed in the Drive list box.

9. To assign a partition to store cache data, select the drive from the list, enter the amount of space to use for caching in the Maximum Size (MB) box, and then click the Set button. Repeat as necessary to assign additional drives to store cached information. Note that only partitions that are formatted with the NTFS file system are accessible for assigning cache storage.

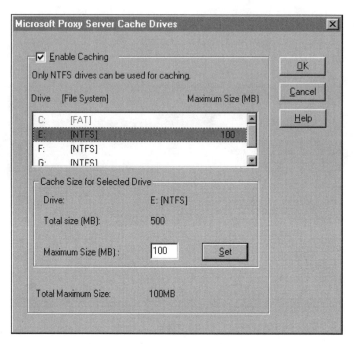

Figure 3.4 Setting disk and space options for caching.

 The minimum requirement for disk caching storage is 100MB plus an additional 0.5MB for each Web Proxy service client. Also note that only local disk drives can be used for caching.

For example, if a server services 24 Web Proxy service clients, you're recommended to allocate 112MB or more to cache. This represents the initial 100MB of initial cache storage, plus 0.5MB for each additional client. The addition of caching space needed to support a given number of clients varies depending on the configuration and load on the system; typically, however, increasing the amount of disk space allocated to cache benefits the cache.

Note: In the event you need to add a new disk to the Web Proxy cache, open the Web Proxy Service Properties dialog box in the ISM. Select the Caching tab and click on Cache Size. This invokes the Microsoft Proxy Server Cache Drives dialog box shown in Figure 3.4.

10. When you're done configuring the cache options, click OK. The Construct Local Address Table dialog box appears (see Figure 3.5). This box is used to identify all internal addresses for your network and to exclude all external addresses.

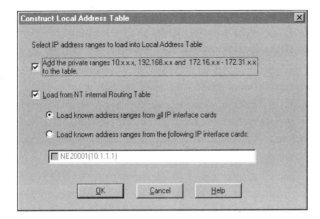

Figure 3.5   Constructing the local address table.

Next, you must construct a table containing the IP addresses of your internal network. Complete the following steps to construct your local address table:

1. Click the Construct Table button. The Construct Local Address Table dialog box appears. The default selections for constructing the local address table are to include the private IP address ranges and to load the known address ranges for all IP interface cards from the NT internal routing table.

2. To include the IP address ranges that are defined as private address ranges, select Add Private Ranges. This includes the address ranges that are defined in the current Request For Comments (RFC) as being for intranet use. If these addresses are used, they will not be routed across the Internet. They are reserved for private, intranet use; one is defined for each address class. The reserved address ranges are as follows:

   ➤ Class A reserved range—10.X.X.X

   ➤ Class B reserved range—172.16.X.X to 172.31.X.X

   ➤ Class C reserved range—192.168.X.X

3. To select the NICs on the server whose IP addresses are included in the LAT, select Load from the NT Internal Routing Table. Here are the two choices available under this option:

   ➤ Load known address ranges from all IP interface cards.

   ➤ Load known address ranges from the listed IP interface cards. Select the card you wish to include.

4. Click OK. Your selections have been made. The entries for the options selected appear in the Internal IP Ranges portion of the Local Address Table Configuration dialog box (see Figure 3.6). You receive a setup warning message asking you to verify the addresses added to the LAT. This ensures all the addresses included are correct.

   Note: The entries included in the LAT should only contain IP addresses for your internal network and the private IP address ranges. At this point, you can add additional IP addresses to the LAT.

5. To add a single entry, under Edit, enter the IP address to be added in the From and To boxes and then click Add. To add a range of addresses, under Edit, enter the starting address in the From box and the ending address for the range in the To box; then click Add.

6. Click OK to accept the default settings. You should receive a setup warning message indicating that you should verify the addresses added to the LAT to ensure all the addresses included are correct. You'll return to the Local Address Table Configuration dialog box.

7. Click OK. The Client Installation/Configuration dialog box appears (see Figure 3.7).

8. Next, you must configure the client setup. Use the choices under WinSock Proxy Client to specify how the client setup program will configure WinSock Proxy clients that install from this server. In this selection, you either provide the computer name (NetBIOS name) or the IP address of the proxy server. The default selection is the computer name.

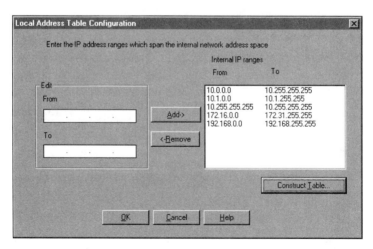

Figure 3.6   The local address table (LAT).

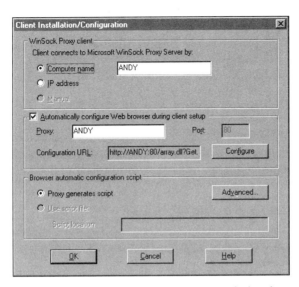

Figure 3.7   The Client Installation/Configuration dialog box.

9. If you select the Automatically Configure The Web Browser During Client Setup checkbox, client setup modifies the client Web browser network setting to send client requests to the proxy server rather than the external network or the Internet. There's a configuration area that allows you to use a custom URL script to configure the client rather than the default one supplied with Proxy Server.

10. Under Browser Automatic Configuration Script, if you click the Advanced button, the Advanced Client Configuration dialog box appears. To return to the Client Installation/Configuration menu, click the OK button to accept the configuration options selected (which are described in the following list):

> You can select whether or not Proxy Server will be used for local servers.

> You can select which IP addresses will be excluded from Proxy Server.

> You can select which domains to exclude from Proxy Server. The entries are typed in the box under the option, and entries are separated by semicolons. The domains mentioned in this area are Internet domains, not Microsoft NT network domains.

> You can enable a backup route either to the Internet or to another proxy server.

11. Accept the default settings by clicking OK. The Access Control dialog box appears. This box allows you to control the Internet access proxy clients have. This option enables the Access Control option. The Access Control settings are modified through the Proxy Server administration tool.

12. Click OK to accept the settings for the Access Control box. Proxy Setup checks for disk space, completes the installation, and restarts the Internet services. After the services are started, the Microsoft Proxy Server 2.0 Setup screen appears and displays a successful installation message. Click OK to end the Microsoft Proxy Server 2.0 Setup.

The installation of Microsoft Proxy Server 2.0 is complete. If desired, you can install just the documentation of Microsoft Proxy Server 2.0. This can be done even if the computer on which you're installing the documentation is not running Microsoft Windows NT Server. To do this, follow these steps:

1. From the root directory of the Proxy Server CD-ROM, run Setup.

2. When the Microsoft Proxy Server 2.0—Installation Options dialog box appears, clear all options except the Install Documentation checkbox.

3. After setup is complete, navigate to the documentation by clicking Start|Programs|Microsoft Proxy Server; then click Microsoft Proxy Server Documentation.

Installing only the documentation provides a way to study and review the online documentation, even if you don't have a computer that meets the requirements for running Microsoft Proxy Server 2.0.

Configuring Proxy Server Auto Dial

Proxy Server can be configured to dial out to an ISP to establish an Internet connection automatically. Proxy Server Auto Dial uses Microsoft Windows NT Server Remote Access Service (RAS) and Dial-Up Networking (DUN) to establish the connection.

Proxy Server Auto Dial is activated when an event occurs that requires a connection to the Internet. The events that activate Auto Dial are configurable through the Auto Dial Configuration tool and are shown in the following list:

➤ When the Web Proxy service requests an object that cannot be located in cache

➤ When the WinSock Proxy service has any client request

➤ When the SOCKS Proxy service has any client request

Proxy Server Auto Dial allows connection time to the Internet to be reduced by establishing a connection only when needed. The Auto Dial feature can also be used as a fault tolerance measure by acting as a backup connection in the event of a failure for a continuous Internet connection. An example of this would be a network with a T1 communications. If the T1 link went down, the backup connection using Auto Dial could be established via ISDN or regular phone lines.

To configure Proxy Server Auto Dial, Windows RAS andDUN must first be installed and configured. To install RAS and configure DUN, follow these steps:

1. Install RAS (through Network Properties).

2. Configure the Phonebook entry.

3. Configure RAS services.

To configure the Auto Dial feature, follow these steps:

1. Configure the Auto Dial credentials.

2. Configure the Auto Dial hours of operation.

3. Restart the Proxy Server services.

RAS is used to configure the modem in a Windows NT computer and can be installed as part of the Windows NT Server installation process or after the operating system is installed through the Network Properties applet in the Control Panel. When installing the RAS service, you need the following information:

➤ The modem manufacturer and model

➤ The type of communication port used for the RAS connection

➤ The TCP/IP configuration information

➤ Any modem settings, such as baud rate, stop bits, and start bits

Dial-Up Security Settings

When configuring the RAS service, it's suggested that the service be configured for Dial Out only. This increases security. If possible, it's also suggested that the RAS service be on a computer other than the Proxy Server computer.

DUN is used to provide the connection information to RAS for establishing a connection with a remote computer. A connection is established by creating a Phonebook entry in the Dial-Up Networking applet, which can be found in My Computer. The following list shows the information you'll need:

➤ A name for the Phonebook entry

➤ The phone number or numbers used to establish the connection

➤ The dial-up server type

➤ Script information (if used)

➤ Security level (plain text, NT challenge/response)

➤ X.25 information

After installing RAS and creating a Phonebook entry, RAS must be config-ured to use the Proxy Server Auto Dial feature. Follow these steps:

1. Stop and disable the Remote Access Auto Dial Manager service. This is done through the Services applet in the Control Panel (see Figure 3.8). To disable the service, select the Remote Access Auto Dial Manager service, click the Startup button, and select Disable. To stop the service, click Stop.

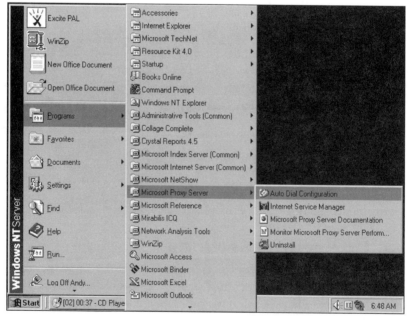

Figure 3.8 Configuring the Remote Access Auto Dial and Connection Manager services.

2. Start the Remote Access Connection Manager service, and set it to Automatic. To set the service for automatic startup, select the Remote Access Connection Manager service, click the Startup button, and select Automatic.

After properly configuring RAS and DUN, you need to configure the Proxy Server Auto Dial credentials used for dialing out, enable dial-up for Proxy Server services, and limit the times the dial-out connection functionality is available. This is done through the Auto Dial Configuration tool. To configure the Auto Dial function (see Figure 3.9), follow these steps:

1. Click Start|Programs|Microsoft Proxy Server and then double-click Auto Dial Configuration.

2. Under the Configuration tab, select the events that will start the Auto Dial feature. Select the times that the Auto Dial feature will be enabled.

3. Under the Credentials tab, configure the RAS phonebook entry, the user name, and the password that will be used to launch and authenticate the connection.

Before the Proxy Server Auto Dial feature can be used to establish a connection to an ISP, the World Wide Web (WWW), Web Proxy, WinSock Proxy, and SOCKS Proxy services must be stopped and restarted if one of two conditions exist:

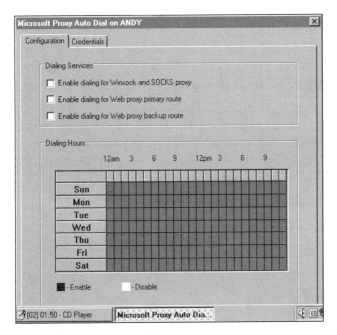

Figure 3.9 Configuring Auto Dial.

➤ When the Proxy Server Auto Dial feature is used the first time, the services must be initialized to use Auto Dial.

➤ When Proxy Server Auto Dial settings are changed, the services must be stopped and restarted before the changes will take effect.

The installation process is complete. Configuring the Microsoft Proxy Server 2.0 environment and clients, as well as setting security are covered in later chapters. The changes that are made to the system by installing Microsoft Proxy Server 2.0 are as follows:

➤ The Web Proxy service is installed on the server and is added to the Internet Service Manager, installed with IIS.

➤ The WinSock Proxy service is installed on the server and is added to the Internet Service Manager.

➤ The SOCKS Proxy service is installed on the server and is added to the Internet Service Manager.

➤ The HTML online documentation is installed and copied to the *system_root*\Help\Proxy directory.

➤ A cache is created on an NTFS partition.

➤ The LAT is created.

➤ Proxy Server Performance Monitor counters are installed.

➤ The client installation and configuration software is copied to the MSP\Clients folder and shared as Mspclnt.

Removing Or Adding Proxy Components

After Proxy Server is installed, components can be added or removed, bad or missing files can be replaced, or the entire Proxy Server product can be removed. The interface to perform these three tasks is similar to the process used with Microsoft Office to perform similar tasks. The directions for performing these tasks are detailed in the following lists.

To add or remove selected Proxy Server components:

1. In the root directory of the Proxy Server CD-ROM, run Setup. The Setup screen appears.

2. Click Add/Remove to add or remove the desired components.

To restore bad or missing files:

1. In the root directory of the Proxy Server CD-ROM, run Setup. The Setup screen appears.

2. Click Reinstall and follow the online instructions. The files that are missing or corrupted are replaced.

To remove Proxy Server:

1. In the root directory of the Proxy Server CD-ROM, run Setup. The Setup screen appears.

2. Click Remove All. A message appears asking you to confirm the removal of Microsoft Proxy Server 2.0.

3. Click Yes. Proxy Server is removed from the server.

Local Address Table (LAT)

The local address table (LAT) is a database containing a series of IP address pairs that define your internal network address space. Each pair of addresses can define one IP address, or an entire range of addresses. Look back at Figure 3.6 to see an example of a LAT with the default entries included.

The LAT installation process was detailed earlier in this chapter. After installation, the LAT can be configured using the Web Proxy service tool located in the Internet Service Manager. Microsoft Proxy Server 2.0 uses the lists of IP addresses found in the NT Server routing table to generate the LAT during installation. It's extremely important that all entries in the LAT be from your internal network and contain no entries from an external network.

When the client Setup program is run, the information contained in the LAT is downloaded to the client and stored in the \Mspclnt directory in a file named MSPLAT.TXT. The server updates the file on the client regularly to keep the file current.

After client setup, each time a WinSock application on a client attempts to establish connection to an IP address, the LAT file is checked to determine if the IP address is local to the internal network or on an external network. If the address is local, a direct connection is established. If the connection is remote, the connection is made through the WinSock Proxy service.

In certain cases, a client may need additional entries placed in the LAT for connecting to internal IP addresses. Because MSPLAT.TXT is copied over by the server on a regular basis, the client should create a custom file named LOCALLAT.TXT and place it in the \Mspclnt directory. The client then uses both files to determine if the destination is local or remote.

 To customize the LAT for individual clients, create a file named LOCALLAT.TXT and place it in the \Mspclnt directory rather than modifying the information in the MSPLAT.TXT file downloaded by Proxy Server.

Multiple Protocol Configuration

Microsoft Proxy Server 2.0 acts as a firewall or gateway by forwarding the packets on the internal network that have external destinations and receiving packets from external sources to forward to the internal client.

The client can run NWLink (Microsoft's version of IPX/SPX used with Windows NT) or TCP/IP, or both. If the packet from the internal client is received using NWLink, Proxy Server will convert the packet to TCP/IP for delivery to the external address.

If a TCP/IP packet is received for an internal client running only NWLink, Proxy Server converts the TCP/IP packet to NWLink for delivery to the internal client.

If both the TCP/IP and IPX/SPX protocols are in use by the client, the client can be forced to use the IPX/SPX protocol to communicate with Microsoft Proxy Server, as shown in Figure 3.10. This screen is reached by opening the MSP Client applet in the Control Panel on the client computer.

On a network running IPX/SPX only, Proxy Server might have only the IPX/SPX protocol configured on the internal network's interface card. Some clients may have both the IPX/SPX and TCP/IP protocols configured on their computer, having installed the TCP/IP protocol for use in connecting to an ISP via the RAS support.

Simply disabling the TCP/IP protocol while on the local area network will not work because the WinSock Proxy client computer will still detect the presence of the TCP/IP protocol, assume it is operational, and attempt to create IP sockets.

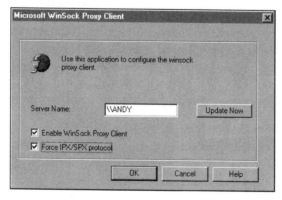

Figure 3.10 Forcing the client to use IPX/SPX.

It's preferable to configure the internal Microsoft Proxy Server client to use only the IPX/SPX protocol, rather than both the IPX/SPX protocol and the TCP/IP protocol, because the use of only the IPX/SPX protocol leaves no chance of an internal address being compromised.

Client Configuration

Microsoft Proxy Server 2.0 Setup creates the MSP\Clients folder and shares it as Mspclnt. The share permissions are set to Read for the group Everyone. Under the Mspclnt share, additional folders are created that contain client-specific files. The creation of the share point is done automatically during the installation process.

The clients that will be supported and which will, consequently, have folders under the Mspclnt share, are configured during the Microsoft Proxy Server 2.0 installation. Step 6 of the installation process, detailed earlier in this chapter, and Figure 3.3 show the selection of the client setup software that will be installed. These are the two ways the client can connect to and be configured to use Proxy Server.

To configure the client by connecting using a Web browser:

1. Start the Web browser on the Client computer.

2. Connect to Proxy Server at http://*proxy_server_computer_name*/ MSProxy.

3. A Web-based WinSock Proxy client installation screen appears. Click the "Click Here" link to begin installation.

To configure the client by attaching to Proxy Server share:

1. Click Start|Run.

2. In the Run Box, type "*proxy_server_computer_name*\Mspclnt" and then click OK. This should connect you to the share on Proxy Server.

3. Double-click Setup. The client installation begins.

The WinSock Proxy client can be removed from the system by selecting Uninstall from the Microsoft Proxy Client group that was created during the installation process. The client installation makes the following changes to the client computer:

➤ The LAT file (MSPLAT.TXT) is copied to the client. Proxy Server updates this file on a regular basis.

- ➤ Windows-based clients (Windows 3.x, Windows 95, Windows NT) have a WSP client icon added to the Control Panel.

- ➤ A Microsoft Proxy Client program group is created.

- ➤ WINSOCK.DLL is renamed WINSOCK.DLX and replaced with Remote WinSock from WinSock Proxy client.

- ➤ MSPCLNT.INI is copied to the client.

Once the WinSock Proxy client is installed, the client can only gain access to the external network (Internet) through Proxy Server. If direct access is needed, the client can temporarily disable the WinSock Proxy client. The procedures to disable and enable the WinSock Proxy client are described in the following lists.

To disable the Winsock Proxy client:

1. In the Control Panel, open the WSP Client applet.

2. Clear the Enable WinSock Proxy Client checkbox and reboot the system.

To re-enable the WinSock Proxy client:

1. In the Control Panel, open the WinSock Proxy Client applet.

2. Select the Enable WinSock Proxy Client checkbox and reboot the system.

Exam Prep Questions

Question 1

You're planning on installing Microsoft Proxy Server 2.0 on your Windows NT Server 4 computer. The server has one NIC and uses NWLink for communications on the local network. Which of the following tasks do you need to do? [Check all correct answers]

❑ a. Install Windows NT Workstation version 4

❑ b. Install a second NIC

❑ c. Configure TCP/IP for the second network card

❑ d. Install IIS, if not installed

❑ e. Apply Microsoft Service Pack 3.0 or later

❑ f. Apply Microsoft Service Pack 2.0 or later

❑ g. Install NetBEUI

The correct answers to this question are b, c, d, and e. A second NIC with TCP/IP, IIS, and Service Pack 3 must be installed for Proxy Server to operate. Proxy Server 2.0 will not run on Windows NT Workstation computers, so answer a is incorrect. Service Pack 2.0 does not include the correct components for Proxy Server, so answer f is incorrect. Proxy Server 2.0 does not support the NetBEUI protocol, so answer g is incorrect.

Question 2

You want to install an additional drive for proxy caching. Which of the following tasks do you need to do? [Check all correct answers]

❑ a. Create a FAT partition

❑ b. Create an NTFS partition

❑ c. Create an HPFS partition

❑ d. Reconfigure caching under WinSock Proxy Service Properties

❑ e. Reconfigure caching under Web Proxy Service Properties

After installing a new disk to be used for caching, it must be formatted as an NTFS partition, then added to the cache through the Web Proxy Service Properties applet. Therefore, answers b and e are correct. Proxy Server caches cannot be installed on FAT or HPFS partitions, so answers a and c are incorrect. Caching is a function of Web Proxy, not WinSock Proxy Server, so answer d is incorrect.

Question 3

> You want to install Microsoft Proxy Server 2.0 to provide support for 200 Web Proxy client computers. What is the minimum recommended disk space you need to allocate for caching?
>
> ○ a. 100MB
>
> ○ b. 200MB
>
> ○ c. 300MB
>
> ○ d. 500MB
>
> ○ e. 1GB

The correct answer to this question is b, 200MB. This takes into account a 100MB base for caching plus 200 multiplied by .5MB per client. 100MB is the minimum required for Proxy Server caching, but does not take into account the number of clients. Therefore answer a is incorrect. Because the question asks for the minimum amount of disk space required for caching, and not the ideal amount of disk space for caching, answers c, d, and e are incorrect.

Question 4

> You're planning to install Microsoft Proxy Server 2.0. The computer you plan to use as the proxy server is running Windows NT Server 4 with Service Pack 2, TCP/IP, and IIS 3.0. The computer has a Pentium 100MHz processor, a 512K pipeline burst cache, and 16MB of RAM with a 4GB disk drive and 500MB of free space. A 10BaseT network adapter connects the computer to your LAN, and an ISDN modem using Microsoft Dial-Up Networking connects it to the Internet. You want to host 100 Web Proxy clients on your LAN. Which of the following Microsoft installation recommended requirements have not been met? [Check all correct answers]
>
> ❑ a. Memory
>
> ❑ b. Software requirements
>
> ❑ c. Web Proxy cache
>
> ❑ d. Processor
>
> ❑ e. Network connection
>
> ❑ f. Internet connection

The computer configuration listed in the question falls short in two areas: memory and software requirements. Therefore, answers a and b are correct. For the number of users listed, at least 32MB of RAM is needed. In addition, Service Pack 3.0 is required for Proxy Server 2.0. The disk space, processor, network connection, and Internet connection for the system are sufficient to support 100 clients, so answers c, d, e, and f are incorrect.

Question 5

> You're configuring the LAT for a proxy server. Which addresses need to be included in the LAT? [Check all correct answers]
>
> ❏ a. IP addresses of your internal network computers
>
> ❏ b. IP address of your ISP's DNS server
>
> ❏ c. IP address of the network card that attaches to your ISP
>
> ❏ d. IP addresses of all external Web sites you want your clients to access
>
> ❏ e. IP addresses on the network cards in your system that attach to the LAN

By default, the LAT consists of IP addresses of the computers on your internal network and the addresses of the NICs in your proxy server attached to the local LAN. Therefore, answers a and e are correct. Neither the IP address of your ISP's DNS server, the IP address of the network card that attaches to the ISP, nor the IP addresses of external Web sites should be included in the local address table. Therefore answers b, c, and d are incorrect.

Question 6

> WinSock Proxy clients can use which naming methods to attach to the Microsoft Proxy Server? [Check all correct answers]
>
> ❏ a. IPX Network Identifier
>
> ❏ b. NetBIOS Scope Identifier
>
> ❏ c. Computer (NetBIOS) name
>
> ❏ d. IP address
>
> ❏ e. IP subnet mask

WinSock Proxy client computers can use either the Proxy Server's computer name or its IP address to connect. Therefore, answers c and d are correct. Although Proxy Server supports IPX, its network identifier cannot be used to connect to Proxy Server, so answer a is incorrect. The NetBIOS Scope ID is used to limit communication between computers, not to identify them, so answer b is incorrect. A computer's IP subnet mask is used to determine whether a destination is local or remote, but has no bearing on the computer's identity, so answer e is incorrect.

Question 7

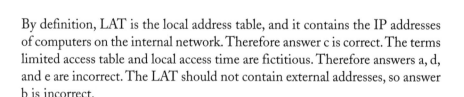

Which of the following is the best definition for the LAT?

○ a. The LAT, or limited access table, defines the IP addresses that belong to the internal network adapters on the MS Proxy Server computer.

○ b. The LAT, or local address table, defines the IP addresses that belong to the external network.

○ c. The LAT, or local address table, defines the IP addresses that belong to the internal network.

○ d. The LAT, or limited access table, defines the IP addresses of all the routers attached to the local network.

○ e. The LAT, or local access time, defines the MS Proxy Server availability hours and user access control list.

By definition, LAT is the local address table, and it contains the IP addresses of computers on the internal network. Therefore answer c is correct. The terms limited access table and local access time are fictitious. Therefore answers a, d, and e are incorrect. The LAT should not contain external addresses, so answer b is incorrect.

Question 8

Which file acts as a custom LAT that can be placed on the client computer?

○ a. LAT.TXT

○ b. MSPLAT.TXT

○ c. MSCLIENT.TXT

○ d. LOCALLAT.TXT

The file LOCALLAT.TXT acts as a custom LAT and is placed on the client computer in the \Mspclnt directory. Therefore answer d is correct. LAT.TXT and MSCLIENT.TXT do not exist, so answers a and c are incorrect. MSPLAT.TXT is the full LAT maintained on the server, but it is not customized for a client computer, so answer b is incorrect.

Question 9

When using Microsoft Proxy Server 2.0 to connect to an external network, you should always configure a default gateway on a network adapter that is used to connect your Proxy Server computer to your internal network.

○ a. True

○ b. False

The default gateway setting should be set to a network adapter on the external network. Therefore answer b is correct.

Question 10

> You administer a 400 client LAN. Your internal network uses IPX/SPX only for communications; however, some clients have TCP/IP installed for RAS to remote clients. You want to install Microsoft Proxy Server and have all client computers connect to the Internet through Proxy Server.
>
> **Required Result:**
>
> - All client computers must use IPX/SPX to connect to the Microsoft Proxy Server.
>
> **Optional Desired Results:**
>
> - Client computers that are using TCP/IP for RAS can continue to do so.
>
> - Client computers will use Proxy Server to publish internal Web pages.
>
> **Proposed Solution:**
>
> Install Microsoft Proxy Server, and configure it to connect to the Internet using TCP/IP and enable IPX/SPX on the proxy server as well. Install the WinSock Proxy client on all the client computers. Check the Force IPX/SPX protocol on the WinSock Proxy client computers.
>
> What results does the proposed solution produce?
>
> ○ a. The proposed solution produces the required result and produces both of the optional desired results.
>
> ○ b. The proposed solution produces the required result, but only one of the optional desired results.
>
> ○ c. The proposed solution produces the required result, but neither of the optional desired results.
>
> ○ d. The proposed solution does not produce the required result.

The proposed solution will continue to allow client computers to use IPX/SPX and allow client computers using TCP/IP and RAS to continue to do so, but it will not provide client computers the ability to use the proxy server to publish Web pages. Therefore answer b is correct.

Need To Know More?

 For more information on the subjects covered in this chapter, consult the online documentation that ships with Microsoft Proxy Server 2.0 or any of the following TechNet articles:

➤ TechNet Article Q164088: "Hardware and Software Requirements."

➤ TechNet Article Q164084: "When Is a Proxy Server Needed?"

➤ TechNet Article Q174922: "Microsoft Proxy Server 2.0 Release Notes."

➤ TechNet Article Q140965: "How to Search for Proxy Server KB Articles by Topic."

Proxy Server Protocols

. . . .

Terms you'll need to understand:

√ IP address

√ Subnet mask

√ CIDR

√ Address class

√ Dotted-decimal format

√ Loopback address

√ InterNIC

√ IANA

√ Port

√ Well-known ports

Techniques you'll need to master:

√ Using subnet masks to determine the network ID and host ID of an address

√ Understanding the structure of the TCP/IP protocol suite

√ Understanding TCP and UDP ports

Because TCP/IP is the protocol of the Internet, you need to understand how TCP/IP operates, how it's addressed, and how it's used to communicate over the Internet. Microsoft has an entire test dedicated to TCP/IP and its implementation. Although it's not necessary to understand all facets of TCP/IP for the Proxy Server exam, TCP/IP and its protocols play a significant role in the Proxy Server environment and should be examined.

The TCP/IP Protocol Suite

As a point of reference, it's important to know how TCP/IP was created and how it's structured. TCP/IP is a suite of protocols developed by the Department of Defense's (DOD) Advanced Research Projects Agency (ARPA). ARPA envisioned a network where researchers at the DOD, corporations, and universities in different parts of the country could share information with one another easily and quickly. Out of the need for interconnectivity and interoperability between the disparate computers running at the different sites, the TCP/IP suite was created. The Internet Protocol (IP) was designed to provide transport across a packet-switched network connecting the sites. The interoperability questions were addressed by the creation of many hardware-independent application protocols that worked together to form a comprehensive group, called a *suite*. Application protocols were created for file transfer and management, email, terminal emulation, printing, and network management.

In September of 1969, four sites were combined to create the Advanced Research Projects Agency Network (ARPANet). This network quickly grew to connect all major colleges and universities, eventually allowing connections from corporations not involved in research. Because the DOD originally funded ARPANet, it was deemed a public domain. This was the beginning of today's Internet.

TCP/IP's vast acceptance has been driven by its use in the Unix environment and its ability to interconnect divergent technologies. TCP/IP is by far the most widely used suite of protocols today and is expected to continue to be number one for the foreseeable future. The TCP/IP suite has grown from just a few protocols in 1969 to over 100 individual protocols today. These protocols do everything from managing files, to providing calendaring and scheduling functions, to transporting for World Wide Web pages, to configuring a computer's IP settings automatically.

TCP/IP Structure

The TCP/IP suite is named for its two primary protocols—the Transmission Control Protocol (TCP) and the Internet Protocol (IP). Its protocols are divided into three categories according to their function:

➤ **Application protocols** Protocols such as FTP (used for file transfer and manipulation), SMTP (provides email transfer), and Telnet (a terminal emulation protocol that provides specific functions and interfaces for the user).

➤ **Network protocols** The most prevalent of these is the IP protocol. They move packets around the network and are responsible for addressing and routing them.

➤ **Transport protocols** TCP and UDP are examples of transport protocols. They ensure delivery between computers. They are responsible for providing a low-layer connection for the applications through mechanisms such as flow control.

You should know how these protocols interrelate and how they're used in a Proxy Server environment. The following list describes some of the most-used TCP/IP protocols:

➤ **Address Resolution Protocol (ARP)** ARP is a Network layer protocol that provides logical (IP) address to physical (MAC) address association. As you know, the network interface card (NIC) in a computer looks for packets with its physical address. IP has no knowledge of this address and, therefore, uses ARP to discover the MAC address for a particular IP address. ARP does this by sending a broadcast that requests the MAC address.

➤ **File Transfer Protocol (FTP)** FTP is an upper-layer protocol that encompasses the Session, Presentation, and Application layers. It's used for file transfer, file manipulation, and directory manipulation.

➤ **Hypertext Transfer Protocol (HTTP)** HTTP is perhaps the most widely used protocol today. This upper-layer protocol is used to deliver World Wide Web (WWW) documents that have been written in HTML and other markup languages.

➤ **Internet Control Message Protocol (ICMP)** ICMP is another Network layer protocol that is used to send control messages. The PING utility uses ICMP to request a response from a remote host. ICMP provides information, such as whether or not the response was received and how long it took to make the trip.

➤ **Internet Protocol (IP)** IP is a Network layer protocol that provides source and destination addressing and routing.

➤ **Routing Information Protocol (RIP)** RIP is used to distribute route information throughout a network. It's a Network layer protocol that uses distance-vector routing algorithms to identify the best path through an internetwork.

➤ **Simple Mail Transport Protocol (SMTP)** Another upper-layer protocol, SMTP is used by messaging programs such as email.

➤ **Simple Network Management Protocol (SNMP)** SNMP is used to manage network devices. It can be used to configure devices, such as bridges, repeaters, and gateways, as well as monitor network events using MIBs and SNMP managers.

➤ **Telnet** Surprisingly not an acronym, Telnet is an upper-layer protocol that is used for remote terminal emulation. It allows users to act as if they were directly connected to the computer. Telnet is most often used as a configuration interface for networking devices, such as routers, and as a terminal program for mainframe and microcomputer systems.

➤ **Transmission Control Protocol (TCP)** TCP is a connection-oriented Transport layer protocol that accepts messages of any length from the upper layers and provides transportation to another computer. TCP is responsible for packet fragmentation and reassembly, and sequencing.

➤ **User Datagram Protocol (UDP)** UDP is the counterpart to TCP. It provides connectionless Transport layer functions for the TCP/IP suite.

IP Addressing And Subnet Masks

As mentioned earlier, IP is responsible for addressing and routing packets through the network. To understand how this works, let's take a look at how all packets are addressed.

Before a packet is placed on a network, it is given a physical source and destination address. These addresses tell the computers on the network where a packet came from and where it's going. The physical address for a computer is its Media Access Control (MAC) address. In most cases, the MAC address is burned into the network interface card's (NIC's) ROM when the card is created.

As the packet traverses the wire, each computer looks at the destination address to determine whether it is the destination. If so, it reads the packet, including the source information, and acts on the data in the packet.

Just knowing the physical address of a computer works fine in a small environment where there are no networking devices, such as routers or gateways. Could you imagine, though, if your computer had to know the physical address of every computer on the Internet to communicate? What if every router that makes up the Internet had this information? In addition, how many people know the MAC address of their computer or even their server? Not many.

IP uses a logical address that is assigned to each computer. Each IP address is 32 bits long and is represented as 4 bytes in decimal format. Hearken back to your binary-to-decimal conversion days. Each bit can be either on (1) or off (0). The decimal value of the number is calculated from right to left with each consecutive bit worth twice the previous bit. The first bit on the right is worth either 0 or 1, the second bit from the right is worth either 0 or 2, the third bit is worth either 0 or 4, and so on through 8, 16, 32, 64, and 128. If there are 8 bits together, the decimal representation can be from 0 (00000000) to 255 (11111111 or 1+2+4+8+16+32+64+128), which gives us 256 combinations of numbers. Table 4.1 shows a few other decimal representations of a byte.

To delineate between each byte in an IP address, the bytes are written in what is called *dotted-decimal format*. Each byte is separated by a period (or *dot*). Therefore, an IP address looks something like this: 205.199.10.1. Remember, though, that this is just a representation of the 32 bits that make up the address.

Table 4.1 Decimal representations of a byte.		
Bit Pattern	**Decimal Equivalent**	**The Math Involved**
10000000	128	0+0+0+0+0+0+0+128
01001100	76	0+0+4+8+0+0+64+0
01011100	92	0+0+4+8+16+0+64+0
11000000	192	0+0+0+0+0+0+64+128
01111111	127	1+2+4+8+16+32+67+0
11111010	250	0+2+0+8+16+32+64+128
00001010	10	0+2+0+8+0+0+0+0
01100011	99	0+2+4+0+0+0+64+128
10101001	169	1+0+4+0+16+0+0+128

Note: Although IP addresses can range from 0–255, certain addresses are reserved for special use. Numbers 0 and 255 are reserved for broadcasts and should be used in host IDs only in special situations. In addition, any address beginning with 127 is treated as a loopback address. If a program, such as PING, uses this address, the traffic does not hit the network.

IP addresses are assigned and maintained by the InterNIC. It is the InterNIC's responsibility to ensure that computers connected to the Internet have unique addresses. However, with the growth of TCP/IP and the Internet, unique addresses are in short supply. InterNIC has taken a number of steps to ease this problem, some of which will be discussed later in this chapter in the section titled "Subnet Masks." One of the biggest steps taken has been to assign particular addresses as private addresses, meaning they cannot be used to connect to the Internet. For companies that have closed and secure environments, these addresses are ideal. Three groups of addresses have been assigned as private addresses according to class, which is discussed in the next section. Here are the private addresses:

➤ Addresses beginning with 10 (one Class A address)

➤ Addresses beginning with 172.16 through 172.31 (16 Class B addresses)

➤ Addresses beginning with 192.168.0 through 192.168.255 (256 Class C addresses)

Private addresses cannot be sent over the Internet. If an Internet router receives a packet with either a source or destination address that is private, it drops the packet.

Address Classes

By definition, an *internetwork* is a group of interconnected networks that operate autonomously. In an internetwork, each network is assigned an address, and it's the responsibility of networking devices, such as routers, to move packets through the internetwork.

In a network using IPX/SPX, the network address is assigned by the administrator and is a hexadecimal representation of the bits in the address field. IPX then uses the MAC address of the NIC to ensure the packet reaches its destination. An IPX packet includes separate fields for the network and host address. In contrast, IP uses a single address for both network and host.

The IP address class system was developed to delineate which bits of the IP address represent the network ID and which bits represent the host ID for a particular computer. The class of an IP address is defined by the value of the first octet of the address. The IP address class system is broken down this way:

➤ **Class A** The first octet is assigned by InterNIC, which leaves the last three octets to be assigned by the administrator. Class A addresses begin with ID numbers between 1 and 126. These addresses were designed with very large corporations in mind. A single Class A address provides for 16,387,064 (254 * 254 * 254) hosts. That's a lot of computers!

➤ **Class B** The first two octets are assigned by InterNIC and begin with IDs between 128 and 191. This leaves the last two octets for host IDs and provides 64,516 hosts per network.

➤ **Class C** The first three octets are assigned by InterNIC and begin with IDs between 192 and 223. A Class C address can have up to 254 hosts.

With internetworks using the class system, the network ID/host ID delineation is along octet lines. Even if a corporation has been assigned a Class B address—if it has no need for more than 254 hosts on a network, or for many networks—it can use a Class C delineation.

Subnet Masks

The delineation between network ID and host ID is made by using a subnet mask. This section of the IP packet specifies which bits of the IP address denote the network ID and which bits denote the host ID. As mentioned earlier, in networks using the class system, this distinction is made along class boundaries. Subnet masks are also written in dotted-decimal format. Let's look at how a computer decides which part of an address is the network ID and which part is the host ID by using a subnet mask. It's important to understand subnet masking because this is where many IP problems start.

Remember that IP addresses are 32 bits long. Subnet masks are also 32 bits long and are used by the computer to determine whether the packet's destination is on the local subnet or a remote subnet by making the delineation between network ID and host ID. Bits in a subnet mask are set to 1 starting at the far left. Each bit that is turned on denotes the network ID of the IP address, either source or destination. For example, an IP address using a Class A subnet mask has the first eight bits set to 1. This means that the first octet denotes the network, whereas the remaining three octets are the host ID. Here are a few examples of how this works:

```
IP address:        100.202.230.99
Subnet Mask:       255.255.255.0 (Class C)
```

```
Binary Address:      01100100   11001010   11100110   01100011
Binary Mask:         11111111   11111111   11111111   00000000
Binary Network ID:   01100100   11001010   11100110
Binary Host ID:                                        01100011
Decimal Network ID: 100.202.230
Decimal Host ID:     99


IP address:          87.104.10.19
Subnet Mask:         255.0.0.0 (Class A)
Binary Address:      01010111   01000100   00001010   00010011
Binary Mask:         11111111   00000000   00000000   00000000
Binary Network ID:   01010111
Binary Host ID:                 01000100   00001010   01100011
Decimal Network ID: 87
Decimal Host ID:     104.10.19


IP address:          87.104.10.19
Subnet Mask:         255.255.0.0 (Class B)
Binary Address:      01010111   01000100   00001010   00010011
Binary Mask:         11111111   11111111   00000000   00000000
Binary Network ID:   01010111   01000100
Binary Host ID:                            00001010   01100011
Decimal Network ID: 87.104
Decimal Host ID:     10.19
```

As you can see, even if a Class A address is used, it can have a different subnet mask to provide more networks with fewer hosts per network. If you think about it from a routing perspective, it makes sense. If, for example, a very large corporation has an internetwork covering the entire U.S. and parts of Europe, it would probably get a Class B address from the InterNIC. If this company used its Class B address with only Class B subnet masks, it would have one very large network. From an IP perspective, every host would be on the same subnet and no routing would take place. All packets would be sent to all sites, thus leading to IP chaos. However, the company could use the Class B address with a Class C mask and have 254 individual subnets with 254 hosts per subnet. This type of configuration is much more manageable and gives the routers something to do. Just imagine what would happen with a Class A address using a Class A mask—16 million hosts across the globe with no routing. For this reason, you'll most often find Class C masks being used.

However, with the growth of the Internet and TCP/IP, even using the class system, there aren't enough IP addresses to go around. How many companies do you know that have less than 100 computers to connect to the Internet? If each of these companies were given a Class C address—in the beginning they were—the addresses would quickly disappear. As mentioned earlier, this is one reason the private IP addresses were reserved for companies not connecting to the Internet. However, something else had to be done to make the most of the available addresses until the next generation of TCP/IP is introduced.

To work around this problem, Classless InterDomain Routing (CIDR) was introduced. CIDR (pronounced *cider*) removes the class boundaries for subnet masks and introduces a new system for determining the network and host ID of an address. Rather than using the dotted-decimal notation, CIDR specifies the exact number of bits representing the network ID. This specification is written as a number following a slash after the IP address: 202.248.130.128 / 26. In this case, the network ID occupies the first 26 bits of the 32-bit address. The following two examples show how CIDR works:

```
IP address:        152.98.212.156
Subnet Mask:       /26 (CIDR)
Binary Address:    10011000   01100010   11010100   10011100
Binary Mask:       11111111   11111111   11111111   11000000
Binary Network ID: 10011000   01100010   11010100   10
Binary Host ID:                                        011100
Decimal Network ID:152.98.212.128
Decimal Host ID:   28

IP address:        129.8.242.156
Subnet Mask:       /21 (CIDR)
Binary Address:    10000001   00001000   11110010   10011100
Binary Mask:       11111111   11111111   11111000   00000000
Binary Network ID: 10000001   00001000   11111
Binary Host ID:                           010        10011100
Decimal Network ID:129.8.240
Decimal Host ID:   2.156
```

By using this method, Internet Service Providers (ISPs) and the InterNIC can provide a company with an address or range of addresses to fit its needs more specifically. This also means that an ISP can get one Class B address from InterNIC and provide addresses for a larger number of companies.

As mentioned earlier, the subnet mask helps the computer determine whether the destination is on the local network or a remote network. When the packet is addressed, the computer looks at the network ID and determines whether it matches its own network ID. If so, it sends the packet down the wire, knowing it will reach its destination. If not, it sends the packet to a gateway.

TCP And UDP Ports

As mentioned earlier, the Transmission Control Protocol (TCP) is the primary transport protocol of the TCP/IP suite. It's a connection-oriented protocol that provides reliable service across a network, including the Internet. TCP also increases its reliability by using acknowledgments, flow control, and checksum information. In contrast, the User Datagram Protocol (UDP), which is not used as often as TCP, is a connectionless protocol that does not provide guaranteed delivery.

Although they approach network communication differently, both protocols utilize the same method to identify which application is sending and receiving data—ports. A *port* is used to name the ends of logical connections that carry on long-term conversations. Most TCP/IP protocols have been assigned their own port between 0 and 1023. These are called *well-known ports* and are assigned by the Internet Assigned Numbers Authority (IANA). Other TCP/IP applications, such as proprietary programs, use ports above 1023. Table 4.2 is a partial list of the well-known ports used in TCP/IP.

Because every packet that uses TCP includes port information, filters can be setup to permit or deny a particular type of application communication on the network. Microsoft Proxy Server takes full advantage of this option, and it's very important to know the most often used ports to successfully configure a proxy server. A complete list of the well-known ports is available at http://www.isi.edu/in-notes/iana/assignments/port-numbers.

Table 4.2 The IANA has assigned well-known port numbers to most TCP/IP protocols and functions.		
Port Number	**Keyword**	**Description**
20	ftp-data	Port used to transfer data using FTP
21	ftp	Control port used by FTP
23	telnet	Port used by Telnet
25	smtp	Port used by SMTP (email)
80	www	Port used by HTTP (WWW)
137	netbios-ns	Port used by the NetBIOS Name Service
161	snmp	Port used by SNMP
532	netnews	Readnews port

Exam Prep Questions

Question 1

> Which type of protocol provides addressing and routing functions?
>
> ○ a. Transport
>
> ○ b. Network
>
> ○ c. Application
>
> ○ d. Routing

The correct answer to this question is b. Network protocols provide addressing and routing functions. Transport protocols ensure delivery between computers. Therefore, answer a is incorrect. Application protocols provide an interface to the user. Therefore, answer c is incorrect. Routing protocols, such as RIP, are a subset of Network protocols, but do not provide addressing information. Therefore, answer d is incorrect.

Question 2

> Which ports are considered well-known ports?
>
> ○ a. Ports greater than 100
>
> ○ b. Ports less than 1000
>
> ○ c. Ports less than 1023
>
> ○ d. Ports greater than 1023

The correct answer to this question is c. Well-known ports are those ports below 1023. All other answers are incorrect.

Question 3

> Which of the following governing bodies of the Internet is responsible for assigning IP addresses?
>
> ○ a. InterNIC
>
> ○ b. IEEE
>
> ○ c. IANA
>
> ○ d. IETF

The correct answer to this question is a. The InterNIC is responsible for assigning IP addresses. Although the IEEE is a governing body, it develops networking standards, not IP addresses. Therefore, answer b is incorrect. The IANA is responsible for well-known ports, whereas the IETF is responsible for RFCs. Therefore, answers c and d are incorrect.

Question 4

Which of the following is the correct binary representation of the number 216?

○ a. 11001000

○ b. 11011000

○ c. 10011000

○ d. 11001100

The correct answer to this question is b. Answer a is the binary representation of 200, answer c is the binary representation of 152, and answer d is the binary representation of 204. Therefore, answers a, c, and d are all incorrect.

Question 5

Which of the following are examples of Application protocols? [Check all correct answers]

❑ a. Telnet

❑ b. RIP

❑ c. FTP

❑ d. IP

The correct answers to this question are a and c. Telnet and FTP are Application protocols. RIP and IP are both Network protocols. Therefore, answers b and d are incorrect.

Question 6

> Which of the following is the CIDR representation of a Class B
> subnet mask?
>
> ○ a. /12
>
> ○ b. /26
>
> ○ c. /24
>
> ○ d. /16

The correct answer to this question is d (/16). Answer c (/24) is the CIDR
representation for a Class C mask, whereas answers a and b are truly classless
masks.

Question 7

> Which of the following is used by a computer to determine the
> network ID portion of an IP address?
>
> ○ a. Subnet mask
>
> ○ b. Gateway
>
> ○ c. DNS server
>
> ○ d. network=

Answer a is correct. A computer uses its subnet mask to determine the network ID portion of its address. A gateway is used to send data to remote
networks. Therefore, answer b is incorrect. A DNS server is used to resolve
host names to IP addresses. Therefore, answer c is incorrect. Finally, there is no
such setting as network=. Therefore, answer d is incorrect.

Question 8

> Which of the following are not valid IP addresses? [Check all cor-
> rect answers]
>
> ❏ a. 199.199.200.200
>
> ❏ b. 156.1.256.2
>
> ❏ c. 1.1.1.1
>
> ❏ d. 299.199.299.1

Answers b and d are correct. IP addresses must be between 0 and 255 because they are a decimal representation of 8 bits. Although they may look odd, 199.199.200.200 and 1.1.1.1 are valid IP addresses. 256 and 299 are not valid IP addresses. Therefore, answers a and c are incorrect.

Question 9

> Which of the following protocols provides connectionless transport for the TCP/IP protocol suite?
>
> ○ a. UDP
> ○ b. TCP
> ○ c. FTP
> ○ d. HTTP

The correct answer to this question is a, UDP. TCP is a connection-oriented protocol. Therefore, answer b is incorrect. FTP and HTTP rely on TCP for transport. Therefore, answers c and d are incorrect.

Question 10

> Using the Class system, which of the following network numbers would be assigned by the InterNIC?
>
> ○ a. 12.199.0.0
> ○ b. 192.134.0.0
> ○ c. 135.119.0.0
> ○ d. 255.255.0.0

The correct answer to this question is c. The network number 135.119.0.0 is a Class B address (indicated by 135 in the first octet) and would be assigned by the InterNIC. The network number 12.199.0.0 is a Class A address; InterNIC would only assign the first octet, not the first two. Therefore, answer a is incorrect. The inverse applies to answer b, 192.134.0.0. This is a Class C address and InterNIC would assign the first three octets, not just two. The network number 255.255.0.0 is a Class B subnet mask and would not be assigned by the InterNIC. Therefore, answer d is incorrect.

Need To Know More?

 Stevens, W. Richard. *TCP/IP Illustrated, Volume 1*. Addison-Wesley Publishing Company, Reading, Massachusetts, 1994. ISBN 0-201-63346-9. The entire book provides detailed information on TCP/IP and how it works.

 Tittel, Ed, Kurt Hudson, and J. Michael Stewart. *MCSE TCP/IP Exam Cram*. Certification Insider Press, Scottsdale, Arizona, 1998. ISBN 1-57610-195-9. Chapters 2, 4, and 5 provide information on the architecture of TCP/IP, IP addressing, and subnet masks.

 Microsoft TechNet. January, 1998. Searches on "TCP," "UDP," "well-known ports," and "subnet masks" will yield a wealth of information.

 A complete list of the well-known ports is available at http://www.isi.edu/in-notes/iana/assignments/port-numbers.

Proxy Server Security

. . . .

Terms you'll need to understand:

✓ Packet filtering

✓ Inbound access

✓ Outbound access

✓ Reverse proxy

✓ Reverse hosting

Techniques you'll need to master:

✓ Planning Proxy Server security

✓ Implementing packet filtering

✓ Implementing Internet service control

✓ Implementing domain filters

✓ Implementing port filters

✓ Configuring logging and alerting

✓ Configuring secure Web publishing

Microsoft Proxy Server 2.0 provides and controls Internet access to internal clients, as well as some level of security by default. However, as you'll see in the following sections, the default security for Proxy Server can be enhanced to limit who has access to specific resources on the Internet, what types of packets are allowed through the server, and also what traffic, if any, is accepted from the Internet.

Proxy Server Security Overview

As you've learned, Microsoft Proxy Server 2.0 acts as a firewall to protect your internal network from the Internet. To provide this functionality in the most effective manner, Microsoft has implemented a very dynamic security model with Proxy Server 2.0.

Many Proxy Server installations are outbound only, which means they provide secure Internet access to clients on the internal network. As you'll see shortly, this traffic can be filtered to restrict access to particular sites, services, domains, ports, and addresses. Implementing outbound filters allows you a high level of control over traffic on your network.

However, Proxy Server also supports Internet access to your internal network. By default, this option is not enabled and must be configured manually. Inbound access controls are as dynamic as outbound controls and provide the most secure access possible. Inbound traffic is controlled by utilizing the Windows NT security structure, such as Challenge/Response authentication, and by filtering packets by packet type.

Finally, Proxy Server supports encryption through Secure Sockets Layer (SSL) tunneling, Point-to-Point Tunneling Protocol (PPTP), and extensions to the ISAPI applications and filters.

By implementing each of these security measures at varying levels, Proxy Server provides granularity to its security structure that fits well in any environment.

Controlling Internet Access (Coming And Going)

When determining the security structure for a Proxy Server implementation, decisions about which direction traffic will be allowed are vital. As mentioned earlier, Microsoft Proxy Server 2.0 provides access control for both inbound (from the Internet to the local LAN) and outbound (from the local LAN to the Internet) traffic. Figure 5.1 illustrates this distinction.

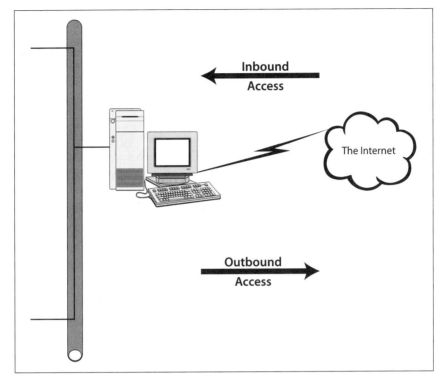

Figure 5.1   Inbound and outbound access can be controlled via Proxy Server.

Controlling Inbound Access

One of the most important considerations when implementing Proxy Server is whether access will be granted to incoming traffic. As mentioned earlier, this configuration is disabled by default, and must be enabled specifically. Once this decision has been made, there are a few ways access to the local LAN can be restricted.

IP Forwarding

IP forwarding takes place when a multihomed computer is configured to pass TCP/IP packets from one network interface card to the other. By default, this option is disabled. The temptation when connecting your LAN to the Internet for services is to enable IP forwarding. By doing this, however, you are opening your LAN to the whole Internet, which is not a safe prospect.

As an alternative to enabling IP forwarding, Microsoft Proxy Server provides a facility to route all IP traffic that is received to specific addresses on your network. This is done by using the local address table (LAT) to restrict access from the Internet to your network. As mentioned in Chapter 3, the LAT is a list of all IP addresses on your local network. However, this can be edited to include only those addresses to which Internet clients will be granted access, thus decreasing the security impact on your network.

Separating Domains

An additional method of limiting Internet client access is to create an Internet-accessible domain. This is done by installing Proxy Server as the Primary Domain Controller (PDC) for a separate domain and then granting a one-way trust between the user domain and the proxy domain. In this configuration, local users are granted access to the proxy server and the Internet, but remote users are only able to access the servers in the Internet-accessible domain, such as the proxy server or an IIS server. In this configuration, the proxy domain is the trusting domain, whereas the user domain is trusted.

Packet Filtering

Finally, inbound access to the network can be controlled on a packet level by enabling packet filtering. Packet filtering evaluates each packet sent from the Internet before it reaches the Proxy Server services. By utilizing this option, you are able to accept or deny traffic based on packet types, datagrams, or packet fragments. This option is configured through the Internet Services Manager (ISM)|Web Proxy Configuration|Security applet, as shown in Figure 5.2.

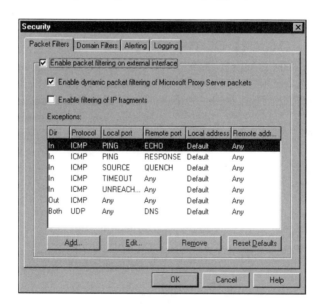

Figure 5.2 Packet filtering is enabled through the Packet Filters tab of the Proxy Server Security applet.

Packet filtering operates in one of two modes—dynamic or static. *Dynamic packet filtering* opens designated ports automatically to transmit or receive, or both, and then closes the ports immediately after a connection has been terminated by one of the Proxy services. This minimizes the number of open ports and provides a high degree of security while requiring little administration.

Static packet filtering allows you to manually configure packet filters through the user interface (refer to Figure 5.2). Although this method is more secure than dynamic filtering, it also requires a high level of administration and is not recommended for most installations. However, if you access the Internet from the same computer that is running Proxy Server, static filters are required.

Controlling Outbound Access

One of the many features of Microsoft Proxy Server 2.0 is its ability to restrict outbound traffic to specific Internet sites. Outbound access can be controlled in three ways:

➤ By Internet service

➤ By IP address, subnet, or domain

➤ By TCP or UDP port number

Internet service control and IP address, subnet, or domain control all work with the Web Proxy service. Port control is a function of the WinSock Proxy service.

Internet Service Control

Internet service control is the most basic of the outbound access controls available. It restricts access by user or group to FTP Read, Gopher, Secure, and Web services, as shown in Figure 5.3. Internet service control is managed through the Permissions tab of the Web Proxy Service Properties applet.

Note that, by default, unlike most NT configurations, no user is granted access to any service. It is recommended that only specific users are granted specific access to the Internet through this control.

IP Address, Subnet, Or Domain Control

Configuring this option requires direct Internet access for the proxy server. It allows you to restrict Internet site access by specifying IP addresses, subnets, or domains to which users are granted or denied access. This configuration is also enabled through the Domain Filters tab of the Security dialog (see Figure 5.4) of the Web Proxy Service Properties applet.

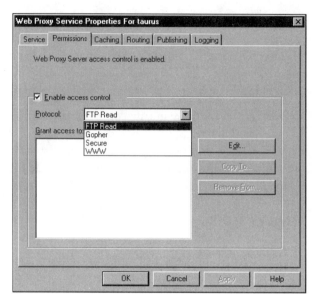

Figure 5.3 Permissions are assigned to users and groups through the Web Proxy Service Properties applet.

Note that the administrator has the option to grant or deny access, by default. An exception list is created by clicking Add. If your security plan calls for limited Internet access, select the Denied option and then create a specific

Figure 5.4 Outbound access can be restricted by IP address, subnet, or domain.

list of domains, subnets, or addresses to which internal users will be granted access.

Port Control

Ports serviced by the WinSock Proxy service are configured through the Protocols tab of the WinSock Proxy Service Properties applet, as shown in Figure 5.5.

This is the most restrictive of the three outbound control types, but it's also the most specific. Note that it is very easy to misconfigure the port control and deny access to all users.

Server Proxy

Server proxy is another method for controlling outbound access. It allows you to place a server, such as Microsoft Exchange Server, using the Internet Mail Connector (IMC) on your private network behind Microsoft Proxy Server. With this configuration, an Exchange Server computer is loaded with the WinSock Proxy client software and provides Internet mail service while relying on features of Proxy Server 2.0 for protection. An added benefit to this type of configuration is that the Exchange Server computer will not require an additional registered Internet IP address.

Figure 5.5   Port access control is configured through the Protocols tab.

The WinSock Proxy client allows you to bind services or applications to the external network interface of the server computer running Microsoft Proxy Server. Once a service or application is bound on the external network interface, it is then available to hosts on the Internet. The proxy server will then "listen" for connections on behalf of the service or application. For example, if you bind an internal SMTP/POP mail server to the proxy server, mail clients or SMTP servers on the Internet would be able to contact this mail server by connecting to the proxy server's Internet IP address. To remote computers on the Internet, these services will appear to be running on the proxy server.

Encryption

Because Proxy Server integrates closely with Internet Information Server (IIS), it supports encryption using Secure Sockets Layer (SSL) tunneling, Point-to-Point Tunneling Protocol (PPTP), and extensions to ISAPI. SSL tunneling is enabled by default on Proxy Server and is invoked when a user is granted access to the Web Proxy service.

Additional Proxy Server Security Measures

As you've seen, Proxy Server security can be implemented on both inbound and outbound packets through the ISM. In addition to the configurations discussed, Proxy Server is able to alert you when specific events occur and log those events to specific log files, the Event Viewer, or an ODBC database.

Proxy Alerts

As mentioned, Proxy Server can be configured to issue alerts when specific events occur. The ability of Proxy Server to issue realtime alerts enables administrators to be aware of critical or potentially damaging situations as they happen. Proxy Server can monitor and issue alerts for several suspicious network events, including frequency of rejected packets, attempted protocol violations, or storage volumes reaching capacity.

Alerts are configured on the Alerting tab of the Security dialog (see Figure 5.6). This is accessed through the Security button listed under Shared services on the Service tab of the Web, WinSock, or SOCKS Proxy Server's Properties dialog of the ISM.

Alerts are automatically recorded in the packet filtering log and the Proxy Server service logs. In addition, you can include alert messages in the System log viewed through the Event Viewer and send an SMTP email message to an administrator.

Figure 5.6   The Alerting tab of the Security dialog.

A rejected packet alert is issued when a specified number of events occur per second. Rejected packets are packets that are sent to an illegal, unknown, or denied port, are frame/packet anomalous, or are dropped due to too much network traffic. A high rate of rejected packets might indicate an active attack on your network.

A protocol violation event is used when filtered packets or frames that violate the standard structure for protocol packets are found. Packet violations are also common indications of network attacks.

A disk full alert is issued when the storage volume hosting any of the service logs or the packet log becomes full. When this alert is issued, you need to free up space on the volume or alter the destinations of the log files.

 For rejected packets and protocol violation alerts to be issued, packet filtering must be enabled.

From the Alerting tab, you can also click the Configure Mail button to configure the SMTP options or the Reset Default button to return all alert settings back to post-installation defaults.

The Configuration Mail button reveals a configuration box where SMTP email message alert parameters are defined. These include the domain name of the SMTP server, the port (the default for SMTP is 25), the email address of the person to notify, and the name to list as the message originator. Once these parameters are defined, the Test button sends a sample message using the provided parameters.

When using email alerts, it is highly recommended that you use only an internal SMTP email server and not an external public SMTP server. This provides you with the highest level of security and prevents external users from intercepting these alert messages.

Windows NT System Log And Alert Events

If the alert option Report To Windows NT Event Log is selected, each occurrence of an alert is recorded in the System log. Using the Event Viewer, you can review the event recorded in the System log. Each event recorded in the System log is tagged with a source name to indicate what type of event was recorded. Table 5.1 details the source names and what they mean.

Proxy Logging

Proxy Server has multiple logs to record the various activities of the proxy system. For example, a Web Proxy log is configured through the Web Proxy Logging tab shown in Figure 5.7. Each Proxy service—Web, WinSock, and SOCKS—has its own log; plus, a security filtering log records packet traffic-related events. The security filter log only records rejected or dropped packet events.

Table 5.1	The source names listed in the System log for alert events. (This table was taken from Proxy Server 2.0 documentation.)
Source Name	**Description**
MSProxyAdmin	Proxy Server administrative events
PacketFilterLog	Packet filter alert events (filtered frames)
SocksProxy	SOCKS Proxy service events
SocksProxyLog	SOCKS Proxy logging events
WebProxyCache	Web Proxy caching events
WebProxyLog	Web Proxy logging events
WebProxyServer	Web Proxy service events
WinSockProxy	WinSock Proxy service events
WinSockProxyLog	WinSock Proxy logging events

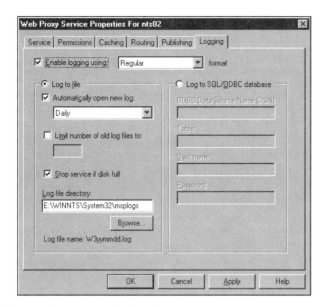

Figure 5.7   The Logging tab of Web Proxy.

Logs are stored in a text file format or in an ODBC-compliant database table format. The database table format is compatible with many database tools, including Microsoft Access and Microsoft SQL Server. Logs can be stored on remote or network drives, but for best performance and security, you should store logs on volumes local to the host server. By default, logging is recorded in a text file when initially enabled.

The configuration tabs for all four of the logs are the same. Logging is enabled by selecting the Enable Logging Using checkbox at the top of the Logging tab.

Logging format can be set to regular or verbose. Regular logging records a limited number of data fields, whereas verbose logging records all available information. Table 5.2 lists the data items that are recorded for each of these log format types.

Table 5.2	The data items recorded in regular or verbose log formats. (This table was taken from Proxy Server 2.0 documentation.)	
Field Name	**Regular Logging**	**Verbose Logging**
Authentication Status (ClientAuthenticate)		X
Bytes Received (BytesRecvd)		X

(continued)

Table 5.2	The data items recorded in regular or verbose log formats. (This table was taken from Proxy Server 2.0 documentation) *(continued)*.

Field Name	Regular Logging	Verbose Logging
Bytes Sent (BytesSent)		X
Client Agent (ClientAgent)		X
Client Computer Name (ClientIP)	X	X
Client Platform (ClientPlatform)		X
Client User Name (ClientUserName)	X	X
Destination Address (DestHostIP)		X
Destination Name (DestHost)	X	X
Destination Port (DestHostPort)	X	X
Log Date (LogDate)	X	X
Log Time (LogTime)	X	X
Object MIME (MimeType)		X
Object Name (URI)	X	X
Object Source (ObjectSource)	X	X
Operation (Operation)		X
Processing Time (ProcessingTime)		X
Protocol Name (Protocol)	X	X
Proxy Name (ServerName)		X
Referring Server Name (ReferredServer)		X
Result Code (ResultCode)	X	X
Service Name (Service)	X	X
Transport (Transport)		X

Log entries may contain extended characters, outside of the normal ASCII characters, supported by text editors and database applications. Make sure the text editor you use to read a text log file is capable of reading and displaying OEM characters (such as Notepad) and that the Data Source Name (DSN) is set to use OEM-to-ANSI conversion for database reading.

Logging To A Text File

Logging to a text file is selected by default. On the Logging tab, the configurations options for text file logging are displayed in the left side. The options are as follows:

➤ Enable new logs to be opened automatically on a daily, weekly, or monthly basis.

➤ Retain only a specified number of old logs.

➤ Stop this service when the disk where log events are recorded becomes full.

➤ Define the directory into which log files are placed. The default is C:\Winnt\System32\Msplogs\.

Here are the automatic names of the log files:

➤ C:\Winnt\System32\Msplogs*W3*<date>.*LOG* for the Web Proxy service

➤ C:\Winnt\System32\Msplogs*WS*<date>.*LOG* for the WinSock Proxy service

➤ C:\Winnt\System32\Msplogs*SP*<date>.*LOG* for the SOCKS Proxy service

➤ C:\Winnt\System32\Msplogs*PF*<date>.*LOG* for packet filter events

The <*date*> portion of the filename is replaced with *yymmdd* for daily logs, W*yymmw* for weekly logs, and M*yymm* for monthly logs, where *yy* is the two digit year (00 through 99), *mm* is the two digit month (01 through 12), *w* is the one digit week within a month (1 through 4), and *dd* is the two digit day of the month (01 through 31).

The data items recorded in a text file are comma delimited. This means each field is separated by a single comma. Be sure that any parsing tools used to convert the log files support CSVs (comma separated values).

Logging To A SQL/ODBC Database

Logging to a SQL/ODBC database file is not selected by default. It must be enabled by selecting the correct radio button on the Logging tab. Open Database Connectivity (ODBC) is a standard API (Application Programming Interface) used to construct platform/application-independent databases. Database logging requires significantly more system resources than text logging; therefore, on heavily trafficked networks, ODBC logging may degrade performance.

The details for creating a SQL or ODBC database are extensive. However, once the database has been created, configuring the Proxy Server service to log to the appropriate database is fairly easy. You must define the ODBC Data Source Name (DSN), Table, Username, and Password parameters for the database, as shown in Figure 5.8.

Service Log Fields

Each of the Proxy Server services—Web Proxy, WinSock Proxy, and SOCKS Proxy—record four types of data in the log files:

➤ Server information

➤ Client information

➤ Connection information

➤ Object information

Server Information Fields

Server information fields contain information that is related to or extracted from the server. These include:

➤ **Log Date** The date of the logged event.

➤ **Log Time** The time of the logged event.

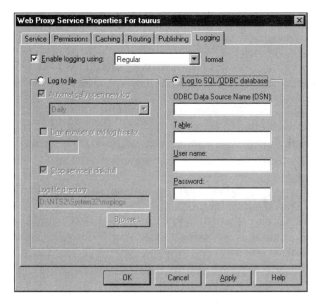

Figure 5.8 Configuration parameters for logging to an ODBC database.

➤ **Proxy Name** The NetBIOS name of the host computer.

➤ **Referring Server Name** The NetBIOS name of the downstream computer that routed the request—only used in chained configurations.

➤ **Service Name** The name of the logged service: "CERNProxy" for Web Proxy; "WSProxy" for WinSock Proxy; and "SOCKS" for SOCKS Proxy.

Client Information Fields

Client information fields contain information that is related to or extracted from the client. The log from Web Proxy contains more client information than the log from WinSock Proxy. Web Proxy clients communicate more information about themselves over HTTP than WinSock applications do. Here are the client log fields:

➤ **Authentication Status** Indicates if an authentic client connection is being used.

➤ **Client Agent** Defines header information from a client browser from Web Proxy or the name of the client application from WinSock Proxy.

➤ **Client Computer Name** The name of the client computer or the proxy name when active caching is transpiring.

➤ **Client Platform** Used only by WinSock to indicate the client operating system, such as 0:3.1 for Windows 3.1 or 2:4.0 for Windows 95 (32 bit).

➤ **Client User Name** The name of the user account currently logged onto the client computer.

Connection Information Fields

Connection information fields contain information that is related to or extracted from the client-to-server or server-to-server connections. They include the following:

➤ **Bytes Received** Used by Web Proxy to indicate the number of bytes received from the client. A hyphen, a zero, or a negative number means this information is not known.

➤ **Bytes Sent** Used by Web Proxy to indicate the number of bytes sent to the client. A hyphen, a zero, or a negative number means this information is not known. Used by WinSock to indicate the number of bytes sent when a connection terminates.

➤ **Destination Address** The IP address for the remote computer providing the requested resource.

> **Destination Name** The domain name for the remote computer providing the requested resource.

> **Destination Port** The reserved port number for the remote computer providing the requested resource.

> **Operation** Used by Web Proxy to indicate the HTTP method used (**GET, PUT, POST,** or **HEAD**). Used by Web Proxy to indicate the current socket API call—**Connect(), Accept(), SendTo(), RecvFrom(), GetHostByName(),** or **Listen()**.

> **Processing Time** Indicates the time, in milliseconds, used by Proxy Server to process a connection.

> **Protocol Name** Used by Web Proxy to specify the protocol used (HTTP, FTP, or Gopher). Used by WinSock to specify the well-known destination port number for the socketed application.

> **Transport** Web Proxy always defined this as TCP/IP. WinSock Proxy can be TCP/IP, UDP, or IPX/SPX.

Object Information Fields

Object information fields contain information that is related to or extracted from the resource object. They include the following:

> **Object MIME** Used by Web Proxy to indicate the Multipurpose Internet Mail Extensions (MIME) type for the current object.

> **Object Name** Used by Web Proxy to indicate the contents of a URL request.

> **Object Source** Used by Web Proxy to indicate the source of the object (for example, cache, the Internet, or an upstream Proxy cache).

> **Result Code** Used by Web Proxy to indicate error and status codes. Windows (Win32) error codes have values less than 100. HTTP status codes have values between 100 and 1000. WinSock error codes have values between 10000 and 11004.

 Most connections have two log entries—one for connection establishment (result code of either 0 or 13301, and a byte count of 0) and a second for connection termination (result code of either 20000 or 20001, and the byte count).

Packet Filter Log Fields

The Proxy Server packet filtering service records five types of data in its log file. As with service logs, packet filter logs can operate as either regular or verbose. Here are the data types available for packet filter logs:

➤ General information

➤ Remote information

➤ Local information

➤ Filter information

➤ Packet information

General Information Fields

General information fields contain information that is related to or extracted from general information. For example, PFLogTime provides the time and date of packet reception.

Remote Information Fields

Remote information fields contain information that is related to or extracted from the remote computer. They include:

➤ **Protocol** Indicates the transport level protocol used by the connection (TCP, UDP, ICMP, and so on).

➤ **SourceAddress** Indicates the IP address of the remote source computer.

➤ **SourcePort** Indicates the service port number (if appropriate to the protocol) on the remote source computer.

Local Information Fields

Local information fields contain information that is related to or extracted from the local computer. They include:

➤ **DestinationAddress** Indicates the IP address of the local destination computer.

➤ **DestinationPort** Indicates the service port number (if appropriate to the protocol) on the local destination computer.

Filter Information Fields

Filter information fields contain information that is related to or extracted from packet filters. They include:

➤ **FilterRule** Has a value of either 1 for an accepted packet or 0 for a dropped packet. Only dropped packets are recorded in the filter log.

➤ **Interface (reserved for future use)** Indicates to the interface that the packet was received, but Proxy Server currently only supports a single interface per instance.

Packet Information Fields

Packet information fields contain information that is related to or extracted from packets. They include:

➤ **IPHeader** Contains the entire IP header, in HEX format, of the packet that caused the alert event.

➤ **Payload** A partial listing, in HEX format, of the data packet that caused the alert event.

➤ **TcpFlags** Indicates the TCP flag value from the culprit packet's IP header (FIN, SYN, RST, PSH, ACK, or URG).

Managing The Internet Publication Process

One of the primary reasons for some companies to connect to the Internet is to provide information to clients—both internal and external. As mentioned, implementing a direct Internet connection without a firewall or proxy server exposes your local network to the dangers of the unsecured Internet. How, then, do you provide information to clients while maintaining the integrity of your network? The answer is through a process Microsoft calls *secure Web publishing*. This system utilizes Proxy Server to provide reverse proxy and reverse hosting services.

Reverse Proxy

When a proxy server is configured for "normal" use, it acts as an agent for internal clients requesting Internet information. As you can imagine, a proxy server configured for reverse proxy takes client requests from the Internet and passes them to an internal Web server while acting as a secure agent for the Internet clients. This allows you to maintain the integrity of your Web server while providing access to external clients.

The reverse proxy system works with IIS on either the same computer or another computer on the network. It is configured through the Publishing tab of the Web Proxy Service Properties applet, as shown in Figure 5.9.

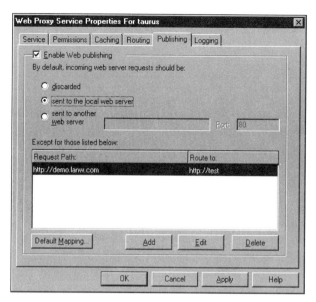

Figure 5.9   Reverse proxy and reverse hosting are configured through the Publishing tab of the Web Proxy Service Properties.

Note that all incoming Web requests are routed to the default option listed at the top of the window (discarded, sent to the local Web server, or sent to a specific Web server). However, an exception list can be created so specific requests can be sent to specific servers. This is convenient when multiple IIS servers are publishing pages for different domains on the same network.

 These configurations only apply to Web (HTTP) requests. To modify the function of FTP or other services, utilize the inbound and outbound filters for the services.

Reverse Hosting

The exception list, which specifies that certain requests are sent to specific servers, is the center of reverse hosting. Reverse hosting allows a number of Web servers to be serviced by a single proxy server by defining each server's specific responsibilities. Proxy Server is able to accept requests for a number of different local domains and forward them to the correct server. This eliminates the need for a single proxy server for each IIS server and can be used to limit your requirements to a single Internet connection.

Exam Prep Questions

Question 1

> What type of Proxy Server logging is enabled by default?
>
> ○ a. Log to text file
>
> ○ b. Log to Event Viewer
>
> ○ c. Log to SQL/ODBC database
>
> ○ d. Do not log

By default, Proxy Server logs to a text file. Therefore, the correct answer to this question is a. Logging to the Event Viewer or an SQL/ODBC database can be configured but is not enabled by default. Therefore, answers b and c are incorrect. Answer d is incorrect because logging is enabled by default.

Question 2

> Which of the following services are part of Microsoft's secure Web publishing system? [Check all correct answers]
>
> ❑ a. WinSock proxy
>
> ❑ b. Reverse proxy
>
> ❑ c. Reverse hosting
>
> ❑ d. Server proxy

The correct answers to this question are b and c. Reverse proxy and reverse hosting combine to create a secure Web publishing environment. WinSock proxy provides access for internal clients to the Internet. Therefore, answer a is incorrect. Server proxy provides a method of shielding an internal server, such as one running Exchange Server, from the Internet. Therefore, answer d is incorrect.

Question 3

> Which of the following methods can you use to efficiently grant
> unlimited and unrestricted access to all protocols and ports via
> WinSock?
>
> ○ a. Assign unlimited access to a user or group via the
> Permissions tab
>
> ○ b. Grant a user or group access to each protocol and port
> individually
>
> ○ c. Add a user to the WinSock Administrators group
>
> ○ d. You cannot grant unlimited and unrestricted access via
> WinSock

Unlimited access can be granted to a user or group through the Permissions
tab of the WinSock Properties applet. Therefore, answer a is correct. Although
it may be possible to grant access to each protocol and port individually, it is
not the most efficient way to provide access. Therefore, answer b is incorrect.
There is no WinSock Administrators group. Therefore, answer c is incorrect.
As you've seen from the previous explanations, it is possible to grant unlimited
and unrestricted access. Therefore, answer d is incorrect.

Question 4

> Which of the following measures can be taken to protect your
> local network from Internet traffic? [Check all correct answers]
>
> ❏ a. Enable port filtering
>
> ❏ b. Enable packet filtering
>
> ❏ c. Enable IP forwarding
>
> ❏ d. Install Proxy Server in its own domain

Enabling packet filtering and installing Proxy Server in its own domain are
two ways to control inbound access. Therefore, answers b and d are correct.
Enabling port filtering is a method of controlling outbound access, not inbound access. Therefore, answer a is incorrect. Disabling IP forwarding protects
your network from the Internet, but enabling IP forwarding actually puts your
network in danger. Therefore, answer c is incorrect.

Question 5

Which of the following are used to define a domain filter? [Check all correct answers]

❑ a. IP address

❑ b. NetBIOS computer name

❑ c. Subnet

❑ d. Domain name

Answers a, c, and d can all be used to define a domain filter. Because the Internet does not use NetBIOS computer names, answer b is incorrect.

Question 6

Which of the following events can trigger alerts? [Check all correct answers]

❑ a. Attempted protocol violations

❑ b. Frequency of rejected packets

❑ c. Invalid name/password combinations

❑ d. Storage volumes reaching capacity

Answers a, b, and d are the only three options available to trigger alerts. Invalid name/password combinations cannot trigger alerts. Therefore, answer c is incorrect.

Question 7

Which of the following cannot be used to define a packet filter?

○ a. Packet type

○ b. Datagram

○ c. IP address

○ d. Packet fragment

A packet filter can be established for a packet type, datagram, or packet fragment, but not an IP address. Therefore, answer c is correct.

Question 8

> Which service utilizes port control to manage outbound access?
>
> ○ a. Web Proxy
>
> ○ b. WinSock Proxy
>
> ○ c. SOCKS Proxy

The WinSock Proxy utilizes port control to manage outbound access. Therefore, answer b is correct. All other answers are incorrect.

Question 9

> Which of the following is required to enable packet filtering on a proxy server?
>
> ○ a. An external network interface
>
> ○ b. Logging to the Event Viewer
>
> ○ c. IIS operating on the same computer as Proxy Server
>
> ○ d. Installing the Packet Filter service in the Network applet

An external network interface is required to enable packet filtering. Therefore, answer a is correct. Although logging to the Event Viewer is convenient, it is not a requirement for packet filtering. Therefore, answer b is incorrect. IIS works closely with Proxy Server, but it is also not a requirement for packet filtering. Therefore, answer c is incorrect. There is no Packet Filter service. Therefore, answer d is incorrect.

Question 10

> Permissions for Web Proxy and WinSock Proxy can be granted on a protocol basis to users and groups.
>
> ○ a. True
>
> ○ b. False

True, permissions for Web Proxy and WinSock Proxy can be granted on a protocol basis for users and groups. Therefore, answer a is correct.

Need To Know More?

 Wolfe, David: *Designing and Implementing Microsoft Proxy Server.* Sams Publishing, Indianapolis, IN, 1996. ISBN 1-57521-213-7. Chapter 8 discusses Proxy Server security and authentication.

 Microsoft TechNet, January, 1998. Searches on keywords within the Proxy Server documentation provide detailed information on security, alerts, and logging. Detailed tables that include all log entries are available.

 The Microsoft Knowledge Base information provides detailed information on all products, including Proxy Server. Searches on "security," "alerts," and "logging" in the Proxy Server section provide detailed information. The Microsoft Knowledge Base is located at http://support.microsoft.com/support/a.asp?M=S.

Managing And Tuning Proxy Server 2.0

6

Terms you'll need to understand:

√ Cache

√ Counter

√ Domain filter

√ Instance

√ Local address table (LAT)

√ Management Information Base (MIB)

√ Object

√ Packet filter

√ Simple Network Management Protocol (SNMP)

Techniques you'll need to master:

√ Tuning and monitoring Microsoft Proxy Server 2.0 hard drive cache

√ Understanding the error-logging functions and interpreting error messages

In this chapter, you'll learn how to perform the administrative tasks necessary to keep Microsoft Proxy Server 2.0 operating at the highest possible performance level. You'll become acquainted with the tools provided with Microsoft Proxy Server 2.0 to maintain Web Proxy, WinSock Proxy, and SOCKS Proxy. You'll also become familiar with the Performance Monitor counters that are used to monitor Proxy Server 2.0 and be introduced to the tool that opens a Performance Monitor chart specifically configured for monitoring Proxy Server components.

To support Microsoft Proxy Server 2.0, you must have a firm understanding of the differences between the Web Proxy service and the WinSock Proxy service, the protocols that can be configured for each service, and a complete understanding of Web Proxy cache configuration.

Internet Service Manager Overview

The Internet Service Manager (ISM) (see Figure 6.1) tool is used to access and administer Microsoft Internet Information Server and Microsoft Proxy Server 2.0. When Proxy Server is installed, the Web Proxy, WinSock Proxy, and SOCKS Proxy icons are added to the ISM tool and are used to manage Microsoft Proxy Server 2.0.

ISM can be accessed through either the Microsoft Internet Server group or the Microsoft Proxy Server group. To open the ISM tool from Microsoft Proxy Server, click Start|Programs|Microsoft Proxy Server|Internet Service Manager.

The ISM screen opens with a list of all installed Internet services. Options that allow connection or identification of other servers on the network that are

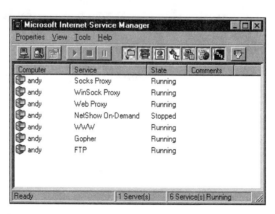

Figure 6.1 The Internet Service Manager.

providing Internet services are located in the Properties menu (see Figure 6.2). A brief explanation of these options follows:

➤ **Connect To Server** This menu selection connects to a remote server, and it provides a way to administer Internet Information Server and Proxy Server computers across a network.

➤ **Find All Servers** This option finds and lists all Internet Information Server computers on the network by polling IPX/SPX routers and WINS servers and by sending broadcast-based messages. Any computers found are listed in the ISM. You must have administrative rights on the remote server to perform remote administration.

➤ **Service Properties** This is where you configure the Internet service.

➤ **Start Service** This is where you start the Internet service.

➤ **Stop Service** This is where you stop the Internet service.

➤ **Pause Service** This is where you pause the Internet service.

Several viewing options are available for ISM. There are three grouped areas, plus a refresh selection and a selection for displaying the toolbar and the status bar. Here's a description of the three grouped areas:

➤ **Services** Each service is listed and can be selected for display. The All option places check marks next to all services.

➤ **Sort** Options allow you to sort by server, service, comment, or state of operation.

➤ **View** The display can be configured for Server view, Services view, or Report view.

Using ISM To Manage Proxy Server

ISM is used to administer all the Internet services installed on the computer. For Microsoft Proxy Server 2.0, that consists of the Web Proxy service, WinSock

Figure 6.2   The Internet Service Manager Properties menu.

Proxy service, and SOCKS Proxy service. Each of these services is described in the following sections.

Web Proxy Management

The Web Proxy service provides a pathway to the Internet for CERN-compliant applications. It also supports requests from any CERN-compliant browsers, such as Microsoft Internet Explorer and Netscape Navigator.

The ISM is used to administer the Web Proxy service. When Microsoft Proxy Server 2.0 is installed, an icon is added to the ISM for Web Proxy service support. To access this tool from the ISM, follow these steps:

1. Select the Web Proxy service from the display window.

2. From the Properties menu, select Service Properties. The Web Proxy Service Properties page appears (see Figure 6.3).

Six tabs are used to configure the Web Proxy service properties. The following sections describe each of these tabs.

Service

When the Service tab is selected, the Proxy revision and ID information is displayed (refer to Figure 6.3). The Current Sessions button lists all connected users for the three proxy services. It also displays the time the clients connected and the length of time each client has maintained the connection. Below the

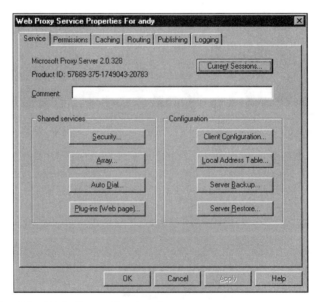

Figure 6.3 The Web Proxy Service Properties page.

Current Sessions button, a comment line allows a comment to be added about the server or one of the services. The central area of the dialog is divided into two parts: Shared Services and Configuration.

The Shared Services area has four buttons—Security, Array, Auto Dial, and Plug-Ins—and is used to configure all three Proxy Server services. The Security button is used to configure the filters, of which there are two types—Domain and Packet. The Array button is used to create an *array*, which is a group of Proxy Server computers that are linked together and use peer-to-peer communication. Arrays provide increased caching performance for the Web Proxy service, as well as increased fault tolerance and load balancing for all the services. The Auto Dial button sets up on-demand dialing of a RAS Phonebook entry by Microsoft Proxy Server. On-demand dialing can be used when one of the Proxy Server services must establish a dial-up connection to the Internet. The Plug-Ins button is used to support the installation of third-party software (plug-ins). When the Plug-Ins button is clicked, it opens your Web browser and loads the Web page www.microsoft.com/proxy/common/plugins.htm.

The Configuration area also has four buttons—Client Configuration, Local Address Table, Server Backup, and Server Restore. The Client Configuration button is used to configure the Proxy Server computer with a share that clients can attach to and to run a setup program that configures them to use the proxy server for Internet access. The Local Address Table button is used to view and modify the local address table (LAT) for the Proxy Server computer. The Server Backup button specifies the directory to which the backup file is saved (by default, it's C:\Msp). The Server Restore button is used to complete a partial or complete restore of an earlier configuration of Proxy Server.

Permissions

The Permissions tab, shown in Figure 6.4, is used to give a user or group permission to use Internet protocols to access the Internet through the Web Proxy service on your proxy server. The permissions are configured and granted for each protocol installed. For example, a user might have permission to use the FTP protocol, but not the WWW protocol. The protocols that can be configured from this box are FTP Read, WWW, Secure, and Gopher.

Caching

The Caching tab, shown in Figure 6.5, is used to enable or disable the caching feature, as well as configure the operation of caching. Two forms of caching can be used—active caching and passive caching. The cache area is actually hard disk space that is set aside for storing Internet sites that have been visited by the client. If the same sites are frequented, this saves time in retrieving the site, because it is stored locally.

Figure 6.4 The Permissions tab of the Web Proxy Service Properties page.

The cache can operate in active mode or passive mode. *Active caching* enables the Web Proxy service to search the Internet for fresh copies of Web pages that are stored in cache, without a request for that object being made by a proxy client. The update frequency for the proxy server is configurable, so the priority

Figure 6.5 The Caching tab of the Web Proxy Service Properties page.

of updating cache can be more important or less important than client requests. By using active caching, the client can access the Web page much quicker because the copy in cache is always kept up-to-date. *Passive caching* stores an Internet object but does not update the Internet site or object until the object is requested by a proxy client. Enabling the caching feature in Proxy Server dramatically increases the proxy server's performance by decreasing the amount of time it takes for a client to retrieve an object from the Internet and reducing Internet traffic from your proxy server to the Internet. It's important to know that the cache file must be created on an NTFS partition. The Enable Caching checkbox is used to enable the caching feature of Proxy Server. Many people install Proxy Server just for its caching feature.

Routing

The Routing tab, shown in Figure 6.6, is used to configure the routing options, which direct client requests for Internet objects. Requests can be configured for routing through the array, to an upstream proxy server, or by directly connecting to the Internet. The Routing tab has two main areas—Upstream Routing and Routing Within Array. Upstream Routing allows you to configure the name of the upstream proxy server computer and port number. Routing Within Array routes Web Proxy clients through the array before sending the client request to an upstream proxy server or to the Internet. This option is available if the proxy server is a member of an array.

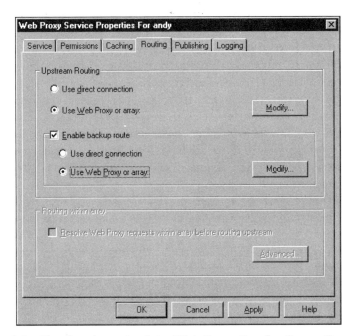

Figure 6.6   The Routing tab of the Web Proxy Service Properties page.

Publishing

The Publishing tab, shown in Figure 6.7, is used to configure reverse proxy and reverse hosting. This enables Proxy Server to respond to external requests by rejecting external requests, sending the requests to the local Web server, or routing the request to another Web server. Downstream servers can be configured to publish Web pages through the proxy server.

Logging

The Logging tab, shown in Figure 6.8, is used to set logging options for the Web Proxy, WinSock Proxy, and SOCKS Proxy services. Logging provides an audit trail and is the key to securing a proxy server. Proxy Server can be configured to log information to a text file or to an ODBC database file. Note that logging to SQL or ODBC database files places a greater strain on the resources than logging to a text file. The default filename used for the Web Proxy service is W3YYMMDD.LOG and is stored in the *System_root*\System32 directory. The logging feature logs server, client, connection, and object information.

Proxy Publishing

Proxy Server allows computers sitting downstream from the Proxy Server computer to publish to the Internet. Proxy Server supports reverse proxying and reverse hosting. These two features enhance security by allowing any computer on the internal network to publish to the Internet. All incoming and outgoing

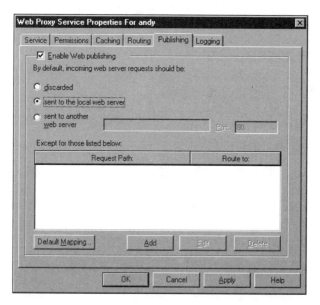

Figure 6.7   The Publishing tab of the Web Proxy Service Properties page.

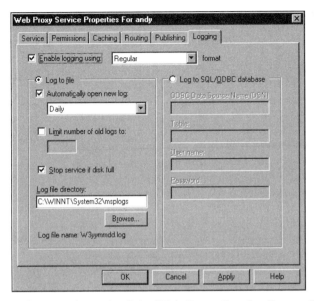

Figure 6.8   The Logging tab of the Web Proxy Service Properties page.

requests are filtered through the Proxy Server computer. In addition, Proxy Server can also cache incoming requests from the Internet, providing safe, easy access. The following points describe how Proxy Server services such requests:

➤ With reverse proxy, the incoming HTTP port of the proxy server "listens" for requests from the Internet and sends the requests downstream to the internal Web server.

➤ With reverse hosting, Proxy Server can maintain a list of several servers that have permission to publish to the Internet. The proxy server "listens" and responds to Internet requests on behalf of the internal Web server.

WinSock Proxy Management

The WinSock Proxy service is used by client Windows applications that use Windows Sockets to communicate on a network. This enables a Windows Sockets-compatible application to perform as it would if directly connected to the Internet. The WinSock Proxy service provides support for applications such as IRC, RealAudio, and Microsoft NetShow.

The WinSock Proxy service is not detected when the Find All Servers command is used on remote server computers. To connect to the WinSock Proxy service on remote server computers, use the Connect To Server command and specify the server name for the connection. In addition, when the WinSock

Proxy service is stopped, you can change the configuration settings, but the changes do not take effect until the service is restarted.

To reach the WinSock Proxy Service Properties page (see Figure 6.9) from ISM, double-click the WinSock Proxy icon, and the WinSock Proxy Service Properties page appears.

Four tabs are available for configuring the WinSock Proxy service—Service, Protocols, Permissions, and Logging. These allow you to control access by port number, protocol, and user or group. Each port can be enabled or disabled for communications by a specific list of users or user groups. The following lists the tabs used to configure the WinSock Proxy service:

➤ **Service tab** The information that can be configured under the Service tab is shared by the Web Proxy, WinSock Proxy, and SOCKS Proxy services and is detailed earlier in this chapter.

➤ **Protocols tab** The Protocols tab, shown in Figure 6.10, is used to determine which Windows Sockets applications will be allowed to access the Internet through the WinSock Proxy service. For each protocol configuration, use the property page to determine which ports can be used for outbound and inbound connections.

➤ **Permissions tab** The Permissions tab is used to configure which users or groups of users can access the Internet using a particular protocol

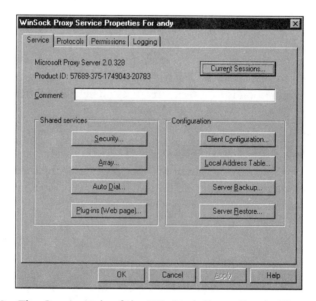

Figure 6.9 The Service tab of the WinSock Proxy Service Properties page.

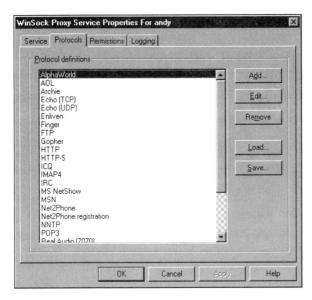

Figure 6.10   The Protocols tab of the WinSock Proxy Service Properties
page.

through the WinSock Proxy service. The setting can be done by protocol or by using the special Unlimited Access selection.

➤ **Logging** The Logging tab is used to set logging options for the Web
Proxy, WinSock Proxy, and SOCKS Proxy services and is described in
the section titled "Web Proxy Management." The default filename used
for the WinSock Proxy service is WSYYMMDD.LOG, and it's stored
in the *System_root*\System32 directory.

SOCKS Proxy Management

The SOCKS Proxy service provides a secure channel between the client and
the server for applications that use SOCKS version 4.3a, and use IP addresses
and the Identification (Identd) protocol to identify and authenticate SOCKS
Proxy clients. To reach the SOCKS Proxy Management screen from ISM,
double-click the SOCKS Proxy icon. The SOCKS Proxy Service Property
page appears.

Three configuration tabs are available for the SOCKS Proxy service—Service,
Permissions, and Logging. A brief explanation of each follows:

➤ **Service** The information that can be configured under the Service tab is
shared by the Web Proxy, WinSock Proxy, and SOCKS Proxy services
and is detailed earlier in this chapter.

➤ **Permissions** SOCKS clients establish a connection to the Proxy Server computer. After the proxy circuit is established, SOCKS relays application data between the client and the server. The Permissions tab, shown in Figure 6.11, on the SOCKS Property page displays an ordered list of entries.

➤ **Logging** The Logging tab is used to set logging options for the Web Proxy, WinSock Proxy, and SOCKS Proxy services and is described in the "Web Proxy Management" section. The default filename used for the SOCKS Proxy service is SPYYMMDD.LOG, and it's stored in the *System_root*\System32 directory.

A SOCKS permission is a rule entry in an ordered list; each rule specifies a source and a destination address, as well as whether a request satisfying the rule entry is permitted or denied. The first rule entry in the list that matches the incoming client request is used to determine whether the request is permitted or denied. If a client request does not match any rule entry in the list, the request is denied. The entries can be arranged by using the Move Up and Move Down buttons.

Performance Monitor Overview

Performance Monitor, shown in Figure 6.12, is provided with Windows NT Server 4.0 to monitor NT Server activities. When Proxy Server is installed,

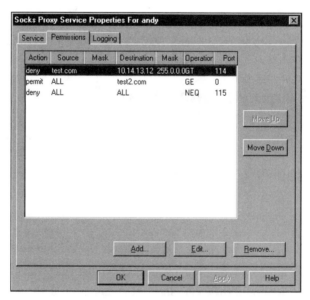

Figure 6.11 The Permissions tab of the SOCKS Proxy Service Properties page.

additional software components are added to Performance Monitor so Proxy Server events can be monitored for optimization and troubleshooting purposes.

A menu option is added under the Proxy Server menu that starts Performance Monitor and displays a chart of indicators that are specific to Proxy Server. Table 6.1 contains a list of counters that are added when Proxy Server is installed or that may be useful in monitoring Proxy Server by using Performance Monitor.

> *Note: The packet filter counters are not currently available but should be available with subsequent releases of Proxy Server.*

Performance Monitor Counters

Several counters can be used to monitor the performance of Microsoft Proxy Server 2.0. A complete list is available with the online documentation that comes with the software. Some of the counters you should be familiar with are listed in Table 6.1.

Monitoring And Tuning Memory

If a network management tool is in use, Microsoft Proxy Server 2.0 comes with SNMP Management Information Base (MIB) files, which are used to enable SNMP monitoring of the Web Proxy and WinSock Proxy services. This service, along with Performance Monitor, can be used to monitor and tune memory settings.

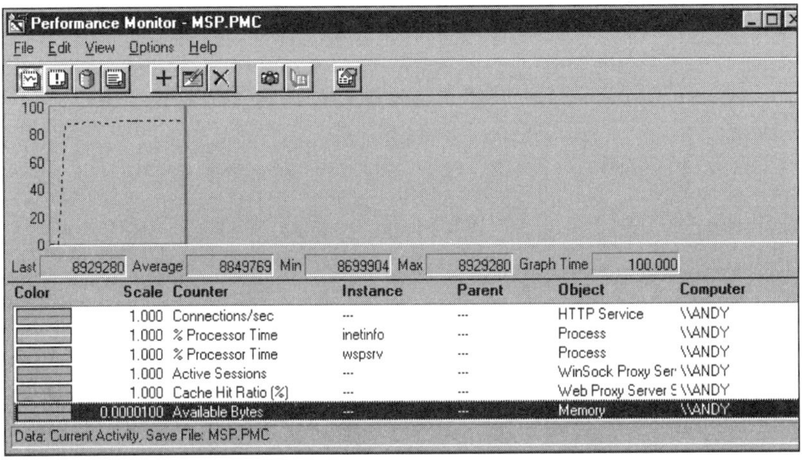

Figure 6.12   The Performance Monitor.

Table 6.1   Performance Monitor counters.

Web Proxy Service Counters	Description
Cache Hit Ratio (%)	The percentage of requests that have been served by using cached data (out of the total number of requests to Web Proxy Server).
Current Users	The number of users currently connected to Web Proxy Server.
DNS Cache Entries	The current number of DNS domain name entries cached by Web Proxy Server.
DNS Cache Hits	The total number of times a DNS domain name was found within the DNS cache.
DNS Cache Hits (%)	The percentage of DNS domain names served by the Web Proxy Server cache (out of the total of all DNS entries that have been retrieved by Web Proxy Server).
FTP Requests	The number of FTP requests that have been made to Web Proxy Server.
HTTP Requests	The number of HTTP requests that have been made to Web Proxy Server.
Maximum Users	The maximum number of users that have connected to Web Proxy Server simultaneously.
Total Cache Fetches	The total number of requests that have been served by using cached data from Web Proxy Server cache.
Total Failing Requests	The total number of Internet service requests that have failed to be processed by Web Proxy Server due to errors. Errors can be the result of Web Proxy Server failing to locate a requested server URL on the Internet, or because of the client being denied access to the requested URL.
Total Users	The total number of users that have ever connected to Web Proxy Server.

Web Proxy Cache Counters	Description
Active URL Refresh Rate	The number of URLs per second that are preemptively refreshed in the URL cache from remote URL sources.
Max Bytes Cached	The maximum number of bytes that have been stored in the URL cache.

(continued)

Table 6.1 Performance Monitor counters *(continued)*.	
Max URLs Cached	The maximum number of URLs that have been stored in the URL cache.
Total Bytes Cached	The cumulative number of bytes that have been stored in the URL cache.
URLs In Cache	The current number of URLs in the URL cache.
WinSock Proxy Service Counters	**Description**
Active Sessions	The number of active sessions.
Active TCP Connections	The number of active TCP connections.
Active UDP Connections	Total number of active UDP connections.
DNS Cache Hits	The total number of times a DNS domain name was found within the DNS cache.
DNS Cache Hits %	The percentage of DNS domain names served from the Web Proxy Server cache (from the total of all DNS entries that have been retrieved by the Web Proxy Server).
SOCKS Proxy Service Counters	**Description**
SOCKS Clients Bytes Total/sec	The sum of **SOCKS Client Bytes Received/ sec** and **SOCKS Client Bytes Sent/sec**. This is the total rate of all bytes transferred between SOCKS Proxy Server and SOCKS Proxy clients.
SOCKS sessions	The total number of SOCKS sessions serviced by the SOCKS Proxy service.

The MIB file for Web Proxy service monitoring is W3P.MIB. The MIB file for WinSock Proxy service monitoring is WSP.MIB. These files are not installed on the server by the Setup program. They are on the Proxy Server CD-ROM and can be copied from the \Perfctrs directory. You must use the correct MIB file for the server's processor architecture, such as the Intel or Alpha chip version of the MIB file.

The SNMP service uses object identifiers (OIDs) for MIB processing. The OID for W3P.MIB is 11. The OID for WSP.MIB is 12.

The Performance Monitor can be used to view the services provided by Proxy Server, but the Processor and Memory objects should also be viewed to gain a better understanding of overall system performance.

Adding more RAM to a Microsoft Proxy Server computer is one of the most effective ways to increase performance. The more RAM installed in the system, the less information has to be cached on the hard drive. If you're considering upgrading the CPU subsystem, install a second processor rather than upgrade to a faster CPU chip. A few simple configuration tips follow:

➤ Limit the number of protocols in use on the system. Ideally, you want to have TCP/IP only or TCP/IP and NWLink only. The fewer protocols installed, the less overhead the operating system needs.

➤ Limit the other services the NT Server performs. If possible, offload WINS, DHCP, DNS, and domain controller support to different computers.

➤ Limit the number of server-based applications running on the Proxy Server computer.

The system configurations vary depending on the number of clients. The recommended system configurations are listed here in the following:

➤ For up to 300 clients:

  ➤ Intel 486 minimum. Pentium 133MHz recommended.
  ➤ 24MB RAM minimum. 32MB RAM recommended.
  ➤ 10MB minimum. From 250MB to 2GB disk space for caching.

➤ For 300 to 1,999 clients:

  ➤ Intel Pentium 133MHz.
  ➤ 64MB of memory RAM.
  ➤ From 2GB to 4GB disk space for caching.

➤ For 2,000 or more clients:

  ➤ Intel Pentium 166MHz or greater.
  ➤ 64MB of memory RAM minimum.
  ➤ From 2GB to 4GB disk space for caching.

Monitoring And Tuning The Proxy Cache

Adding RAM or decreasing any additional services that are running can dynamically increase the performance of the Proxy Server computer, but there are not many other options for configuring RAM. The Proxy Server cache has several configuration options available to increase performance. Some of the hardware techniques that can employed include the following:

➤ **Implement hardware RAID or the Microsoft NT Server software implementation of RAID 0 or RAID 5** RAID 0 is striping and RAID 5 is striping with parity. Both increase read performance greatly, but RAID 5 also provides some fault tolerance and can survive a single disk failure.

➤ **Upgrade the hard disk controller subsystem** A bus-mastering controller makes fewer CPU calls and provides several times the throughput as standard hard disk controllers.

➤ **Install faster hard drives** If possible, for best performance install SCSI drives. If faster drives cannot be installed, make sure you have enough hard drive space available to support the clients that are accessing the Internet through the proxy server.

Enabling caching on the proxy server and providing enough hard drive space to store Web sites is critical to the overall performance of the proxy server. The amounts of disk space recommended for the number of proxy clients were listed earlier, but those are only recommendations. Be sure to use Performance Monitor to view the usage of cache listed in the Web Proxy Cache object. Here are some things that should be checked when tuning cache:

➤ **Verify there's enough available hard drive space for the cache.** This is done by viewing available hard disk space and comparing that with the calculated number of users attaching to the proxy server.

➤ **Use Performance Monitor to verify effectiveness of cache settings.** This is done by viewing the counters under the Web Proxy Server Cache object. Distribute the cache files across multiple physical disk drives, if possible. Use Performance Monitor to see how effective the changes are.

➤ **Customize the TTL (Time To Live) settings for objects in cache.** The TTL settings are configured from the Advanced Cache Policy screen located under the Caching tab for the Web Proxy properties. Set the TTL objects to be flushed in a timely manner.

➤ **Limit the size of cached objects to increase the number of objects that can be cached.** This configuration is also done on the Advanced Caching Policy screen.

Two forms of caching can be implemented and configured—passive caching and active caching. Passive caching does not refresh sites stored in cache, whereas active caching does. Active and passive caching are configured under the Caching tab of the Web Proxy Server Properties page (refer to Figure 6.5). A brief explanation of the setting follows:

➤ **Cache Expiration Policy** This setting is used to set the freshness of the objects in cache. Freshness is a measurement of how long an object is used that is stored in local cache, as compared to retrieving the object remotely. Here are the three settings that are available for selection:

➤ Updates are more important (more update checks)

➤ Equal importance

➤ Fewer network accesses are more important (more cache hits)

➤ **Enable Active Caching** This setting is used to enable active caching (allowing the server to make network requests to update objects stored in cache), and configure how often and when active caching will take place. One of three selections can be made:

➤ Faster user response is more important (more prefetching)

➤ Equal importance

➤ Fewer network accesses are more important (less prefetching)

The Cache Size button allows you to adjust the size and location of the cache. Remember that the cache can only be placed on NTFS partitions. The size of the cache space that should be allocated depends on the amount of clients that the proxy server is expected to support.

The Advanced button allows you to perform the following tasks:

➤ Specify a maximum size allowed for cached objects.

➤ Return expired objects from the cache when the requested Internet site is unavailable and the cache does not contain an expired copy of the requested object.

➤ Filter the cache, listing specific URLs, sites, or directories that should either always be cached (subject to other caching rules) or can never be cached.

➤ Set the TTL parameters for HTTP and FTP cached objects.

Advanced techniques of distributing cached information can be employed by configuring arrays and downstream proxy servers. These topics are covered in Chapter 8.

Error Logging And Interpretation

The Logging tab, (refer to Figure 6.8), is used to set logging options for the Web Proxy, WinSock Proxy, and SOCKS Proxy services. Logging provides an audit trail and is the key to securing a proxy server. Each of the services (Web Proxy, WinSock Proxy, and SOCKS Proxy) has an associated log file. These logs do not provide error information, but they are used to provide a "paper trail" for auditing purposes.

Errors that occur after Microsoft Proxy Server is installed are recorded in the System Event log and the Application Event log, and they are viewed with the Event Viewer. If errors occur during the setup process, view the MPS SETUP.LOG file created by the Setup program and store it in the root directory. A list of the error messages can be found in the online documentation.

Web Proxy service event messages are viewed through the Event Viewer and stored in the Windows NT System log. The source names used by the Web Proxy Server service are WebProxyServer and WebProxyLog. A complete list of the error messages can be found in the online documentation for Proxy Server. The following is a list of some of the more common errors:

➤ **HTTP/1.0 500 Server Error (-*number*).** This error occurs when Windows NT Challenge/Response authentication is used on Microsoft Proxy Server to validate proxy clients. Microsoft Proxy Server uses the password authentication specified in the WWW service properties to validate Web Proxy clients.

➤ **HTTP/1.0 500 Server Error. (The specified module could not be found.)** This error occurs when certain proxy binaries are not installed in the correct directory for proxy scripts.

➤ **115—W3Proxy failed to start because the system time is incorrect.** The date and time on the server's system clock is not correct and must be adjusted before the service can be restarted.

➤ **127—The Web Proxy service failed to initialize.** This is a generic error message and provides no detail to the problem.

Web Proxy service cache event messages are also listed in the online documentation. Here are two of the error messages. Both include a brief explanation of the event that generated the log entry. The source name for the events is WebProxyCache:

➤ 112—WebProxyCache corrected a corrupted or old format URL cache by removing all or part of the cache's contents. Some cached objects have been deleted or removed from the cache and no further action is required.

➤ 114—The hard disk used by the Web Proxy server to cache popular URLs is full. Space needs to be freed or the WebProxyCache reconfigured to resume normal operation. This is the error message that indicates the cache hard disk is full.

WinSock Proxy service event messages are stored under the source names WinSockProxy and WinSockProxyLog. A complete list is available in the online documentation. Here are a few of the errors and indications that can appear:

➤ 4—WinSock Proxy service was unable to initialize due to a shortage of available memory. The server computer cannot initialize the service due to lack of available memory on the server.

➤ 6—WinSock Proxy service was unable to initialize performance counters. The data is the error. System DLLs needed for performance monitoring of the service may be missing or cannot be located on the system.

➤ 7—WinSock Proxy service has failed due to a shortage of available memory. The data is the number of connections. The server computer cannot support additional connections for the server due to lack of available resources. Check the number of connections in use on the server and server memory usage.

➤ 17—Incorrect network configuration. None of the server's addresses are internal. An IP address configured for the internal network adapter card for the server needs to be included within the local address table (LAT) for the server.

➤ 28—The WinSock Proxy service failed to initialize the network dial-out. Dial-Up Networking would appear to have failed in this case. Check modem settings.

SOCKS Proxy service creates two log entries for each connection—one establish and one terminate message. SOCKS Proxy service event messages are in the Windows NT system log under the source names SocksProxy and SocksProxyLog. The following is a list of a few of the messages:

➤ 2222—The network is down.

➤ 2317—Out of memory.

➤ 2320—Bind failed.

➤ 2321—Unknown host.

A complete list of error messages is available in the online documentation. The problems indicated by a proxy server failure can be caused by any number of other services on which the proxy service depends. Therefore, you should always start with the Event Viewer messages that immediately preceded the error you are troubleshooting.

Exam Prep Questions

Question 1

> Your users access a stock quote page that is updated every night. They are complaining that the first time the page is accessed in the morning, it takes an unusually long time to come up on the screen and they want to know if you can "fix" it. What can you do to try and help your users?
>
> ○ a. From the WinSock Proxy Service Properties page, select the Caching tab and select the Enable Caching checkbox. Select the Updates Are More Important option.
>
> ○ b. From the SOCKS Proxy Service Properties page, select the Caching tab and select the Enable Caching checkbox. Select the Updates Are More Important option.
>
> ○ c. From the Web Proxy Service Properties page, select the Caching tab and select the Enable Caching checkbox. Select the Updates Are More Important option.
>
> ○ d. From the Web Proxy Service Properties page, select the Routing tab and select the Aggressive Caching checkbox.

The correct answer to this question is c. Caching is configured from the Caching tab of the Web Proxy Service Properties page. There is no Caching tab available on the WinSock Proxy Service and SOCKS Proxy Service Properties pages. Therefore, answers a and b are incorrect. Caching is not configurerd on the Routing tab of the Web Proxy Service Properties page. Therefore, answer d is incorrect.

Question 2

> You are receiving complaints that access to the current pricing information (which changes several times a day) on an external server is extremely slow. How can you speed up access to that site?
>
> ○ a. Disable caching.
>
> ○ b. Enable active caching and add a cache filter for the URL of the sales site forcing the site to be cached.
>
> ○ c. Set the Cache Expiration Policy for Equal Importance.
>
> ○ d. Enable active caching and add a cache filter for the URL of the sales site forcing the site to not be cached.

The correct answer to this question is d. By enabling active caching and adding a filter for the site, you force the site to be cached and updated without a client requesting the site. Disabling caching or enabling active caching and forcing the site to not be cached will not retrieve the site from the Internet until a user requests the site. Therefore, answers a and b are incorrect. Setting the Cache Expiration Policy for Equal Importance only changes the amount of time the system spends providing information to clients and updating cached information. Therefore, answer c is incorrect.

Question 3

You administer a 300 client local area network. Your internal network uses IPX/SPX only for communications. You want to configure the cache to provide the quickest response to user requests. You want to configure the Microsoft Proxy Server on your Windows NT Server, which meets or exceeds all installation requirements, so WinSock Proxy clients can benefit from its caching capabilities.

Required Result:

- Internet objects must be stored locally and updated every hour.

Optional Desired Results:

- Provide the best user response and maximize cache hits.
- Internet objects that are larger than 2MB should not be cached.

Proposed Solution:

- In the Web Proxy Service Properties page's Caching tab, select the Enable Caching checkbox. For the Cache expiration policy, select Fewer Network Accesses Are More Important. Select the Enable Active Caching checkbox and then select the Faster User Response Is More Important option. Click the Advanced button and then select the Limit Size Of Cached Object To checkbox and set the limit to 200K. For the Object Time To Live options, select the Enable HTTP Caching checkbox; then set the Maximum TTL to 60 minutes.

Which results does the proposed solution produce?

- ○ a. The proposed solution produces the required result and produces both of the optional desired results.
- ○ b. The proposed solution produces the required result, but only one of the optional desired results.
- ○ c. The proposed solution produces the required result, but neither of the optional desired results.
- ○ d. The proposed solution does not produce the required result.

The correct answer to this question is a. The proposed solution satisfies the required result and both optional desired results. By enabling caching, Web objects are stored in the local proxy cache. By selecting Faster User Response Is More Important, the cache is maximized for user response. By setting the maximum TTL to 60 minutes, all sites stored in cache will update hourly. All other answers are incorrect.

Question 4

You're installing Microsoft Proxy Server 2.0 on your network and want the users on your network to configure their Web browser software to use the Proxy Server. How can you do this?

○ a. Have the clients reinstall the Web browser software, selecting the Use Proxy selection in the Advanced options.

○ b. Do nothing at all. Client computers will automatically attempt to use the Proxy Server to connect to the Internet.

○ c. From the Web Proxy Service Properties page, select the Client Configuration button and set the options so the clients will automatically be configured during client setup.

○ d. From the WinSock Proxy Service Properties page, select the Client Configuration button and set the options so the clients will automatically be configured during setup.

The correct answer to this question is c. By configuring the Client Configuration information found on the Web Proxy Service Properties page, a client setup share is created. The clients do not have to reinstall the browser. The browser can be modified after installation. Therefore, answer a is incorrect. The client computers will not know there is a proxy server available unless configured to look for a proxy. Therefore, answer b is incorrect. Client configuration is not available from the WinSock Proxy Server Properties page. Therefore, answer d is incorrect.

Question 5

You have a user that connects to a site that provides news updates on a regular basis. The user tells you that before the proxy
server was installed, there was audio on the site, such as a radio
station. The site uses RealAudio to send the audio information.
You need to verify that all the proxy server clients are able to use
the RealAudio protocol. Select the screen that will provide this
information.

○ a. The Protocols tab in the Web Proxy Properties page

○ b. The Protocols tab in the WinSock Proxy Properties page

○ c. The Protocols tab under the SOCKS Proxy Properties page

○ d. The Protocols tab under the Network Properties page on
each client's computer

The correct answer to this question is b. RealAudio is configured under the
WinSock Proxy Properties page. The RealAudio protocol cannot be configured from the Web Proxy Properties page, the SOCKS Proxy Properties page,
nor the Network Properties page. Therefore, answers a, c, and d are incorrect.

Question 6

You want to configure your Microsoft Proxy Server 2.0 computer
to cache Internet objects, but you want to limit the size of the
objects stored to 1.5MB each. How do you do this?

○ a. From the WinSock Proxy Service Properties page, select
the Caching tab, click the Advanced button, then select
the Limit Size Of Cached Objects checkbox and set the
limit to 1.5MB.

○ b. From the Web Proxy Service Properties page, select the
Caching tab, click the Advanced button, then select the
Limit Size Of Cached Objects checkbox and set the limit
to 1.5MB.

○ c. From the SOCKS Proxy Service Properties page, select
the Caching tab, click the Advanced button, then select
the Limit Size Of Cached Objects checkbox and set the
limit to 1.5MB.

○ d. From the System Properties page, select the Performance tab. Under Virtual Memory, click the Change
button. Select the Limit Size Of Cached Objects checkbox
and set the limit to 1.5MB.

The correct answer to this question is b. Caching information is configured under the Web Proxy Service Properties page. The Caching tab is only accessible from the Web Proxy Service Properties page, and size limits on cached information can be configured under the Advanced button. Therefore, all other answers are incorrect.

Question 7

You want the Internet Information Server (IIS) on your proxy server to be able to publish Web pages for use by your traveling sales force. To configure the proxy server to allow this, what do you need to do?

- ○ a. Install a proxy server that is on the external network.
- ○ b. In the Web Proxy Service Properties page, under the Routing tab, select Use Direct Connection.
- ○ c. In the Web Proxy Service Properties page, under the Publishing tab, place a check in Enable Web Publishing.
- ○ d. Install an IIS server on the internal network.

The correct answer to this question is c. By enabling Web publishing under the Web Proxy Service Properties page, an internal IIS server can publish Web pages. There is no such configuration as Use Direct Connection. Therefore, answer b is incorrect. Installing a proxy server on the external network wouldn't help solve the problem, and installing an internal IIS server will not enable the proxy server to forward external requests on the internal network. Therefore, answers a and d are incorrect.

Question 8

You have just installed a new hard disk for use as a cache storage area by the Proxy Server services. Which of the following tasks would you need to do? [Check all correct answers]

❑ a. Format the partition as NTFS.

❑ b. Format the partition as FAT.

❑ c. From the WinSock Proxy Properties page, select the Caching tab, click the Cache size button, and add the volume and space for the new drive.

❑ d. From the Web Proxy Service Properties page, select the Caching tab, click the Cache Size button, and add the volume and space for the new drive.

❑ e. Reinstall the Proxy Server software. During the installation, select the new drive as the cache area.

The correct answers to this question are a and d. Caching has to be on an NTFS partition and is configured from the Web Proxy Service Properties page Cache Size button. Caching cannot be configured on a partition that has been formatted FAT, and the WinSock Proxy Service Properties page does not have a caching configuration button. Therefore, answers b, c, and e are incorrect.

Question 9

While reviewing the event logs for your Microsoft Proxy Server 2.0 computer, you notice that the FTP server is being heavily used. You need to limit the use of FTP to the Programmers local group only. How can you do this?

○ a. Open the Web Proxy Service Properties dialog, select the Permissions tab, and enable access control, listing only the local group Programmers under the FTP protocol.

○ b. Under the Security tab for Web Proxy Server Properties window, click the FTP Protocol button and type in "Programmers".

○ c. Open the Network Properties window's Protocol tab; then select FTP and add the Programmers local group.

○ d. Open User Manager For Domains, select the local group Programmers, and then add the FTP service to the group.

The correct answer to this question is a. The FTP protocol can be configured for limited use. This configuration is not done through the Network Properties or User Manager For Domains areas. Therefore, answers c and d are incorrect. There is no FTP Protocol configuration button under the Security tab. Therefore, answer b is incorrect.

Question 10

Users are complaining that Web pages accessed once a week are very slow to come up, but the Web pages that are used every day are quick to come up. You want to configure the Web Proxy service to update objects that are stored in cache after half the TTL has expired in an attempt to update the cached pages more often and speed up access to the pages less frequently accessed. How do you do this?

○ a. From the Web Proxy Service Properties page, select the Caching tab and select the Enable Active Caching checkbox. Set it for Equal Importance.

○ b. From the Web Proxy Service Properties page, select the Caching tab and click the Advanced button. Under Object Time To Live, select TTL=__% and set the percentage box to 50%.

○ c. From the WinSock Proxy Service Properties page, select the Caching tab and click the Advanced button. Under Object Time To Live, select TTL=__% and set the percentage box to 50%.

○ d. From the SOCKS Proxy Service Properties page, select the Caching tab and click the Advanced button. Under Object Time To Live, select TTL=__% and set the percentage box to 50%.

The correct answer to this question is b. TTL information is configured under the Web Proxy Service Properties page by selecting the Caching tab and clicking the Advanced button, and then selecting TTL=__% and setting the percentage box to 50 percent. Enabling active caching and setting equal importance will have an effect of active caching, but will not change the TTL setting for cached objects. Therefore, answer a is incorrect. The WinSock Proxy Service Properties page and the SOCKS Proxy Service Properties page don't have the Caching configuration tab available. Therefore, answers c and d are incorrect.

Need To Know More?

 For more information on the subjects covered in this chapter, refer to the following TechNet articles (these articles are also contained in the Microsoft Knowledge Base at www.microsoft.com):

➤ TechNet Article Q 135982. "Configuring Internet Explorer for Use with Proxy Server."

➤ TechNet Article Q 164084. "When Is a Proxy Server Required?"

➤ TechNet Article Q 164085. "The Difference Between Active and Passive Caching."

➤ TechNet Article Q 164051. "Proxy Server Fails if Virtual Memory Is Set Below Recommended Size."

➤ TechNet Article Q 163696. "WinSock Proxy Logging Limited in Comparison to Web Proxy."

Internet Access Via Proxy Server

Terms you'll need to understand:

- √ Local address table (LAT)
- √ Client configuration scripts
- √ Auto Dial
- √ Proxy Server arrays
- √ Cache
- √ Web Proxy service
- √ WinSock Proxy service
- √ SOCKS Proxy service

Techniques you'll need to master:

- √ Understanding the structure of the local address table (LAT) and what information it should or should not contain
- √ Configuring the Web Proxy cache
- √ Backing up and restoring the Proxy Server configuration

Because connecting to the Internet is a major reason to install Microsoft Proxy Server, you need to become very familiar with some if its configuration options. You must also have a good understanding of the local address table (LAT) and how to configure it. In addition, you must configure Auto Dial and cache settings properly to have a successful implementation of Microsoft Proxy Server.

Proxy Server's Role On The Internet

Microsoft Proxy Server provides an easy, secure, and cost-effective way to connect every desktop in an organization to the Internet (see Figure 7.1). Proxy Server "listens" to your internal computers. When a client application makes a request to the Internet, Proxy Server translates the request and passes it to the Internet. When a computer on the Internet responds, Proxy Server passes that response back to the client application on the computer that made the initial request.

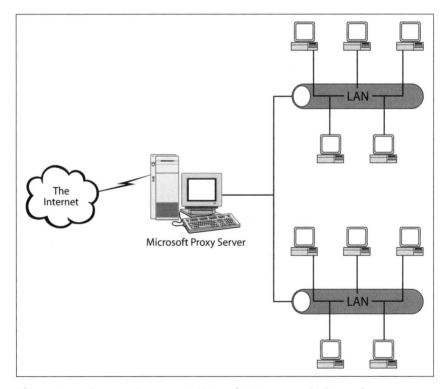

Figure 7.1 Connecting your LAN to the Internet via Proxy Server.

Configuring And Managing Client Internet Access

You can configure clients in two ways. The first is by modifying the default settings specified during the Proxy Server or client setup. The second is by modifying the configuration parameters of existing clients using the Internet Service Manager (ISM) or by using the Microsoft Management Console (MMC) with the Windows NT Option Pack. The following sections cover several of the configuration and management tasks you can perform for the clients. Here are some examples:

➤ Changing client configuration parameters

➤ Using client configuration scripts

➤ Editing the client configuration file

➤ Creating a client LAT file

➤ Configuring Web Proxy client applications

➤ Configuring WinSock Proxy client applications

Changing Client Configuration Parameters

Within the Client Installation/Configuration dialog (shown in Figure 7.2), you can specify how WinSock Proxy client applications and Web browsers

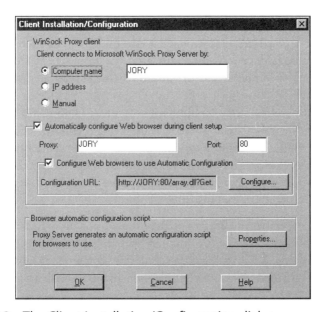

Figure 7.2   The Client Installation/Configuration dialog.

connect to the proxy server. The information within this dialog is initially configured during the server installation process.

The Client Installation/Configuration dialog is divided into three sections:

➤ WinSock Proxy Client

➤ Automatically Configure Web Browser During Client Setup

➤ Browser Automatic Configuration Script

Under WinSock Proxy Client, you specify how the WinSock clients connect to the proxy server. This connection can be made in one of three ways: by computer name, by IP address, or by manually entering the array name or the group of IP addresses for an array. If Manual is selected, you have to edit the client configuration file MSPCLNT.INI.

You also have the ability to specify that Web browsers use a configuration script, written in JavaScript, to designate how client requests are routed to the proxy server. You can route a client request to a proxy server, a proxy server array, or directly to the Internet. This eliminates the single point of failure by allowing you to automatically transfer from one proxy server to another.

The default location for this script is http://*servername*/array.dll?Get. Routing.Script, where *servername* is the name of the proxy server. This is the location of the script that is automatically generated based on the configuration options set in the Advanced Client Configuration dialog. You can access the Advanced Client Configuration dialog (shown in Figure 7.3) by clicking the Properties button.

You can specify IP addresses that should not be routed through the proxy server by adding these addresses to the list in the Advanced Client Configuration dialog. The client computer will attempt to access the Internet directly for any IP address specified in this list. Because clients must be able to resolve each URL to an IP address, they should have access to a DNS server that can resolve Internet names. Clicking the Add button and entering the IP address and the subnet mask configures this feature. You can also specify that all internal requests to internal servers pass through the proxy server. This is done by selecting the Use Proxy For Local Servers option. This allows you to improve browser performance by caching internal objects.

You can also specify domain names that should not be routed through the proxy server. Again, the client computers will attempt to access the Internet directly, bypassing the proxy server. Just enter the domain name to be excluded in the space provided. Separate multiple domain names with a semicolon (;).

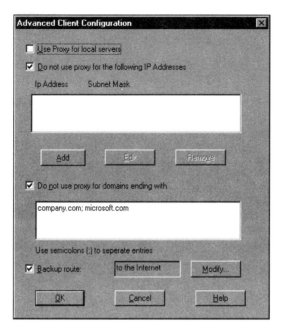

Figure 7.3   The Advanced Client Configuration dialog.

You can configure a backup route in case the primary route is unavailable. You can either specify that you want a direct connection to the Internet, or you can specify a route to another proxy server.

Using Client Configuration Scripts

You can optionally specify that each time a Web browser is opened, a client configuration script located on the proxy server is downloaded. This allows you to improve browser performance and to update browser configuration parameters. This downloaded script is executed each time the browser requests a URL. This helps to offload some of the routing work performed by the array. You can easily update all browser settings for your clients without having to manually reconfigure each of them. The client browser must be either Microsoft Internet Explorer 3.02 or higher, or Netscape 2.0 or higher.

Editing The Client Configuration File

The client configuration information is stored in the MSPCLNT.INI file. A master copy of this file is generated during the Microsoft Proxy Server installation process and is stored in the C:\Msp\Clients directory (or the drive letter where Proxy Server is installed if other than the C drive). Every client computer that is configured to use the proxy server has a copy of this file in its Mspclnt directory. The following code shows a sample MSPCLNT.INI file:

```
[Master Config]
Path1=\\JORY\mspclnt\
[Servers Ip Addresses]
Addr1=11.0.0.1
[Servers Ipx Addresses]
[Common]
WWW-Proxy=JORY
Set Browsers to use Proxy=1
Set Browsers to use Auto Config=1
WebProxyPort=80
Configuration Url=http://JORY:80/array.dll?Get.Routing.Script
Port=1745
Configuration Refresh Time (Hours)=6
Re-check Inaccessible Server Time (Minutes)=10
Refresh Give Up Time (Minutes)=15
Inaccessible Servers Give Up Time (Minutes)=2
Setup=Setup.exe
```

By default, this file is updated and copied to the client each time a client computer is restarted and every six hours after the initial refresh is made. When the
refresh is made, the client computer scans the MSPCLNT.INI file for the
server share paths listed in the **[Master Config]** section. There has to be at
least one path entry, and it is tried first. The only time additional path entries
are tried is if the preceding path did not supply updated files during a download.

You can modify the server's copy of the MSPCLNT.INI file in one of
two ways:

➤ Reinstall the server and specify new information in the Client Installa-
tion/Configuration dialog.

➤ Use a text editor to modify the MSPCLNT.INI file found in the
C:\Msp\Clients directory on the server.

You can also modify the client's copy of the MSCPCLNT.INI file in one of
two ways:

➤ Refresh the client's copy of the file by downloading the new version
from the server.

➤ Use a text editor to modify the MSPCLNT.INI file.

If you modify the MSPCLNT.INI file using a text editor, it will be
overwritten when refreshed by the server.

Creating A Client LAT File

When the client Setup program is executed, it installs a file named MSPLAT.TXT into the Mspclnt directory on the client computer. This file contains the LAT, which defines the IP addresses of the internal network. Like the client configuration file, the LAT configuration file is updated regularly from the proxy server. When a Windows Socket application tries to connect to an IP address, the LAT is checked to determine whether the IP address is on the internal or the external network. If the address is internal, the connection is made directly. If the address is external, the connection is made through the WinSock Proxy service on the proxy server.

Sometimes you'll be required to define different internal addresses so that specific clients can gain access to certain internal servers. However, the server copy will overwrite any changes that you make to the MSPLAT.TXT file when the file is refreshed. Therefore, you have the ability to create a custom LAT file for the client. To do so, use a text editor to create this file; then name it LOCALLAT.TXT and place it in the client's Mspclnt directory. The client then uses both MSPLAT.TXT and LOCALLAT.TXT to determine which IP addresses are internal and which are external.

When you create the LOCALLAT.TXT file, enter the IP addresses as ranges or as a single IP address. Here's an example:

```
192.168.12.0      192.168.12.255
192.168.12.50     192.168.12.50
```

Configuring Web Proxy Client Applications

A Web Proxy client is a client that uses a CERN application, such as a Web browser, and is configured to use the Web Proxy service. The client setup program configures the client's Web browsers. You can also configure the clients manually by changing the browsers' configuration parameters.

Configuring WinSock Proxy Client Applications

A WinSock Proxy client is a client that has Windows Sockets applications configured to use the WinSock Proxy service. The client setup program installs the WinSock client software. You should note that the client Setup program does not configure the individual Windows Sockets applications, instead it replaces the existing Windows Sockets DLL file that the applications use.

The WinSock Proxy service supports Windows Sockets 1.1 applications. You'll have to permit user access for specific protocols and service ports by configuring the WinSock service.

Configuring And Managing Server Internet Access

The following sections describe the following Proxy Server parameters that you can set and how to configure the other information in the dialogs:

➤ Configuring Auto Dial

➤ Changing The Local Address Table

➤ Configuring The Cache

➤ Backing Up And Restoring Configuration

Configuring Auto Dial

Auto Dial is an on-demand dial-out feature of Microsoft Proxy Server. It works in conjunction with the Windows NT Remote Access Service (RAS) to schedule dial-out connection times to the Internet.

The proxy server makes an Internet connection in the following situations:

➤ **Web Proxy Service** When the object being requested is not located in cache, or when active caching is automatically refreshing cached objects.

➤ **WinSock Proxy Service** All client requests are processed using a dial-up connection.

➤ **SOCKS Proxy Service** All client requests are processed using a dial-up connection.

You can schedule the times at which the proxy server uses the Auto Dial feature. To do this, you have to configure the times in the Configuration tab of the Auto Dial dialog (shown in Figure 7.4). You'll also be required to enter the connection information (RAS Phonebook entry to use, user name, password, and domain) in the Credentials tab of this dialog.

Changing The LAT

As previously stated, the LAT is contained in the MSPLAT.TXT file and is created initially during Proxy Server installation. The internal network information you provided during the installation is used to create the LAT. Any external networks are excluded from this list. You can modify the existing LAT

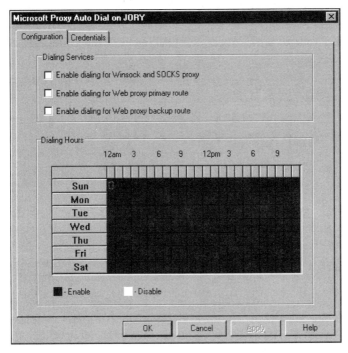

Figure 7.4   The Configuration Tab of the Auto Dial dialog.

by adding or removing IP address pairs manually. The Local Address Table Configuration dialog, where this is done, is shown in Figure 7.5.

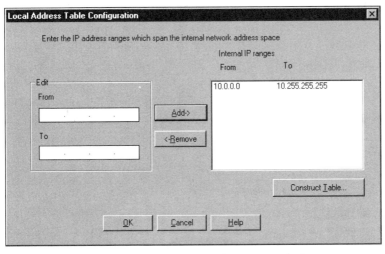

Figure 7.5   The Local Address Table Configuration dialog.

You can add a single IP address or a range of IP addresses:

➤ To add a single IP address to the LAT, enter in the same address in both From and To.

➤ To add a range of IP addresses to the LAT, enter the first address in the range in From and enter the last address in the range in To.

Configuring The Cache

The Web Proxy service of Proxy Server uses caching to store copies of HTTP and FTP objects on the local machine. This is done to improve performance (as the user sees it) and to reduce the bandwidth by accessing these cached objects from the local cache, rather than from the Internet. The Web Proxy Caching tab is shown in Figure 7.6.

 To use caching with Microsoft Proxy Server 2.0, you must install it on a computer that has at least one partition formatted as an NTFS volume. In Microsoft Proxy Server 1.0, you could place the cache on a FAT partition.

Some Internet objects are difficult to cache properly. These include objects that require authentication or are dynamically created. Proxy Server uses pre-defined criteria to determine if an object can be cached or not.

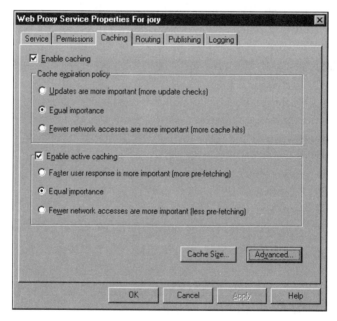

Figure 7.6   The Web Proxy Caching tab.

Internet objects that require authentication, or the Secure Sockets Layer (SSL), are not cached.

Several configuration options are available when you configure the cache on the proxy server:

➤ You can set passive caching parameters and a general expiration policy for object "freshness."

➤ You can set active caching parameters.

➤ You can change the cache drives and the total cache size.

➤ You can set advanced caching parameters, such as object Time To Live (TTL) and size.

Backing Up And Restoring Configuration

All server configuration information can be backed up to a locally stored text file. By default, this information is stored in the C:\Msp\Config directory. The filename is created using the form

```
MSPyyyymmdd.MCP
```

where *yyyy* is the year, *mm* is the month, and *dd* is the day.

You may restore (or roll back) to a previous configuration if you have backed the server configuration up to the file previously described. You may perform a *partial restore* or a *full restore*. A partial restore only restores the noncomputer-specific configuration parameters, such as user permissions. A full restore restores all configuration parameters that belong to the server (including the ones for the partial restore).

Be aware that to upgrade from Microsoft Proxy Server 1.0 to version 2.0, you should backup the 1.0 configuration, install 2.0, and then restore the configuration files.

Several configuration parameters are not restored during a partial restore:

➤ The Web Proxy cache size and disk location

➤ The disk location for all service logs and the packet filter log

➤ The packet filter configuration

➤ The Auto Dial configuration

➤ The server intra-array IP address

➤ The server alias used in the "HTTP Via" header for routing

➤ The Registry keys that cannot be configured through the ISM user interface

Tuning And Controlling Internet Access Performance

It can be difficult to tune your Proxy Server performance. Therefore, you need to take several different criteria into consideration: for example, number of users, the protocols used to access the Internet, and your available Internet bandwidth.

A nice feature of Microsoft Proxy Server 2.0 is the ability to set up a proxy array. With arrays, a group of Proxy Server computers can be configured and administered as a single entity with a large cache. Arrays also provide scalability and ease of administration.

Table 7.1 has Microsoft's recommended specifications for running Proxy Server. Remember, these recommendations are based on a server running just Windows NT and Microsoft Proxy Server.

To select the amount of cache needed, use the following formula: 100MB + 0.5MB for each Web Proxy client. For example, if you have 250 desktops that will be using the Web Proxy service, you'll need at least 225MB for cache.

Table 7.1   Microsoft Proxy Server minimum recommendations.

Scenario	Processor	Disk Space	RAM
Minimum	Intel 486 or faster	10MB	At least 24MB
Small office (up to 299 desktops)	Pentium 133	250MB to 2GB	At least 32MB
Medium office (300 to 1,999 desktops)	Pentium 166	2 to 4GB	At least 64MB
Large (2,000+ desktops)	1 Pentium 166 per 2,000	2GB to 4GB per server	At least 64MB per server
ISP (1,000+ dial-up users)	Pentium 166 per 1,000	2GB to 4GB per server	At least 64MB per server

Internet-Specific Proxy Server Logging

Three service logs record events generated by the Web Proxy, WinSock Proxy, and SOCKS Proxy services. Also, a separate packet log records network packet events. You may have this information logged to a text file or to an ODBC-compliant database. Although you can log to a remote drive, it is recommended that you have the information logged to a local drive to improve performance.

By default, all information is logged to a text file. Each service can be configured separately for logging to a text file or to a database. You also have the ability to select two logging modes—*regular* and *verbose*. The regular logging method has a smaller number of information fields to be logged. The verbose logging method logs all available information.

Because Proxy Server is a Microsoft Back Office product, it uses the Windows NT system event log to record events. You can use this information to monitor or troubleshoot a server problem. Table 7.2 lists the event source names that appear in the NT system event log and the source names that correspond to them.

When the proxy information is logged to a text file (the default), the file locations for each log are as follows:

➤ C:\Winnt\System32\Msplogs\W3*filname*.LOG for the Web Proxy service

➤ C:\Winnt\System32\Msplogs\WS*filename*.LOG for the WinSock Proxy service

Table 7.2   Microsoft Proxy Server source names.

Source Name	Description
MSProxyAdmin	Proxy Server administrative events
PacketFilterLog	Packet filter alert events
SocksProxy	SOCKS Proxy service events
SocksProxyLog	SOCKS Proxy logging events
WebProxyCache	Web Proxy caching events
WebProxyLog	Web Proxy logging events
WebProxyServer	Web Proxy service events
WinSockProxy	WinSock Proxy service events
WinSockProxyLog	WinSock Proxy logging events

➤ C:\Winnt\System32\Msplogs\SP*filename*.LOG for the SOCKS Proxy service

➤ C:\Winnt\System32\Msplogs\PF*filename*.LOG for packet filter events

The name itself depends on how logging is configured. You can configure logging to create a new log each day, week, or month. For example, here are the log files for the SOCKS Proxy service:

➤ SP*yymmdd*.LOG for daily logs

➤ SP*yymmw*.LOG for weekly logs

➤ SP*yymm*.LOG for monthly logs

In these log filenames, *yy* is a number between 00 and 99 (indicating the year), *mm* is a number between 01 and 12 (indicating the month), *w* is a number between 1 and 5 (indicating the week of the month), and *dd* is a number between 01 and 31 (indicating the day of the month).

You can also log to any ODBC-compliant database, such as Microsoft SQL Server. Proxy Server has an SQL logging table tool, called MKPLOG.EXE, that creates a Microsoft SQL Server table with the required field name, data type, and field length settings. MKPLOG.EXE must be executed from a Web browser on the same computer where the SQL server is located. This tool can be found in the IIS scripts directory (C:\Inetpub\Scripts\Tools) of a computer running Proxy Server. Be sure to remember that this tool creates the database table only for Microsoft SQL Server; all other database tables must be created manually, and you cannot use this tool to create a packet filter log table.

Troubleshooting Proxy Server Internet Connections

Proxy Server ships with a utility called MSPDIAG. It is installed by default in the C:\Msp directory. You can use this utility to detect common configuration problems on the server. Many of these will help you diagnose Internet connection problems. Here are some of the conditions that MSPDIAG checks for:

➤ Verify that Internet Information Server (IIS) 3.0 or later is installed

➤ Verify that Windows NT Service Pack 3 or later is installed

➤ Verify that valid IP addresses are assigned in the LAT

➤ Check the status of the IIS WWW service

➤ Check the status of the Proxy services

➤ Check to see if IP forwarding is disabled

➤ Check to see if the default gateway is specified

Make sure the LAT only contains internal network addresses. If an external network address is located in the LAT, both the clients and the proxy server will search for these addresses internally, rather than on the Internet. Often, if the LAT is incorrectly configured, you'll notice slow connections from the client.

Exam Prep Questions

Question 1

> You have several network interface cards in your Microsoft Proxy
> Server computer. There are two internal networks (192.168.12.0
> and 192.168.13.0) and two external networks (204.35.4.0 and
> 207.54.34.0). Which networks would you place in the LAT? [Check
> all correct answers]
>
> ❑ a. 192.168.12.0
>
> ❑ b. 192.168.13.0
>
> ❑ c. 204.35.4.0
>
> ❑ d. 207.54.34.0

The correct answers to this question are a and b. Only internal addresses are
entered in the LAT. Both c and d are external addresses. Therefore, answers c
and d are incorrect.

Question 2

> You have 550 client desktops that will access the Internet via the
> proxy server. You would like to configure the proxy server to cache
> common URLs. What is the minimum recommended cache size
> needed?
>
> ○ a. It doesn't matter, cache will be dynamically allocated as
>   needed
>
> ○ b. 200MB total
>
> ○ c. 375MB total
>
> ○ d. 5MB per URL accessed

The correct answer to this question is c. Use the formula 100MB + 0.5MB per
client desktop. The cache has to be manually configured and is not dynamic.
Therefore, answer a is incorrect. Two hundred megabytes is not sufficient for
cache in this situation. Therefore, answer b is incorrect. It is impossible to
know how many URLs are accessed; also, at 5MB per URL, the cache would
grow to unmanageable levels rather quickly. Therefore, answer d is incorrect.

Question 3

One of your managers needs to gain access to a private internal network (10.100.20.0). You do not want other users to have access to it through the LAT. What would you do?

○ a. Create a LOCALLAT.TXT file on the manager's computer with the network range (10.100.20.0 to 10.100.20.255)

○ b. Edit the manager's copy of the MSPLAT.TXT file and add the network range

○ c. Create a LOCALLAT.TXT file on everyone's computer denying access to the network range

○ d. Edit everyone's MSPLAT.TXT file and deny access to the network range

The correct answer to this question is a. You would need to create a local LAT file for the manager so that he/she may have access to this network. If you add the network range to the manager's MSPLAT.TXT file, the server copy at the next refresh will overwrite it. Therefore, answer b is incorrect. You cannot deny access to a range within the LAT (server or client)—you can only grant access. Therefore, answers c and d are incorrect.

Question 4

You upgraded your server from Microsoft Proxy Server 1.0 to Microsoft Proxy Server 2.0, and now caching does not work. Why?

○ a. Microsoft Proxy Server 1.0 is completely different from Microsoft Proxy Server 2.0; therefore, you cannot upgrade.

○ b. The old caching directory was on a FAT partition. Microsoft Proxy Server 2.0 only supports logging to NTFS partitions.

○ c. You are out of disk space. Add a drive.

○ d. Add more memory.

The correct answer to this question is b. You can upgrade from version 1.0 to 2.0. Therefore, answer a is incorrect. Caching worked before and the only change is the upgrade. Therefore, answer c is incorrect. Although adding more RAM solves a lot of problems, it does not in this case. Therefore, answer d is incorrect.

Question 5

You have 5,000 client desktops. How would you configure your Microsoft Proxy Server?

○ a. One server for all 5,000 clients.

○ b. Two servers. Manually configure half the clients to each.

○ c. Three servers. Manually assign an equal number of clients to cach.

○ d. Three servers in an array. Assign the clients to the array.

The correct answer to this question is d. When you have more than 2,000 client desktops, it is recommended that you create an array. One server would not be able to manage 5,000 desktops efficiently. Therefore, answer a is incorrect. Again, it is recommended that you install one proxy server for every 2,000 clients. Therefore, answer b is incorrect. Although you have enough servers in this configuration, you would not want to manually assign 5,000 clients. Therefore, answer c is incorrect.

Need To Know More?

 Search the online documentation installed with Proxy Server.

 Microsoft TechNet. February, 1998. A search on "Proxy Server 2.0" will yield a wealth of information.

 Many resources and documents are available on Microsoft's Web site at http://www.microsoft.com/proxy.

Managing Multiple Proxy Servers

8

. . . .

Terms you'll need to understand:

√   Distributed proxying

√   Hierarchical proxying

√   Proxy chaining

√   Cascading proxying

√   Proxy server array

√   Proxy route

Techniques you'll need to master:

√   Configuring a proxy server array

√   Configuring an upstream proxy server or array

√   Configuring a proxy server route

In this chapter, you'll learn how to configure proxy server arrays and routes to distribute proxy server workloads, provide higher client performance, and provide fault tolerance to the Microsoft Proxy Server environment. Proxy server arrays are configured and maintained using the Internet Service Manager (ISM) tool. Note that WinSock Proxy and SOCKS Proxy clients are not able to take complete advantage of the proxy server array environment.

An Overview Of Multiple Proxy Server Scenarios

Microsoft Proxy Server 2.0 provides the ability to connect multiple proxy servers logically. This provides fault tolerance for the client, distributes the client request workload, and subsequently distributes cached information, all of which provide better client request servicing by the proxy server array. When multiple proxy servers are connected logically, the structure can be distributed or hierarchical.

Distributed Proxying

In *distributed proxying*, multiple proxy servers are connected in a logical peer-to-peer fashion to form an array (see Figure 8.1). Each server in the array is known as an *array member*. By connecting proxy servers in this fashion, the cache of each server is combined to form one large, logical cache. When one server in an array is configured, all servers in the array are updated; therefore, virtual management of all proxy servers is accomplished. Fault tolerance is provided because when one proxy server goes down or is removed from the array, the other computers in the array are aware of the failure and "listen" for the return of the inoperative array member. Through a synchronization process, every member of the proxy server array is aware of the other members and their configuration. All members of a proxy server array must be running Microsoft Proxy Server 2.0.

When a proxy server array is configured, all members of the array pass configuration information to each other. By doing this, all array members have a current list of operational array members. The synchronization process can be configured for automatic synchronization. Here's a list of the information that is shared with other array members:

➤ Web Proxy service caching information (which includes the standard and advanced caching options)

➤ Web Proxy service protocol configuration (which includes access control information)

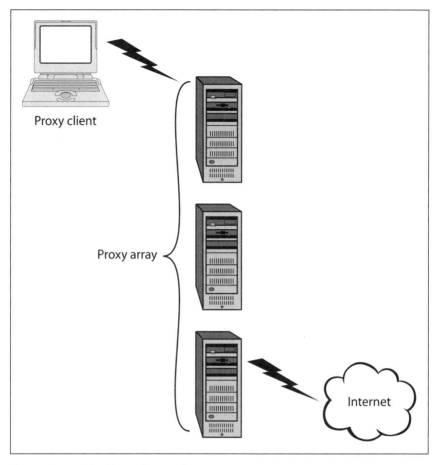

Figure 8.1   Distributed proxying.

➤ Web Proxy service publishing information (support for reverse proxying and reverse hosting)

➤ Web Proxy service security information

➤ Web Proxy service upstream routing options

➤ WinSock Proxy service protocol configuration

➤ WinSock Proxy service security information

➤ SOCKS Proxy service permissions

➤ Client configuration information

➤ Domain filters

➤ Logging information for each service (except packet filter logging)

➤ Local access table (LAT) information

Because the hashing method is used to determine the location of cached information, there isn't a cache contents list that has to be distributed among the proxy server array. Other information that is not passed includes the following:

➤ Web Proxy service Enable Caching flag status

➤ Web Proxy service cache size, disk, and directory location

➤ Logging directory information

➤ Packet filters, filter alerts, and logging information

The replication process takes place on the proxy server that is being altered. If someone else is modifying data at the same time you are, a conflict can occur. If the other proxy server changes have been applied and the synchronization process begins before your changes have been applied, a message appears on your screen and you can do one of two things:

➤ **Refresh** If you select Refresh, all the changes you made will be discarded.

➤ **Overwrite** If you select Overwrite, your changes will remain and be replicated across the array.

If you have applied the changes to your proxy server and you receive changes from another proxy server, an Array Configuration Conflict message box appears. You have two choices:

➤ **Synchronize Now** If this option is selected, you select an array member with which all of the Proxy Server computers in the array synchronize.

➤ **Cancel** If this option is selected, you are returned to the Internet Service Manager and effectively ignore the warning message.

 The best policy is to attempt to avoid conflicts. This can be done by scheduling time intervals when changes can be implemented by members of your administrative team.

Hierarchical Proxying

In *hierarchical proxying*, individual Proxy Server computers or arrays are "chained" together (see Figure 8.2). Rather than the communications path being peer-to-peer, as in distributed proxying, the communications path is hierarchical in structure. The Internet is at the top of the communications path, and the client is at the bottom. The Proxy Server computers or arrays between the top and the bottom are considered *upstream* if they are above other proxy servers in the communications path. The lower proxy servers in the structure are known as *downstream proxy servers*. Hierarchical proxying is also referred to as *proxy chaining* or *cascaded proxying*. Hierarchical proxying provides load balancing and improved cache performance, but it doesn't offer fault tolerance.

When multiple proxy servers are used, either chaining, distributed proxying, or a combination of both can be configured. In chaining, if a proxy server cannot fulfill a client request, it passes the request to an upstream proxy server. If the upstream proxy server cannot fulfill the client's request, the request is passed to the Internet. Every Proxy Server computer in the chain is its own entity; therefore, information about the individual computers is not passed between proxy servers.

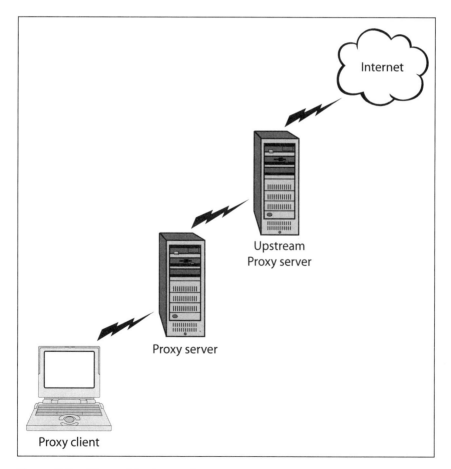

Figure 8.2   Hierarchical proxying.

With upstream routing, a primary upstream route can be configured, as well as a secondary (or backup) upstream route, in the event the primary upstream route is unavailable. To configure an upstream route, follow these steps:

1. In Internet Service Manager, select the Web Proxy service for the computer you're configuring an upstream route for. From the Properties menu, select Service Properties. The Web Proxy Service Properties menu appears.

2. Select the Routing tab. In the Upstream Routing area of the dialog, select Use Web Proxy Or Array. The Modify button then becomes active and you can configure an upstream proxy server or array. The Enable Backup Route option also becomes active, and you can configure an upstream backup route.

The Use Direct Connection option can be selected if you want the request routed directly to the Internet. While configuring the upstream proxy server, you can configure your proxy server to gather proxy server array information automatically for the upstream array membership. You can also provide a valid user name and password to be used for authentication by the upstream proxy server if the proxy server is in a different domain.

In a proxy server array, which is distributed proxying, the array acts as one logical entity, and each array member shares information about its configuration with other array members. When a client makes a request, the request goes to the configured array member. If the array member doesn't have the requested object, a hash function is performed to determine the array member the object should be stored on, and the request is forwarded to that array member. If that array member doesn't have the object, the request is passed to an upstream proxy server (if configured) and then forwarded to the Internet.

CARP And Hashing

Hashing is the technique the Cache Array Routing Protocol (CARP) uses to determine the location of stored objects in distributed proxying. The precursor to the CARP protocol was the Internet Cache Protocol (ICP), which couldn't scale very well to large proxied environments. CARP can be configured on the client using the Proxy Auto-Config (PAC) file so that the client sends the request for a stored object to the correct proxy server array member.

The hash technique performs a mathematical algorithm on all the proxy server names and the requested URL. The URL hash and proxy server hashes are combined, and the information is stored on the proxy server with the highest combined number. Because all the proxy servers in the array are using CARP, each computer uses the same algorithm and comes up with the same answer. This eliminates the need for large cached object location tables.

Balancing The Load Among Multiple Proxy Servers

Balancing the load among multiple proxy servers is accomplished by distributing the clients that use them evenly, which effectively distributes the information stored in the proxy server array's collective cache. For Web Proxy service clients, the distribution of clients can be automated, whereas the WinSock Proxy service and SOCKS Proxy service clients have to be assigned to a specific Proxy Server computer. This means WinSock Proxy and SOCKS Proxy clients can't take full advantage of the fault tolerance provided by a proxy server array. Three methods can be used to distribute clients evenly across a proxy server array: DNS Server, WINS Server, or a client-side configuration script.

Balancing Client Distribution Using DNS

Web Proxy client distribution can be accomplished by using Microsoft DNS server. This can be done by adding a CNAME (canonical name) resource record for each Proxy Server computer on your network. The CNAME, or *alias record*, would have the same name for all proxy server records.

When DNS provides IP address resolution for a client request, the first record in the list is used. For the next request made, the DNS server provides the address of the second proxy server in the list. This continues until the bottom of the list is reached; then DNS returns to the first resource record listed. This is known as a *round-robin* fashion of providing response to the client. For more information on DNS and configuring multiple CNAME resource records, refer to the *Windows NT Server Resource Kit* and the *Windows NT Server Resource Kit Supplement 1*.

Balancing Client Distribution Using WINS

Client distribution can also be accomplished using the Microsoft WINS service. To accomplish this task, make a multihomed entry in the WINS server database, with the IP address of all array members listed. When a client request for the IP address of a proxy server array member is received, the WINS server attempts to send back the address of a proxy server on the same subnet that the request came from. If this is not possible, the WINS server will provide the IP address for a proxy server on the same network as the client. If that is not possible, the WINS server will select a proxy server array member for the array at random.

Dealing With Geographical Distribution

When the network that the proxy server array supports is spread over a large geographical area, the preferred method for the discovery of a member of a proxy server array is through the WINS service.

As previously noted, DNS uses a round-robin method of providing the address of an array member back to the client, whereas the WINS service uses a method of attempting to provide the IP address of the array member that is closest to the client. The DNS method of distributing the client workload could have a negative impact on overall network performance by providing the client with the IP address of an array member that might not be located on the client's local subnet.

Reverse Hosting With Proxy Server

As stated in earlier chapters, reverse hosting with Microsoft Proxy Server 2.0 allows the proxy server to receive external requests, forward those requests to an internal Internet Information Server (IIS) computer, and send back responses on behalf of the IIS computer. This makes it possible for an internal Web server to accept incoming requests and publish objects on the Internet. To configure reverse hosting, follow these steps:

1. From the ISM, select the Web Proxy Service icon. From the Properties menu, select Service Properties. The Web Proxy Service Properties dialog appears.

2. Select the Publishing tab and then select the Enable Web Publishing box. If the proxy server is the IIS Web server to which you want to pass the Internet requests, select Sent To The Local Web Server. If the IIS server is a downstream server, select Sent To Another Web Server and provide the computer name and port used. The default port number is 80.

All requests will be sent to the listed Web server. Exceptions to this can be configured by adding the original URL and a new path to the Except For Those Listed dialog.

Best Practices For Multiple Proxy Servers

Here are some best practices to follow when using multiple proxy servers:

➤ Configure clients to use a proxy server array rather than a single proxy server. This provides the client better proxy performance and fault tolerance.

➤ If possible, all the proxy servers should be members of the same domain. This makes the authentication process much easier to configure and provides another layer of protection against unauthorized external detection of your internal network.

➤ Use WINS rather than DNS to distribute client workload. WINS attempts to provide the client with the IP address of the closest proxy server, whereas DNS uses a round-robin approach to distribute the workload with no regard to physical location of the client.

➤ Create a distributed proxying environment by setting up a proxy server array rather than a chained proxy environment. This provides better overall support for the proxy client.

➤ If multiple administrators are assigned to modify the configuration in an array, assign times when each administrator can perform administrative tasks to avoid synchronization conflicts.

➤ If only one administrator is responsible for maintaining and configuring a proxy server array, modify only one proxy server array member at a time to avoid synchronization conflicts.

Troubleshooting Multiple Proxy Server Situations

Several problems can arise when dealing with multiple proxy servers in an array. If you're in a multidomain environment, create a domain for all of the proxy servers for your network. This will help limit some of the user authentication problems that can occur when a downstream proxy server attempts to contact an upstream proxy server in a chained proxy environment.

As always, troubleshooting should follow a logical path, gathering information from a higher level and working down to more precise information. For instance, if a proxy server array problem is indicated, look in Event Viewer first to gather information about anything that may have occurred to cause the proxy server array problem. This can save you hours of troubleshooting time due to looking in the wrong place for a problem.

For problems that manifest themselves with a dialog when you're attempting to make changes, such as applying the changes you have just made to a proxy server array member, be sure to read the dialog before making a selection. Also, make sure you know what the selection you choose will do to overcome an error. In the case of making changes to an array member, two different message boxes come up:

➤ **Configuration Changed** This message box appears if a change has been made by another array member and has been implemented before your changes have been applied. The choices you have in this scenario are Refresh, in which case your changes are discarded and you will have to reconfigure after the synchronization is complete, and Overwrite, in which case your changes will overwrite the changes made to the array by the other person. In this case, it's advisable to find out who was making the changes and explain that you have overwritten the changes.

➤ **Array Configuration Conflict** This message box appears if you have made and applied changes to a member server and someone else has done the same thing. One option you can choose is Synchronize Now, which allows you to select an array member with which to synchronize the entire array. You can select the array member you're in conflict with, in which case your changes will be discarded, and the other member's changes will be implemented. You can also select your array member, in which case the other array member's changes will be lost, or you can select a different array member, in which case both updates will be lost. The second option you have is Cancel, which cancels the message box but does not discard your changes.

Here's a list of some of the more common error messages that can appear when working with an array problem:

➤ **130—The Web Proxy service detected that the upstream proxy *servername* is down.** This indicates that an upstream server is down. Attempt to connect to the server using ISM and determine what the problem is. If you cannot establish communications in this manner, attempt to view the event log for the upstream proxy server.

➤ **131—The Web Proxy service detected that the upstream proxy *servername* is back up.** This indicates that the problem with the upstream server has been resolved.

➤ 132—The Web Proxy service detected that the array member *servername* is down. This indicates that an array member is down. Use the same troubleshooting technique as you would for the 130 error message.

➤ 133—The Web Proxy service detected that the array member *servername* is back up. This indicates that the problem with the array member has been resolved.

➤ 139—Proxy server *servername* requires proxy-to-proxy authentication. Proxy server *servername* is not configured. This indicates that the user name and/or password used for authentication on the remote proxy server is invalid. To troubleshoot this error, verify that the user name and password have not changed on the remote server.

➤ 141—Proxy server detected a proxy chain loop. Please check the proxy server routing configuration on all chained proxies. This indicates that an upstream router points back to the downstream route, which causes a virtual loop between proxy servers.

A complete list of error messages is available in the online documentation for the Proxy service, broken into categories for WinSock Proxy, SOCKS Proxy, packet filtering events, RAS errors, logging errors, and miscellaneous errors. The error messages listed indicate errors with the proxy server array specifically, and they give a general idea of the problem and how to begin troubleshooting it.

Exam Prep Questions

Question 1

Which of the following statements is the best definition of a proxy server array?

○ a. A distributed, peer-to-peer-type multiple proxy server configuration that provides fault tolerance and better client response for the client when accessing the Internet.

○ b. A hierarchical-structured multiple proxy server environment that provides better client response when accessing the Internet.

○ c. A distributed, single proxy server environment with multiple clients connecting to a specific proxy server when accessing the Internet.

○ d. A hierarchical proxy client configuration that allows clients to connect to a proxy server through other proxy clients.

The correct answer to this question is a. A proxy server array is a distributed proxying environment. Answer b is the definition of a chained proxy environment. Answer c is incorrect because it's the definition of a proxy server, not a proxy server array. Answer d is incorrect because it describes a fictional proxy structure.

Question 2

Which of the following apply to a chained proxy server environment? [Check all correct answers]

❑ a. Provides better client response for Internet requests by filling more client requests locally.

❑ b. Has a hierarchical structure.

❑ c. Has a distributed structure.

❑ d. Updates upstream and downstream Proxy Server computers.

The correct answers are a and b. A chained proxy environment places multiple proxy servers in a hierarchical structure to provide better client response to

Internet requests. Answer c describes a proxy server array configuration, and is, therefore, incorrect. Answer d is incorrect because upstream and downstream proxy servers don't update each other.

Question 3

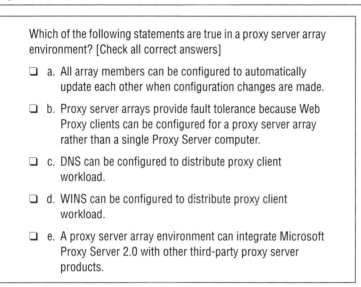

Which of the following statements are true in a proxy server array environment? [Check all correct answers]

❑ a. All array members can be configured to automatically update each other when configuration changes are made.

❑ b. Proxy server arrays provide fault tolerance because Web Proxy clients can be configured for a proxy server array rather than a single Proxy Server computer.

❑ c. DNS can be configured to distribute proxy client workload.

❑ d. WINS can be configured to distribute proxy client workload.

❑ e. A proxy server array environment can integrate Microsoft Proxy Server 2.0 with other third-party proxy server products.

The correct answers to this question are a, b, c, and d. In a proxy server array, all proxy members update each other's configuration information, and clients can use DNS or WINS to access any available proxy server array member. By doing this, the workload is distributed evenly to all proxy server array members and fault tolerance is provided. Only Microsoft Proxy Server 2.0 servers can join or form a proxy server array. Therefore, answer e is incorrect.

Question 4

> Which of the following statements best describes a chained proxy environment?
>
> ○ a. A distributed, peer-to-peer-type multiple proxy server configuration that provides fault tolerance and better client response for the client when accessing the Internet.
>
> ○ b. A proxy server configured to respond to requests from the Internet and forward the requests to an IIS server located on the internal network.
>
> ○ c. A hierarchical proxy client configuration that allows clients to connect to a proxy server over proxy clients.
>
> ○ d. A hierarchical-structured multiple Proxy Server environment that provides better client response when accessing the Internet.

The correct answer to this question is d. In a chained proxy environment, client requests that cannot be fulfilled by the proxy server or array are forwarded to an upstream proxy server. Answer a is incorrect because it's the definition of a proxy server array. Answer b describes a proxy server that's configured to support reverse proxying. Answer c is incorrect because it's not a valid proxy configuration.

Question 5

> In a proxy server array, not all information is replicated to each proxy member. Select the information that is replicated to all proxy server array members. [Check all correct answers]
>
> ❑ a. A list of cached items
>
> ❑ b. Web Proxy service protocol information
>
> ❑ c. Local access table (LAT) information
>
> ❑ d. Proxy cache size

The correct answers to this question are b and c. The Web Proxy service protocol information is shared along with the LAT information. A list of cached items doesn't have to be distributed because the CARP hashing algorithm determines where items will be located, and all proxy servers in an array use CARP. Therefore, answer a is incorrect. The proxy cache size on each array member is privileged information and does not need to be shared. Therefore, answer d is incorrect.

Question 6

Which of the following statements best describes the role of hashing in a proxy server array environment?

○ a. Hashing is the protocol used by downstream clients to access upstream proxy servers.

○ b. Hashing is the protocol used by array members to communicate.

○ c. Hashing is performed on all available array members and on the URL the client requests. The array member with the highest hashed total is used to cache the Internet site locally.

○ d. Hashing is the method DNS uses to distribute clients evenly to all proxy server clients.

The correct answer to this question is c. Hashing is the mathematical algorithm used to determine which array member will provide the cache area for an Internet URL when retrieved. Hashing is not a protocol. Therefore, answers a and b are incorrect. DNS uses a round-robin method to distribute client workload to all members of a proxy server array. Therefore, answer d is incorrect.

Question 7

You receive a Synchronization Conflict message and have the choice to Synchronize Now or Cancel. What does this indicate?

○ a. You were making changes to an array member but hadn't applied the changes, and someone else made changes to a different array member and did apply the changes.

○ b. You were making changes to an array member and applied the changes, and someone else made changes to a different array member and hadn't applied the changes.

○ c. You were making changes to an array member and applied the changes, and someone else made changes to a different array member and applied the changes.

○ d. You were making changes to an array member but haven't applied the changes, and someone else made changes to a different array member and hadn't applied the changes.

The correct answer to this question is c. If you apply changes to an array member and someone else has also made changes to a different array member and applied the changes, a synchronization conflict occurs. Answer a provides a different error message. In answer b, the other array member will receive the error message when the changes are applied. Therefore, answers a and b are incorrect. Answer d is incorrect because none of the array members have been modified yet.

Question 8

While modifying an array member, you receive a message stating you can Refresh or Overwrite, yet you haven't applied your changes. What does this indicate?

○ a. You were making changes to an array member but hadn't applied the changes, and someone else made changes to a different array member and did apply the changes.

○ b. You were making changes to an array member and applied the changes, and someone else made changes to a different array member and hadn't applied the changes.

○ c. You were making changes to an array member and applied the changes, and someone else made changes to a different array member and applied the changes.

○ d. You were making changes to an array member but haven't applied the changes, and someone else made changes to a different array member and hasn't applied the changes.

The correct answer to this question is a. If another array member has been modified and the changes have been applied, the synchronization process starts. If you are making changes to your array member, a message will appear on the screen that allows you to accept the refresh from the other array member and lose your changes or to overwrite the changes made on the other array member. Answer b is incorrect because the message would appear on the other array member's screen. Answer c is incorrect because a different message would appear on your screen. Answer d is incorrect because no changes have been applied, so the synchronization process would not have started.

Question 9

> You want to evenly distribute clients across all array members on your local area network. You have decided to use the Microsoft DNS Server to define all your proxy server array members and send back IP address resolution to the array in a round-robin fashion. How would you configure the DNS server?
>
> ○ a. Make an "A" type resource record for each array member and select the Enable Round Robin selection box under DNS Properties.
>
> ○ b. Make a CNAME resource record with the same name and the IP address of each array member.
>
> ○ c. Make a PROXYA resource record and add the IP address of each array member to the record.
>
> ○ d. Do nothing at all. Proxy Server will automatically add resource records to the DNS server for you.

The correct answer to this question is b. A CNAME record is an alias record. Make a CNAME resource record for each array member with the IP address of each but use the same alias name. Answer a is incorrect because a CNAME resource record is created, not an "A" resource record. Answer c is incorrect because there is no PROXYA-type resource record defined in DNS. Answer d is incorrect because the proxy servers do not attempt to contact the DNS server.

Question 10

> Which of the following protocols replaced the Internet Cache Protocol (ICP), was designed by Microsoft, and is an integral part of the multiple proxy server capability?
>
> ○ a. RARP
>
> ○ b. Hash
>
> ○ c. TCP
>
> ○ d. CARP

The correct answer to this question is d. CARP was designed by Microsoft to manage caching for proxy servers. RARP is reverse ARP and is used to boot remote computers that have no boot device. Therefore, answer a is incorrect.

HASH is the mathematical algorithm that helps determine where information is stored in a proxy server array. Therefore, answer b is incorrect. TCP is the Transmission Control Protocol, which is an integral part of connection-oriented communications using IP. Therefore, answer d is incorrect.

Need To Know More?

 For more information on the subjects covered in this chapter, refer to the following TechNet articles (these articles can also be found in the Microsoft Knowledge Base at www.microsoft.com):

➤ TechNet Article Q 174922: "Proxy Server 2.0 Release Notes."

➤ TechNet Article Q 177063: "Proxy Server 2.0: Error 12201 Proxy to Proxy Authentication."

➤ TechNet Article: "MS Proxy Server Security Evaluation."

➤ TechNet Article: "Cache Array Routing Protocol And Proxy Server Version 2.0"

➤ TechNet Article: "Proxy Server Reviewers Guide: Array Administration."

9

Troubleshooting
. . . .

Terms you'll need to understand:

√   Counter

√   MIB (Management Information Base)

√   SNMP (Simple Network Management Protocol)

√   Registry

√   Registry tree

√   Event logs

Techniques you'll need to master:

√   Understanding the Windows NT Registry Editor

√   Using the Microsoft Performance Monitor application

√   Using the Microsoft Event Viewer

In this chapter, we'll cover one of the most important aspects of any operating system—troubleshooting. It's important to know how to determine a problem, where to look for solutions, and how to fix the problem. We'll cover some basic troubleshooting techniques, as well as techniques specific to troubleshooting Microsoft Proxy Server 2.0.

The Basics Of Troubleshooting

Troubleshooting a combined Microsoft NT Server and Proxy Server configuration is one of the most difficult and challenging tasks you might perform as a network administrator. It is a four-step process that includes identifying a problem, diagnosing the problem, implementing a solution, and verifying that the implemented solution has solved the problem.

Identifying a problem is usually straightforward and easy. Diagnosing the problem is much more challenging. Use the resources you have at hand—these include TechNet, the online documentation, the Internet, and most important, other administrators. Subscribe to a mailing list, such as NTSYS ADMIN-list or NTools E-News (subscribe at www.sunbelt-software.com). You'll be amazed as to how far other NT administrators will go to assist an administrator they have never met (and will probably never meet).

When you implement a solution, document every task you perform. This will help you reverse the changes made, if required. Once a task is performed, verify whether the problem has been fixed. If it has not, reverse the change and try a different solution. Try not to implement change after change without first checking the results. If your system fails in other ways, you'll have a tough time figuring out which of your changes caused the problem. Once you have verified that a problem has been solved, document the problem and the change you made to solve it. By doing this and storing the information in a text file or a database, you'll save you and your colleagues time should the same problem occur again.

Resources For Shooting Trouble: Where To Look For Help

Because Proxy Server is part of Microsoft BackOffice, it ties in very closely with the Windows NT Event Viewer. If you're experiencing problems with Proxy Server, the system event log in the Windows NT Event Viewer is a good place to start. Proxy Server logs many messages in the format

Messagetext Errornumber

where *Messagetext* is the explanatory message and *Errornumber* is a Windows NT error code number. Figure 9.1 shows the Event Viewer's Event Detail dialog.

You can also use the Server Diagnostic utility (MSPDIAG.EXE) to troubleshoot common configuration problems. Several other tools are available to you to help you troubleshoot Proxy Server installation and performance. These include:

➤ **Microsoft TechNet** A monthly subscription of CD-ROMs that contain an impressive amount of information on the evaluation, implementation, and support of Microsoft products. This product also contains the same Microsoft Knowledge Base that the Microsoft support engineers use to troubleshoot customer problems. Also included are the Microsoft *Resource Kits*, as well as service patches, hot fixes, and evaluation copies of many Microsoft products, including Proxy Server 2.0. You can find more information about TechNet on the Web at www.microsoft.com/technet.

➤ **Microsoft Knowledge Base** An online version of the same database used by Microsoft support engineers when they troubleshoot customer problems. Also included are troubleshooting wizards and downloadable files (such as printer and video drivers). You can access the Microsoft Knowledge Base at http://support.microsoft.com.

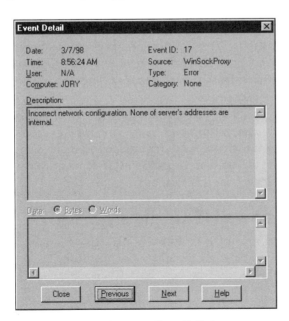

Figure 9.1   The Event Viewer's Event Detail dialog.

➤ **Microsoft Proxy Server Home Page** This Web site contains a wealth of information specific to Microsoft Proxy Server. Most of the information available on this page is also available on TechNet CD-ROM. It is, however, a good idea to check this page regularly because new information is posted here before it is added to TechNet. You can access the Microsoft Proxy Server home page at www.microsoft.com/proxy.

➤ **Microsoft Proxy Server Online Documentation** An online manual for Microsoft Proxy Server 2.0 (it requires Internet Explorer 4.0 to use all its features). You can choose to install this documentation when you install Proxy Server. The online documentation has a complete listing of the Proxy Server Registry entries and event messages.

Proxy Server Registry Entries (And Related Data)

All configuration information for Windows NT (and Proxy Server) is stored in a database known as the Registry. The *Registry* is made up of sections (called *subtrees*) such as HKEY_LOCAL_MACHINE and HKEY_CURRENT_CONFIG, at the top of the hierarchy. Below these sections are keys (such as HARDWARE, SOFTWARE, and SYSTEM), and below the keys are the subkeys. Each key and subkey has an entry assigned to it. These entries consist of entry names, data types, and values. You can choose from two Registry editors (REGEDT32.EXE or REGEDIT.EXE) to view, change, or delete these entries directly. REGEDT32.EXE has more menu items, and you can only search for Registry keys and subkeys. REGEDIT.EXE allows you to search for Registry strings and values, as well as keys and subkeys.

 Do not edit the Registry unless it is absolutely necessary *and* you know what you're doing. Try to use the Windows NT Control Panel applets to make any system changes. If the Registry is edited incorrectly, you may have to reinstall some or all of your system's software.

The Windows NT Registry Editor

By default, when you install Windows NT, no icons are created for the Registry Editor. You must execute the application manually. To do this, select Run from the Start menu and type "regedt32" (shown in Figure 9.2) or "regedit" (shown in Figure 9.3).

When you make changes to the Registry, try to limit the number of changes you make at one time; it will be much easier for you to troubleshoot if something

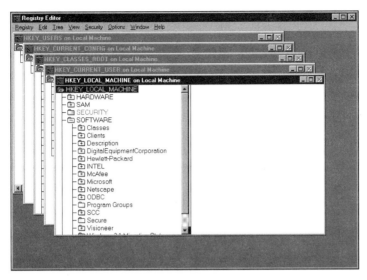

Figure 9.2   REGEDT32.EXE.

goes wrong. If, for example, you change one entry in the Registry and Proxy Server (or any other application) stops working, you know to change the entry back to its original value. However, if you change several different entries and Proxy Server stops working, you have to figure out which of the entries caused the failure.

You should use the administrative tools in the Internet Service Manager (ISM) or the Microsoft Management Console (MMC) whenever possible. Use the

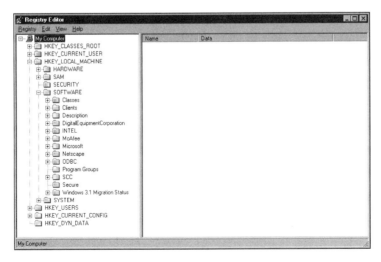

Figure 9.3   REGEDIT.EXE.

Registry Editor only if the changes you require cannot be performed through the ISM or the MMC. Changes made using the ISM or the MMC take effect immediately, whereas values made using the Registry Editor do not take effect until you start and stop the proxy service.

We won't detail every one of the Registry entries for Proxy Server (there are just too many of them). However, we will cover the different types of entries as well as where the Proxy Server Registry information is stored. Value entries in the Registry appear as a string, which consists of three components:

➤ The name of the value

➤ The class or type of the value entry

➤ The value itself

Also, here are the five different value classes or data types:

➤ **REG_BINARY** Identifies a value entry as binary

➤ **REG_SZ** Identifies a value entry as a data string

➤ **REG_DWORD** Identifies a value entry as a DWORD entry

➤ **REG_MULTI_SZ** Identifies a value entry as a multiple string

➤ **REG_EXPAND_SZ** Indicates that a value entry is an expandable string

Several Registry values apply to the Web Proxy service, the WinSock Proxy service, and the SOCKS Proxy service. Their location in the Registry is covered in the following sections.

Domain Filtering Keys

Domain filtering keys determine which Web sites the clients have permission to access. The Registry entries are located in HKEY_LOCAL_MACHINE\ SYSTEM\CurrentControlSet\Services\W3Proxy\Parameters\DoFilter.

Additional Registry entries exist for domains and IP addresses where access has been granted or denied. They are located in HKEY_LOCAL_ MACHINE\SYSTEM\CurrentControlSet\Services\W3Proxy\Parameters\ DoFilter\DenySites\GrantSites.

Packet Filtering Keys

The packet filtering Registry keys are located in HKEY_LOCAL_ MACHINE\SYSTEM\CurrentControlSet\Services\mspadmin\Filters.

Proxy Server Alerting Keys

The Registry keys used to configure mail notification of alerts are located in HKEY_LOCAL_MACHINE\SYSTEM\CurrentControlSet\Services\msp admin\ Parameters\Alerting.

Proxy Server Array Keys

If you change the Registry for one member of the proxy array, you must also change the Registry entries for all the other members of the array; otherwise, the array members will be out of synchronization and will not perform properly. There are three important Registry keys: the array membership, the chained array, and the backup route.

The array membership keys are located in HKEY_LOCAL_MACHINE\ SYSTEM\CurrentControlSet\Services\W3Proxy\Parameters\MemberArray\ *computername*, where *computername* is the name of the array member.

The chained array keys are located in HKEY_LOCAL_MACHINE\ SYSTEM\CurrentControlSet\Services\W3Proxy\Parameters\ChainedArray.

The backup route keys are located in HKEY_LOCAL_MACHINE\ SYSTEM\CurrentControlSet\Services\W3Proxy\Parameters\BackupRoute.

Logging Values

The logging value entries affect Proxy Server packet filtering. They are located in HKEY_LOCAL_MACHINE\SYSTEM\CurrentControlSet\ Services\ mspadmin\Parameters.

Storing Logs On A Network Share

You have the ability to change the log directory of the Proxy Server computer so that it logs all its information to another computer on the network. You are required to permit access to null sessions on the computer that contains the log files by accessing the Registry keys located in HKEY_LOCAL_ MACHINE\ SYSTEM\CurrentControlSet\Services\LanmanServer\Parameters.

Handling Web Proxy Service Problems

This section is divided into two subsections. The first covers the Web Proxy service event messages. The second section lists where the keys for the Web Proxy service are stored in the Registry. (You will not need to know the details about the individual entries within those keys.)

Event Messages

Web Proxy has three different types of event messages: service event messages, cache event messages, and array and chain event messages. These messages and a brief description of each are covered in the following sections.

Web Proxy Service Event Messages

The Web Proxy service event messages (including arrays and chains) appear in the system event log with the WebProxyServer and WebProxyLog source names.

The Web Proxy service logs the following event messages:

➤ HTTP/1.0 500 server error (an attempt has been made to operate on an impersonation token by a thread that is not currently impersonating a client).

➤ HTTP/1.0 500 server error (-number).

➤ HTTP/1.0 500 server error (the specified module could not be found).

➤ 115—W3Proxy failed to start because the system time is incorrect.

➤ 116—W3Proxy failed to start because the Microsoft Proxy Server RC program expired on date. Please contact Microsoft about this product.

➤ 118—The Web Proxy service was halted. The 60-day free evaluation period has expired.

➤ 125—The Web Proxy service received *number* requests from the Internet port during the past *number* seconds while Internet publishing was disabled.

➤ 126—The Web Proxy service configuration has been modified *number* time(s) during the past *number* seconds.

➤ 129—The Web Proxy service is continued.

Web Proxy Cache Event Messages

The Web Proxy service cache event messages appear in the system event log with the WebProxyCache source name.

 If caching does not occur, make sure there's sufficient disk space available on the cache drive.

The Web Proxy service logs the following cache event messages:

➤ 111—Web Proxy cache initialization failed due to an incorrect configuration. Please use the administration utility or manually edit the Registry to correct the error and restart the service.

➤ 112—Web Proxy cache corrected a corrupted or old format URL cache by removing all or part of the cache's contents.

➤ 113—Web Proxy cache failed to initialize the URL cache on disk.

➤ 114—The hard disk used by the Web Proxy Server service to cache popular URLs is full. Space needs to be freed, or the Web Proxy cache needs to be reconfigured to resume normal operation.

Web Proxy Array And Chain Event Messages

The Proxy Server array and chain event messages appear in the system event log with the WebProxyServer and WebProxyLog source names. The Web Proxy service logs the following array and chain event messages:

➤ 130—The Web Proxy service detected that the upstream proxy *servername* is down.

➤ 131—The Web Proxy service detected that the upstream proxy *servername* is back up.

➤ 132—The Web Proxy service detected that the array member *servername* is down.

➤ 133—The Web Proxy service detected that the array member *servername* is back up.

➤ 139—Proxy Server *servername* requires proxy-to-proxy authentication. Proxy Server *servername* is not configured with this type of authentication.

Web Proxy Service Registry Keys

Web Proxy has four different types of values: service, service MIB, service cache, and service publishing values. These values are covered in the following sections.

Web Proxy Service Values

The Web Proxy service Registry keys are located in HKEY_LOCAL_MACHINE\SYSTEM\CurrentControlSet\Services\W3Proxy\Parameters.

Web Proxy Service MIB Values

The path to the dynamic link library (DLL) for the Web Proxy service Management Information Base (MIB) is located in HKEY_LOCAL_MACHINE\ SOFTWARE\Microsoft\W3Proxy\CurrentVersion.

> *Note: The MIB is a set of objects that can be used by the Simple Network Management Protocol (SNMP) to manage Proxy Server. SNMP works by sending messages, called Protocol Data Units (PDUs), to the proxy server. The server then returns a list of its manageable objects to the SNMP requesters.*

Web Proxy Service Cache Values

The three important Registry keys are the cache parameters, the cache path, and the cache filters. The cache parameter keys are located in HKEY_ LOCAL_MACHINE\SYSTEM\CurrentControlSet\Services\W3Pcache\Parameters.

The cache path keys are located in HKEY_LOCAL_MACHINE\SYSTEM\ CurrentControlSet\Services\W3Pcache\Parameters\Paths.

The cache filters keys are located in HKEY_LOCAL_MACHINE\SYSTEM\ CurrentControlSet\Services\W3Pcache\UrlData.

Web Proxy Service Publishing Values

The parameters that define the reverse proxy (publishing) values of the Web Proxy service are located in HKEY_LOCAL_MACHINE\SYSTEM\ CurrentControlSet\Services\W3Proxy\Parameters\Reverse Proxy.

Mapping routes an incoming Internet request from the system identified in the request to another system located behind the proxy server. The Registry keys for mapping are located in HKEY_LOCAL_MACHINE\SYSTEM\ CurrentControlSet\Services\W3Proxy\Parameters\Reverse Proxy\Mapping.

Managing WinSock Proxy Service Problems

This section is divided into two parts. The first covers the WinSock Proxy service event messages. The second lists where the keys for the WinSock Proxy service are stored in the Registry. (You will not need to know the details about the individual entries within those keys.)

Event Messages

The WinSock Proxy service event messages appear in the system event log with the WinSockProxy and WinSockProxyLog source names.

The WinSock Proxy service logs the following event messages:

➤ 1—The WinSock Proxy service failed to initialize. The data is the internal error code.

➤ 2—The WinSock Proxy service failed to initialize the network. The data is the error.

➤ 3—The WinSock Proxy service started.

➤ 4—The WinSock Proxy service cannot initialize due to a shortage of available memory. The data is the error.

➤ 5—User *username* at host *hostname* has timed out after *number* seconds of inactivity.

➤ 6—The WinSock Proxy service cannot initialize performance counters. The data is the error.

➤ 7—The WinSock Proxy service has failed due to a shortage of available memory. The data is the number of connections.

➤ 9—The performance counters DLL for the WinSock Proxy service failed because the function *functionname* failed. The data is the error.

➤ 10—The WinSock Proxy service failed to initialize because of missing or corrupted Registry settings. The data is the error.

➤ 11—The WinSock Proxy service failed to bind its socket to *unknown* port *portnumber*.

➤ 12—Client from unknown attempts to access WinSock Proxy service by using control protocol version *versionnumber*. The server supports version *versionnumber*.

➤ 13, 14—The WinSock Proxy service requires Windows NT Server 4.0.

➤ 15—The WinSock Proxy service failed to load security DLL.

➤ 16—The WinSock Proxy service failed to determine network addresses.

➤ 17—Incorrect network configuration. None of the server's addresses are internal.

➤ 18—The WinSock Proxy service failed to start because the system time is incorrect.

➤ 19—The WinSock Proxy service failed to start because the Microsoft Proxy Server RC program expired on date. Please contact Microsoft for details about this product.

➤ 20—Warning: the Microsoft Proxy Server RC program expired on date. Please contact Microsoft for details about this product.

➤ 36—*Address* address is missing from the configuration file.

WinSock Proxy Service Registry Keys

The WinSock Proxy Service Registry key has two types of values: service and MIB.

WinSock Proxy Service Values

The WinSock Proxy service Registry keys are located in HKEY_LOCAL_MACHINE\SYSTEM\CurrentControlSet\Services\WSPSrv\Parameters.

WinSock Proxy Service MIB Values

The path to the DLL for the WinSock Proxy service MIB is located in HKEY_LOCAL_MACHINE\SYSTEM\CurrentControlSet\WSPSrv\SNMP.

Managing SOCKS Proxy Service Problems

This section is divided into two sections. The first covers the SOCKS Proxy service event messages. The second section lists where the keys for the SOCKS Proxy service are stored in the Registry. (You will not need to know the details about the individual entries within those keys.)

Event Messages

The SOCKS Proxy service logs two entries to the event log for each successful connection—one when the connection is established and the other when the connection is closed. When the connection is closed, the number of bytes sent and received is logged. The SOCKS Proxy service event message appears in the system event log with the SocksProxy and SocksProxyLog source names.

SOCKS Proxy Service Registry Keys

The SOCKS Proxy service Registry keys are located in HKEY_LOCAL_
MACHINE\SYSTEM\CurrentControlSet\Services\W3Proxy\ Pa-
rameters\ SOCKS.

Troubleshooting Proxy Server Performance

Microsoft Windows NT has an incredibly powerful tool for monitoring system (and service) performance. This tool is called Performance Monitor, and it
has many built-in counters, such as processor, memory, disk, network, services,
and so on, that allow you to monitor objects.

When Proxy Server is installed, several counters are installed into the Performance Monitor. These counters are used to monitor the different components
of Proxy Server:

➤ **Web Proxy Server Service** Includes counters to monitor the Web Proxy
   and SOCKS Proxy services.

➤ **Web Proxy Server Cache** Includes counters to monitor the Web Proxy
   service cache.

➤ **WinSock Proxy Server** Includes counters to monitor the WinSock
   Proxy service.

➤ **Packet Filtering** Includes counters to monitor Proxy Server packet
   filtering.

To run the Microsoft Performance Monitor, follow these steps:

1. Select Start|Microsoft Proxy Server from the Programs menu.

2. Select Monitor Microsoft Proxy Server Performance. This starts a
   Performance Monitor session, as shown in Figure 9.4, with some
   predetermined counters specific to Microsoft Proxy Server.

To add, modify, or delete counters, follow these steps:

1. Select Add To Chart from the Edit menu or click on the plus (+) icon.

2. In the Add To Chart dialog, in Object, select a Proxy Server object (see
   Figure 9.5).

3. In Counter, select a counter and then click Add.

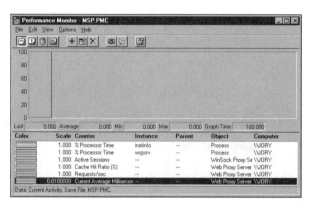

Figure 9.4   The Performance Monitor.

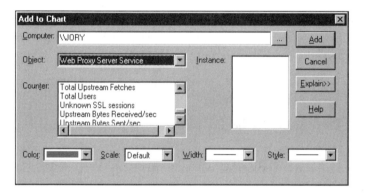

Figure 9.5   The Add To Chart dialog.

Some of the Proxy Server counters rely on monitoring disk activity. Because monitoring the hard drives in a computer can affect the performance of that system, disk counters are disabled by default. You can enable the disk counters by using the **diskperf -y** command (you must reboot your system for disk monitoring to occur). You can then disable the disk counters by using the **diskperf -n** command.

Exam Prep Questions

Question 1

> Your Web Proxy service is having some caching problems. Which source name should you look for in the Microsoft Event viewer?
>
> ○ a. WebProxyServerCache
>
> ○ b. WebCache
>
> ○ c. WebProxyCache
>
> ○ d. CacheEvent

The correct answer to this question is c. Any Web Proxy service event messages that deal with caching will by logged under the WebProxyCache source name. WebProxyServerCache, WebCache, and CacheEvent are not valid source names. Therefore, answers a, b, and d are incorrect.

Question 2

> Your Web Proxy service caching has stopped working. What should be your first step for troubleshooting?
>
> ○ a. Run Performance Monitor and monitor the cache objects.
>
> ○ b. Reinstall Microsoft Proxy Server.
>
> ○ c. Check the WPS.LOG file created in the \Systems32\Logs directory.
>
> ○ d. Check the Event Viewer for event messages.

The correct answer to this question is d. Any event messages (including error messages) are logged in the Event Viewer. Once caching has stopped, running the Performance Monitor will not give you any useful information. Therefore, answer a is incorrect. Reinstalling Proxy Server is a last resort and may not fix the problem. Therefore, answer b is incorrect. The Web Proxy service does not create or log information to a log file called WPS.LOG. Therefore, answer c is incorrect.

Question 3

What is the Registry?

- ○ a. A database of Microsoft-specific configuration information
- ○ b. A database of all Windows NT configuration information
- ○ c. A database of Proxy Server–specific configuration information
- ○ d. A database that stores all informational and error messages logged by Windows NT

The correct answer to this question is b. By definition, all configuration information for Windows NT and its applications is stored in the Registry. The Registry is a global database of configuration information and is not specific to one application or to one application developer. Therefore, answers a and c are incorrect. The informational and error messages are logged to the Event Viewer's event log, not the Registry. Therefore, answer d is incorrect.

Question 4

Which of the following Registry entries are shared by all the Proxy Server services? [Check all correct answers]

- ❏ a. Packet filtering keys
- ❏ b. Alerting keys
- ❏ c. Logging values
- ❏ d. SOCKS Proxy service values

The correct answers to this question are a, b, and c. The SOCKS Proxy service values only control configuration for the SOCKS Proxy service. Therefore, answer d is incorrect.

Question 5

You run Performance Monitor and attempt to log hard disk activity. All disk activity counters read zero, why?

○ a. You have to run the **diskcount -start** command.

○ b. You have to run the **diskperf -start** command.

○ c. You have to run the **diskperf -y** command.

○ d. You have to run the **diskcount -y** command.

The correct answer to this question is c. By default, the disk counters are disabled; you must enable them by running the **diskperf** -y command. There is no **diskcount** command. Therefore, answers a and d are incorrect. The **diskperf** command does not have a -**start** option. Therefore, answer b is incorrect.

Need To Know More?

 Search the online documentation that is installed with Proxy Server. Using search strings such as "troubleshooting," "counter," "MIB," "SNMP," "Registry," "Registry tree," and "event logs" should lead you in the right direction.

 Microsoft TechNet. February, 1998. Searches on "Proxy Server 2.0" and "Troubleshooting" will yield a wealth of information.

 Many resources and documents are available on Microsoft's Web site at www.microsoft.com/proxy.

 Many troubleshooting documents are available on Microsoft's Knowledge Base site at www.microsoft.com/kb.

Planning Your Proxy Server Implementation

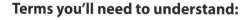

Terms you'll need to understand:

- √ Bandwidth
- √ Capacity analysis
- √ Needs analysis

Techniques you'll need to master:

- √ Identifying the capacity needs for your network
- √ Knowing the right questions to ask your ISP
- √ Choosing the right connection for your network
- √ Choosing the right hardware for your proxy server

A key factor in determining the success of any installation is planning. Planning involves several phases—from understanding your current capabilities, to determining your current needs, anticipating your future needs, and, ultimately, finding a viable solution. We have all been in situations where the immediate need surpassed the need for planning and the installation was rushed. More often than not, the installation had to be repeated to correct problems. Microsoft stresses successful planning techniques, both to ease the initial installation and as a preventative troubleshooting task.

The Site Analysis Process

A key consideration of planning future network capacity is determining what services, users, and data will be present on the network. Take the time to complete a thorough site analysis. A bit of formal analysis now will ease the process of upgrading and configuring the system later. Don't succumb to the "easy way out." Planning can be a long and arduous task that is overlooked far too often, but one that pays off ultimately.

Network Capacity Analysis

The *capacity* of a network is that network's ability to support the amount of data transmitted over it. A network that can support the activity of your organization today may not be able to support the increased activity level when Internet access is offered via Proxy Server. You need to carefully consider the performance ramifications of adding new information services to an already overtaxed network.

Although Proxy Server's ability to cache resources saves on performance over the Internet communication link, it does not decrease the amount of data ultimately transferred to the client. Even if 100 percent of requested data is stored in the proxy server's cache, it will still be sent across your local network to the client computer, increasing network traffic significantly.

The first step in network capacity analysis is to define a baseline profile of the performance levels of your current network by using Performance Monitor and Network Monitor. This involves sampling various aspects of your network over several days. Examine these readings to decipher what is normal and abnormal about how your network performs. This includes pinpointing which areas of your network experience the heaviest load, which users or applications cause the most traffic, and if there are failure points (for example, broken cables, bad connectors, failed links, or misconfigured protocols).

Compare the actual traffic and performance levels on your network with the known capacity of the hardware that composes your network. For example, if you're using 10Mbps NICs and hubs on your network and the average network load is around 7 or 8Mbps, you have little room for additional traffic. A network consistently operating at 70 percent of available capacity would experience severe performance degradation if Internet information services were added to the existing system.

As mentioned earlier, adding one or more Internet services to your current network will increase network traffic levels significantly. Often, adding Internet services requires an increase in the capacity of your network. Some considerations involved in expanding the capacity of your network include the following:

➤ The number and type of services provided by the proxy server

➤ The number of users accessing those services

➤ The restrictions that will be implemented (particular users or groups, time of day, or amount of data)

➤ The number of users that may be added in the next year

Needs Analysis

Determining your current needs involves making a list of services and features required on your network to improve or expand its current capabilities. This list can range from information services, to security restrictions, to content sources. To help you focus on this process, the following questions related to this process have been included. The needs analysis questions are divided into three categories:

➤ **Why** Why do you need Internet access?

➤ **Connectivity** What hardware do you have? Does it need to be upgraded?

➤ **Security** What type of access will you allow through Proxy Server?

Why Grant Internet Access?

If you've come to this section of the book, you've probably already decided to connect to the Internet using Microsoft Proxy Server. However, the following are some questions to help you justify this implementation:

➤ What are the top three reasons you need to add Internet access to your network?

➤ How will your products and/or services be improved with Internet access?

➤ Is Internet access just today's latest business fad or does it really offer solid, tangible benefits?

➤ What exactly are you expecting to happen once Internet access is added to your system?

➤ What capabilities and services are you expecting to deploy or derive from Internet access?

➤ Will the majority of information flow out from your network or in from the Internet?

Connectivity Concerns

As mentioned earlier, the specifics of how to connect, and whether your network can handle the traffic generated by connecting, to the Internet must be addressed. Answers to the following questions will grant you insight into this area:

➤ What network or communications technologies have recently been deployed within your organization?

➤ Ultimately, who is responsible for the deployment of Internet access on your network?

➤ Are improvements to the network properly funded? Are they included in the budget?

➤ Which is more important—service, reliability, or speed of access?

➤ What compromises are you willing to make to sustain reliability over speed (or vice versa)?

➤ To improve your network's performance, what services or capabilities are you willing to sacrifice?

➤ If your Internet access links go down, what projects, tasks, or abilities will be affected?

➤ Is your current network media (NIC, hubs, repeaters, cables, and so on) upgradeable, expandable, or replaceable?

➤ Do you need a dedicated or on-demand Internet connection?

Security

Perhaps the most important set of questions involves security and how information will be guarded on your network:

➤ Which Internet information services will be supported, allowed, or deployed?

➤ Which capabilities and services will you prevent or deny in relation to Internet access?

➤ If full open access is not granted, what restrictions will be in place and who will determine them?

➤ What content filters will be put into place? Who is responsible for implementation and maintenance of these filters?

➤ What penalties will be enforced against users who violate (or attempt to violate) access restrictions?

➤ Have you documented the logic used to construct or describe your security or restriction system?

➤ What restrictions on "outsiders" do you plan to implement?

➤ How important is it to restrict or control access to your internal information?

➤ What does your organization consider a security breach?

From these lists of questions, you can formulate a clear picture of your present situation and what you want, need, or can afford in terms of Internet access. This knowledge is an important step in the process of deploying any new technology, including Proxy Server 2.0.

Connecting With An Internet Service Provider

Connecting your network to the Internet involves working with an *Internet Service Provider (ISP)*. As you know, ISPs are service companies that sell network access to the Internet. They purchase bandwidth in bulk and, in turn, resell it in smaller packages. You should evaluate an ISP in the same manner as you would any other supplier or vendor.

Types Of ISPs

There are three basic types of ISPs: global/national corporations, small local businesses, and hobbyists/amateurs.

Global/national corporations ISPs are those ISPs that have points of presence across the country, or even around the world. Typically, you'll not deal with ISPs of this level directly because they are most often in the business of whole-saling access to local business ISPs instead of end users. However, if your organization is of significant size, this type of ISP may be the only one that can adequately supply your connection needs. The cost for service from these large ISPs is often high, with little or no room for negotiation. In addition, although technical support may be available 24 hours a day, seven days a week, your specific issue or problem may not be as important to them as it is to you.

The small local business ISPs generally have one or only a few points of presence. Local ISPs are often more responsive to customer needs and can be flexible on service costs. The scope and value of services provided by a local ISP vary greatly, but with a little time and effort (as you'll see in the next section), you can find a provider to meet your needs.

A hobbyist or an amateur access provider is often a small or upstart business. Most ISPs of this nature offer little in the way of value-added services, have limited bandwidth choices, and have unreliable service. We do not recommend using an amateur ISP for business Internet access.

Locating An ISP

Finding the right ISP for your organization involves some work on your part. Mainly, it requires you to seek out possible ISPs, interview them, and then make an informed decision. You should be looking for a quality provider that is currently supporting professional or business customers. There are several ways to locate or discover ISPs initially; but just because an ISP is easy to find doesn't mean its service is acceptable. We suggest you make a list of four or five ISPs, then evaluate them in light of the specific criteria discussed throughout this chapter.

Listed here are a few methods for finding an ISP:

➤ **Word of mouth** Ask friends or colleagues for references to ISPs with which they have had experience. Because a relationship with an ISP is typically very important, most customers will not hesitate in letting you know what they think about the service they are paying for.

➤ **Newspaper and magazine advertisements** Print advertisements are common methods of obtaining attention by ISPs. Check business and technology sections in your local newspaper to see who wants your business.

➤ **Businesses/competition** Ask other business owners, or even your competitors, who they use for their Internet service.

➤ **Vendors** Ask your hardware and software vendor/supplier/retailer for recommendations for ISPs. It's not uncommon for technical salespeople to be aware of related products and services available locally.

➤ **Yellow pages** The phone book is now a great place to look for ISPs. Check out the entries under the headings of Internet, Computers, Computer Services, Network, Access Providers, or Online Access.

➤ **Radio and television** Many well-to-do ISPs are spending the money to advertise on radio and television. However, just because an ISP can afford the expense doesn't mean it should be your only choice. It does mean, however, that the ISP is making a profit, which is a good sign.

➤ **Search engines** All of the Web-based search engines can provide you with an extensive list of ISP possibilities. Just search with the keywords "Internet Providers," "Internet Service Providers," and "Internet Access Providers."

➤ **www.thelist.com** This Web site is a comprehensive database of ISPs. This well-organized collection of ISP information is worth taking a look at.

➤ **Dlist** This is another online resource worth looking into. Dlist or "Definitive listing of ISPs" is an email distribution of ISP information. To get the Dlist, just send an email to mj@ora.com. In the body of the message, include "request dlist." Within minutes, you'll receive an automated response that contains the list.

Test Your ISP

Once you've made a short list of ISP possibilities, run the list through the following gambit of tests. Switching from one provider to another is not impossible, but the switch can be fairly difficult and confusing. We recommend you take the time to ensure that everything you need in the foreseeable future is provided for with the ISP you select. You should examine every potential ISP using the criteria covered in the next sections.

Technical Support

Your ISP should be able to provide you with technical support, advice, and consultation. Find out what technical support assets are available from an ISP, including any technical certification or education, length of experience, and troubleshooting success history. Find out the size of the technical support staff and the hours of availability. Ultimately, you'll need to make a judgment call— if you have an emergency, will your ISP be able to offer a helping hand?

You need to know if technical support is provided as part of normal service or if it's provided on a paid basis only. Most often there's a sliding scale of basic technical support.

Here are a few more items to ponder when making your ISP selection:

➤ What is covered by the ISP's technical support?

➤ What isn't covered by the ISP's technical support?

➤ Does technical support stop on the ISP's end of the communications link or on your network's communications device? Does it cover your clients?

Geographic Location

Because you'll be using the link between you and your ISP a great deal, it is unwise to select an ISP located a great distance from your network. Connecting to an ISP in a different area code, city, or state will cost more in line charges. Most likely, you'll not be using a telephone line dial-up connection; however, other dedicated digital subscriber lines also have distance costs. If you have a choice, closer is always better.

Internet Information Services

Usually, having a connection to the Internet through an ISP enables you to access every information service type available anywhere in the world. However, some ISPs have taken the liberty of restricting or blocking some of these services for various reasons—illegal activity, too much bandwidth waste, not enough storage capacity, or nonprofessional content. Often, the restrictions imposed by an ISP will correspond to your organization's desired access limitations, but you should inquire about them all the same.

Communication

Unlike most vendors from whom you purchase a product or service, you'll develop a close relationship with your ISP. This is mainly because, from your perspective, it is the one link in the configuration of Internet communication that can bring everything to a halt when it fails. Look into the ability to contact the ISP by phone, email, and the Web. If you fail to get a human on the phone or don't get a response to your email within 24 hours, you should look elsewhere for Internet service. An ISP that communicates with its customers is one that values customer satisfaction.

Remote Connectivity

If members of your organization travel frequently, you may want to inquire about out-of-town access methods. Some ISPs have contracts with other ISPs across the country to provide their users with consistent access while on the road. If you plan to implement virtual private network (VPN) services, discuss your technologies with the ISP to guarantee that its routers, gateways, and servers can handle the load and will allow the specialized connections to take place.

Downtime

Even the largest ISPs have one problem in common with small local ISPs—humans run the computers and problems do occur. No service is 100 percent guaranteed. What is important is how an ISP deals with system failures and downtime. Ask the ISP about downtime history and the efforts that were made to restore service. Plus, ask if refunds or discounts are available for serious lapses in connection time.

Business Background

Never hook up your organization's network to an ISP that is less than two or three years old. Success comes with maturity, and experience has no substitute when dealing with the Internet. Plus, the longer an ISP has been in business, the more information you can find about it. Inquire with the Better Business Bureau, request customer references, ask to speak with customers who stopped working with the ISP, and look for any business report or study about the ISP. Ask to see a business plan, financial statement, and any documents about the goals or future of the business.

Compatibility

Even the best ISPs will be worthless to you if their hardware and software are incompatible with yours. Generally, because the communication link will be a TCP/IP connection, there's very little chance that a communication problem will exist. But if your ISP uses only Unix systems and you use Windows NT, it may not be able to offer you much in the way of useful technical support if something on your end goes awry.

One way to improve the compatibility of your ISP is to use the same type of communication device on your end of the link as it uses. Whenever possible and practical, duplicate the computer setups and networking hardware employed by the ISP—any equipment you have in common with the ISP is another area where you can leverage its expertise.

ISP Peak Time

ISPs have hundreds or even thousands of customers. You need to know when the ISP experiences its highest level of network traffic. This will be a combination of the Internet's peak times and the use patterns of the ISP's customers. There's little you can do to completely avoid peak time, but you can use this information to schedule your automated services and caching systems. Most ISPs maintain bandwidth and throughput statistics for its own use. It shouldn't be any great effort to obtain this information.

Bandwidth Options

Your network needs will grow, and it will eventually require larger connection pipelines to your ISP. Make sure your ISP already has available the next level of bandwidth you'll eventually need. In addition, make sure the ISP has an ongoing plan for expansion to add new levels of service as they become available at a reasonable cost. Don't get stuck with an ISP that can only offer you modem and ISDN access if you anticipate the need for a T1 or Asynchronous Transfer Mode (ATM).

Fine Print

Always get everything regarding your account with the ISP in writing, signed by you and the ISP. This is the only way to get what you ask (and pay) for. If it's not in writing when you sign the contract and hand over the first payment, you have no basis to demand it. Special services, unique configurations, technical support depth, and any added services must be spelled out. Every time either you or the ISP needs to alter or change the inventory of services, this document needs to be re-created or at least properly amended.

Choosing The Right Internet Connection For Your Network

A *pipeline* is a slang term referring to the communications link between your network and your ISP, which is appropriate because the ability for a connection to support significant amounts of data is dependent upon the size of the link. Choosing the most appropriate link for your network can be a bit of a guessing contest. Until you actually get everything deployed, you won't know for sure exactly how much traffic will move over the link and how popular Internet access will be.

Although the caching services of Proxy Server 2.0 can limit the amount of traffic sent over your Internet connection, bandwidth calculations should be made for a worst-case scenario. The following formula can give you an indication of the bandwidth you will need:

```
Number of users X bandwidth per user X 1.4 = pipeline size
```

The number of users in this equation should be the actual user count of individuals who will be given access to resources over the Internet. The bandwidth required, per user, equals how much data, per second, is minimally required for each user based on the information services (email, FTP, and so on) used on the network. If users only have email, a bandwidth of .75Kbps per user is sufficient. However, if FTP, Web, or streaming multimedia is retrieved from the Internet, 7.5Kbps per user is required—effectively, 10 times the requirement for email-only connections. Multiply the resulting number by 1.4 adds in 40 percent for growth.

By using this formula, a 700Kbps link would be sufficient for a network with 100 Internet users, needing 5Kbps each. This equates to five or six ISDN connections or a fractional T1. Remember that this is a worst-case calculation. It may be that this is too much bandwidth for such a small network because Proxy Server will be used and rarely will all 100 users be accessing Internet resources simultaneously. Discuss your needs and plans with the ISP before making a decision to deploy less than what this formula recommends. When it comes to networking, especially when connecting to the Internet, you can never have too much bandwidth. No matter what size pipeline you install, your Internet use will grow to consume every last bit of available bandwidth. Look ahead, take precautions, discuss options in-depth with your ISP, but don't spend more than you can afford.

Most ISPs will offer several options in communication link sizes and cost. Here is a list of some of the more common options:

➤ **POTS (plain old telephone service)** An analog communications link with a maximum bandwidth of 56Kbps.

➤ **ISDN (Integrated Services Digital Network)** A digital communications link with a maximum bandwidth of 128Kbps per dual-channel line.

➤ **56Kbps leased line** A digital communications link with a bandwidth of 56Kbps.

➤ **T1 and fractional T1** A digital communications link with a bandwidth of 1.544Mbps for a full T1. This link is also available in 56 or 256Kbps fractional T1 chunks.

➤ **Others** Several other digital communication link technologies may be available in your area with a wide variety of bandwidths. These include cable modems, ATM, Frame Relay, Switched Multimegabit Data Service (SMDS), Digital Subscriber Line (DSL), and Synchronous Optical Network (SONET).

Most of these options are available in either dedicated or nondedicated form. Dedicated service means you're assigned exclusive access to a specific communications port, which guarantees your connection, but at a price. Nondedicated service means you must compete with other users to gain access to a pool of communications ports. Nondedicated service does not guarantee access at any time and, therefore, is much less expensive. We recommend dedicated service for a business network connection. Nondedicated service can impose complications on a network and, therefore, should only be considered if dedicated service is cost prohibitive.

Choosing The Right Hardware For Your Proxy Server

When selecting hardware for your proxy server, the amount of data to be transferred must be taken into account. The physical size and the number of computers on your network are related, but are ancillary considerations. You should also take note that no two networks are the same. They vary in an infinite number of possibilities. Consequently, our recommendations and the recommendations of Microsoft may not be the absolute best fit for your specific situation. Take the time to examine every aspect of your network before accepting the recommendations of experts who have no direct experience with your system.

With that in mind, we'll still review some common or basic configurations for networks of various workloads (which, coincidentally, corresponds to geographic size and number of computers).

 In all of the following computer configurations, it is assumed you are using a dedicated Windows NT Server, NT-compatible components, and that NT Server is already installed.

Low-Volume Network

A low-volume network is typically a network in a SOHO (Small Office/Home Office) environment with 10 or fewer computers. Low-volume networks can obtain adequate Internet access using a single proxy server connected to a single ISDN line.

Microsoft recommends that the computer hosting Proxy Server meet the following minimum requirements:

➤ Intel Pentium 133 or faster

➤ 2GB of storage space for caching

➤ 32MB of RAM, or more

Moderate-Volume Network

A moderate-volume network is typically a network in a mid-size company with under 1,000 computers. Moderate volume networks can obtain adequate Internet access using two or more proxy servers arranged in an array or chain connected to multiple ISDN lines or a fractional T1.

Microsoft recommends that the computer hosting Proxy Server meet the following minimum requirements:

➤ Intel Pentium 166 or faster

➤ 2 to 4GB of storage space for caching

➤ 64MB of RAM, or more

High-Volume

A high-volume network is typically a network in an enterprise corporation with thousands of computers. High volume networks can obtain adequate Internet access using multiple proxy servers in a combined array and chain combination connected to a T1 line or greater.

Microsoft recommends that the computer hosting Proxy Server meet the following minimum requirements:

➤ Intel Pentium 200, Pentium Pro 166 or faster

➤ 8 to 16GB of storage space for caching

➤ 128 to 256MB of RAM, or more

Exam Prep Questions

Question 1

> In calculating capacity requirements, what percentage should be added for future growth?
>
> ○ a. 20 percent
>
> ○ b. 40 percent
>
> ○ c. 60 percent
>
> ○ d. 80 percent

Answer b is correct. 40 percent should be added to calculations to provide room for future growth. Answers a, c, and d are incorrect.

Question 2

> What is the minimum RAM size for a moderate volume network?
>
> ○ a. 32MB
>
> ○ b. 128MB
>
> ○ c. 64MB
>
> ○ d. 1GB

A network that sees moderate network volume requires at least 64MB in the proxy server. Therefore, answer c is correct. 32MB is insufficient to run a proxy server with a fair volume of traffic. Therefore, answer a is incorrect. Of course, more is always better when dealing with Microsoft and the Internet. Although 128MB or 1GB of RAM might be preferable, the question asked for the minimum. Therefore, answers b and d are incorrect.

Question 3

> Which of the following are methods for learning about ISPs in your area? [Check all correct answers]
>
> ❑ a. www.microsoft.com
>
> ❑ b. www.thelist.com
>
> ❑ c. Word of mouth
>
> ❑ d. Search engines

Answers b, c, and d are all methods for learning about ISPs in your area. Microsoft does provide ISP services through the Microsoft Network; however, it doesn't provide information on ISPs in your area. Therefore, answer a is incorrect.

Question 4

> What is the minimum bandwidth requirement for a network with 350 users using only email?
>
> ○ a. 367.5Kbps
> ○ b. 262.5Kbps
> ○ c. 3675Kbps
> ○ d. 2625Kbps

Three hundred and fifty users that use only email require at least 367.5Kbps, including room for growth. Therefore, answer a is correct. Answer b is incorrect because 262.5Kbps is the current requirement for 350 users, but does not take expansion into account. Answers c and d are incorrect because they are the calculations for full Internet access.

Question 5

> Which of the following provide at least 56Kbps transmission speeds? [Check all correct answers]
>
> ❑ a. POTS
> ❑ b. ISDN
> ❑ c. Fractional T1
> ❑ d. T1

All of the answers provide at least 56Kbps transmission. POTS has a maximum of 56Kbps, ISDN operates at either 64Kbps or 128Kbps, a fractional T1 is divided into 56Kbps channels, and a full T1 operates at 1.544Mbps (much higher than 56Kbps). Therefore, answers a, b, c, and d are correct.

Question 6

Which of the following is not a question to be asked during network capacity planning?

○ a. What level of growth is anticipated in the next year?

○ b. Which Internet services will be used and what are their bandwidth requirements?

○ c. How many users will be connecting to the Internet from your network?

○ d. What operating systems are used on desktop computers on your network?

Operating systems are not a consideration for network capacity planning. Therefore, answer d is correct. Each of the other questions must be asked during the planning stage of a proxy server installation. Therefore, answers a, b, and c are incorrect.

Need To Know More?

 Wolfe, David: *Designing and Implementing Microsoft Proxy Server.* Sams Publishing. Indianapolis, IN, 1996. ISBN 1-57521-213-7. Chapter 4, "Planning Your Installation and Configuration," covers all the issues you need to consider when planning and installing Microsoft Proxy Server.

 Microsoft TechNet. January, 1998. There is a section on the TechNet CD entitled "The Proxy Server Reviewer's Guide and Technical Notes" that provides extensive information on planning your Proxy Server installation.

 The Microsoft Knowledge Base provides detailed information on all products, including Proxy Server. Search on "planning" brings up the Proxy Server FAQ, which includes capacity planning information. The Microsoft Knowledge Base is located at http://support.microsoft.com/support/a.asp?M=S.

Sample Test

In this chapter, we provide a number of pointers for developing a successful test-taking strategy, including how to choose proper answers, how to decode ambiguity, how to work within the Microsoft framework, how to decide what to memorize, and how to prepare for the test. At the end, we provide a number of questions that cover subject matter that is pertinent to the Implementing and Supporting Microsoft Proxy Server 2.0 exam. Good luck!

Questions, Questions, Questions

There should be no doubt in your mind that you are facing a test full of questions. The Proxy Server 2.0 exam is comprised of 68 questions; you are allotted 105 minutes to complete the exam. Remember, questions are of four basic types:

➤ Multiple-choice with a single answer

➤ Multiple-choice with multiple answers

➤ Multipart with a single answer

➤ Picking the spot on the graphic

Always take the time to read a question twice before selecting an answer, and be sure to look for an Exhibit button. The Exhibit button brings up graphics and charts used to help explain the question, provide additional data, or illustrate layout. You'll find it difficult to answer this type of question without looking at the exhibits.

Not every question has a single answer; a lot of questions require more than one answer. In fact, for some questions, all the answers should be marked. Read the question carefully so you know how many answers are necessary and look for additional instructions for marking your answers. These instructions are usually in brackets.

Picking Proper Answers

Obviously, the only way to pass any exam is by selecting the correct answers. However, the Microsoft exams are not standardized like SAT and GRE exams; they are more diabolical and convoluted. In some cases, questions are strangely worded, and deciphering them is nearly impossible. In those cases, you may need to rely upon answer-elimination skills. Almost always at least one answer out of the possible choices can be immediately eliminated due to one of the following reasons:

➤ The answer doesn't apply to the situation.

➤ The answer describes a nonexistent issue.

➤ The answer is already eliminated by the question text.

Once obviously wrong answers are eliminated, you must rely on your retained knowledge to eliminate further answers. Look for items that sound correct but refer to actions, commands, or features not present or not available in the described situation.

If after these phases of elimination you still are faced with a blind guess between two or more answers, reread the question. Try to picture in your mind's eye the situation and how each of the possible remaining answers would alter the situation.

If you have exhausted your ability to eliminate answers and are still unclear about which of the remaining possible answers is the correct one—guess! An unanswered question offers you no points, but guessing gives you a chance of getting a question right; just don't be too hasty in making a blind guess. Wait until the last round of reviewing marked questions before you start to guess. Guessing should be a last resort.

Decoding Ambiguity

Microsoft exams have a reputation for including questions that are at times difficult to interpret, confusing, and ambiguous. In our experience with numerous exams, we consider this reputation to be completely justified. The Microsoft exams are difficult.

The only way to beat Microsoft at its own game is to be prepared. You'll discover that many exam questions test your knowledge of things that are not directly related to the issue raised by the question. This means that the answers offered to you, even the incorrect ones, are just as much part of the skill assessment as the question itself. If you don't know about all aspects of Proxy Server cold, you may not be able to eliminate obviously wrong answers because they relate to a different area of Proxy Server than the one being addressed by the question.

Questions often give away the answer, but you have to be better than Sherlock Holmes to see the clues. Often, subtle hints are included in the text in such a way that they seem like irrelevant information. You must realize that each question is a test in and of itself, and you need to inspect and successfully navigate each question to pass the exam. Look for small clues, such as the mention of times, group names, and configuration settings. Little items such as these can point out the right answer; if missed, they can leave you facing a blind guess.

Another common difficulty with the certification exams is that of vocabulary. Microsoft has an uncanny knack of naming utilities and features very obviously in some instances and completely inanely in others. Be sure to brush up on all of the terms presented at the beginning of each chapter. You may also want to review the Glossary before approaching the test.

Working Within The Framework

The test questions are presented to you in a random order, and many of the elements or issues are repeated in multiple questions. It's not uncommon to find that the correct answer to one question is the wrong answer to another. Take the time to read each answer, even if you know the correct one immediately. The incorrect answers may spark a memory that helps you on another question.

You can revisit any question as many times as you like. If you're uncertain of the answer to a question, make a mark in the box provided so that you can come back to it later. You should also mark questions you think may offer data you can use to solve other questions. We've marked 25 to 50 percent of the questions on exams we've taken. The testing software is designed to help you mark an answer for every question, so use its framework to your advantage. Everything you want to see again should be marked; the software will help you return to marked items.

Deciding What To Memorize

The amount of rote memorization you must do for the exams depends on how well you remember what you've read. If you are a visual learner and can see the drop-down menus and the dialogs in your head, you won't need to memorize as much as someone who is less visually oriented. The tests will stretch your recollection of commands and functions of Proxy Server.

Here are the important types of information to memorize:

➤ The difference between an array and a chain

➤ The well-known ports

➤ The role and location of the LATs

➤ The types of security supported by each service

If you work your way through this book while sitting at a Proxy Server machine, you should have little or no problem interacting with most of these important items.

Preparing For The Test

The best way to prepare for the test—after you've studied—is to take at least one practice exam. We've included a practice exam in this chapter; the test questions are located in the following pages. You should give yourself 105 minutes to take the test. Keep yourself on the honor system and don't cheat by looking at the text earlier in the book. Once your time is up or you finish, you can check your answers in Chapter 12.

Taking The Test

Relax. Once you're sitting in front of the testing computer, there's nothing more you can do to increase your knowledge or preparation. Take a deep breath, stretch, and attack the first question.

Don't rush; there's plenty of time to complete each question and to return to skipped questions. If you read a question twice and are clueless, mark it and move on. Both easy and difficult questions are dispersed throughout the test in a random order. Don't cheat yourself by spending so much time on a difficult question early on that it prevents you from answering numerous easy questions positioned near the end. Move through the entire test, and before returning to the skipped questions, evaluate your time in light of the number of skipped questions. As you answer questions, remove the mark. Continue to review the remaining marked questions until your time expires or you complete the test.

That's it for pointers. Here are some questions for you to practice on.

Sample Test

Question 1

Which of the following files contains IP address information required by a specific client and is therefore located in the \Mspclnt directory on the client computer?

○ a. LOCALLAT.TXT

○ b. MSPLAT.TXT

○ c. MSCLIENT.TXT

○ d. MSPCLLAT.TXT

Question 2

Which of the following partition types can be used for caching on your proxy server?

○ a. FAT32

○ b. VFAT

○ c. NTFS

○ d. HPFS

Question 3

Microsoft's secure Web publishing system is comprised of which of the following services? [Check all correct answers]

❑ a. Reverse proxy

❑ b. Web Proxy service

❑ c. Server proxy

❑ d. Reverse hosting

Question 4

In a proxy server array, what information is replicated to all proxy array members? [Check all correct answers]

❑ a. The Web Proxy service cache directory location

❑ b. Packet filter logging information

☑ c. Web Proxy security information

☑ d. WinSock Proxy service protocol configuration

Question 5

Which of the following is used to configure your proxy server to allow RealAudio onto your network?

○ a. The Protocols tab in the Web Proxy Properties dialog

○ b. The Protocols tab in the WinSock Proxy Properties dialog

○ c. The Protocols tab in the SOCKS Proxy Properties dialog

○ d. The Protocols tab in Network Properties dialog on each client's computer

Question 6

Which of the following configurations could be used to grant access to a network for a particular client but deny access for all other clients?

○ a. Create a LOCALLAT.TXT file on all computers that will be denied access.

○ b. Edit the MSPLAT.TXT file on all computers that will be denied access.

○ c. Create a LOCALLAT.TXT file on the client computer that will be granted access.

○ d. Edit the MSPLAT.TXT file on the client computer that will be granted access.

Question 7

While modifying an array member, you receive a message stating you can refresh or overwrite, yet you haven't applied your changes. What does this indicate?

○ a. You were making changes to an array member but hadn't applied the changes, and someone else made changes to a different array member and did apply the changes.

○ b. You were making changes to an array member and applied the changes, and someone else made changes to a different array member and hadn't applied the changes.

○ c. You were making changes to an array member and applied the changes, and someone else made changes to a different array member and applied the changes.

○ d. You were making changes to an array member but hadn't applied the changes, and someone else made changes to a different array member and hasn't applied the changes.

Question 8

You administer a 300-client local area network. Your internal network uses IPX/SPX only. You want to configure the cache to provide
the quickest response to user requests. You want to configure
Microsoft Proxy Server on your Windows NT Server machine,
which meets or exceeds all installation requirements, so WinSock
Proxy clients can benefit from its caching capabilities.

Required Result:

- Internet objects must be stored locally and updated every hour.

Optional Desired Results:

- Provide the best user response and maximize cache hits.

- Internet objects that are larger than 2MB should not be cached.

Proposed Solution:

In the Caching tab of the Web Proxy Service Properties page, select the Enable Caching checkbox. For the Cache Expiration Policy
option, select Fewer Network Accesses Are More Important. Select the Enable Active Caching checkbox and then select the Faster
User Response Is More Important option. For the Object Time To
Live options, select the Enable HTTP Caching checkbox and then
set the Maximum TTL option to 60 minutes.

- ○ a. The proposed solution produces the required result and
     produces both of the optional desired results.

- ⊙ b. The proposed solution produces the required result but
     only one of the optional desired results.

- ○ c. The proposed solution produces the required result but
     neither of the optional desired results.

- ○ d. The proposed solution does not produce the required
     result.

Question 9

You have been asked to ensure that the FTP traffic is not accepted by your proxy server. Which of the following well-known ports are assigned to FTP? [Check all correct answers]

❑ a. TCP 25

❑ b. TCP 21

❑ c. TCP 20

❑ d. TCP 23

Question 10

What is the minimum RAM size for a low-volume network?

○ a. 32MB

○ b. 128MB

○ c. 64MB

○ d. 1GB

Question 11

Which of the following protocols was designed by Microsoft to replace the Internet Cache Protocol (ICP) in a multiple proxy server environment?

○ a. ICMP

○ b. CARP

○ c. RRAS

○ d. HASH

Question 12

> When Proxy Server is combined with RRAS, which of the following secure Internet functions is enhanced?
>
> ○ a. VPNs
>
> ○ b. SSL
>
> ○ c. HTTPS
>
> ○ d. Secure16

Question 13

> Which of the following types of communication are employed by TCP? [Check all correct answers]
>
> ❑ a. Connection-oriented communication
>
> ❑ b. Point-to-point communication
>
> ❑ c. Stream-oriented communication
>
> ❑ d. Datagram-oriented communication

Question 14

> Select the answer that best describes the role of hashing in a proxy server array environment.
>
> ○ a. Hashing is the protocol used by downstream clients to access upstream proxy servers.
>
> ○ b. Hashing is the protocol used by array members to communicate.
>
> ○ c. Hashing is performed on all available array members and on the URL the client requests. The array member with the highest hashed total is used to cache the Internet site locally.
>
> ○ d. Hashing is the method DNS uses to distribute clients evenly to all proxy server clients.

Question 15

Which of the following measures can be taken to control outbound access on your network?

○ a. Enable port filtering

○ b. Enable packet filtering

○ c. Enable IP forwarding

○ d. Install Proxy Server in its own domain

Question 16

Users on your network connect to an investment site that is updated every two hours. However, the users are complaining that access is slow when the information is updated. Which of the following answers would provide the greatest increase in performance for your clients?

○ a. Disable active caching

○ b. Set the Cache Expiration Policy option to Equal Importance

○ c. Enable active caching

○ d. Disable all caching

Question 17

The term LAT is most accurately described by which of the following statements?

○ a. The LAT, or limited access table, defines the filters for access to the Internet.

○ b. The LAT, or local address table, contains the IP addresses for all computers on the local network.

○ c. The LAT, or local address table, contains the IP addresses for computers on the Internet that will be granted access to the local network.

○ d. The LAT, or limited access table, contains the IP addresses for firewalls attached to the Internet.

Question 18

You have started getting calls from internal users saying that access to the Web is significantly slower than normal. You suspect caching errors. What should be your first step in resolving this problem?

❍ a. Check the Event Viewer for event messages.

❍ b. Run Performance Monitor and monitor the cache objects.

❍ c. Stop and restart the Web Proxy service.

❍ d. Check the WPS.LOG file created in the \Systems32\Logs directory.

Question 19

Which of the following questions should be asked during network capacity planning? [Check all correct answers]

❏ a. What level of growth is anticipated in the next year?

❏ b. Which Internet services will be used and what are their bandwidth requirements?

❏ c. How many users will be connecting to the Internet from your network?

❏ d. What operating systems are used on desktop computers on your network?

Question 20

Which of the following settings will decrease the access time for a number of clients that request the same online news information throughout the day?

○ a. From the WinSock Proxy Service Properties page, select the Caching tab and select the Enable Caching checkbox. Select the Updates Are More Important option.

○ b. From the SOCKS Proxy Service Properties page, select the Caching tab and select the Enable Caching checkbox. Select the Updates Are More Important option.

○ c. From the Web Proxy Service Properties page, select the Caching tab and select the Enable Caching checkbox. Select the Updates Are More Important option.

○ d. From the Web Proxy Service Properties page, select the Routing tab and select the Aggressive Caching checkbox.

Question 21

Which of the following settings can be used to improve access time for sites that are updated and accessed weekly?

○ a. From the SOCKS Proxy Service Properties page, set TTL% to 50%.

○ b. From the Web Proxy Service Properties page, set the Active Caching checkbox option to Equal Importance.

○ c. From the WinSock Proxy Service Properties page, set TTL% to 50%.

○ d. From the Web Proxy Service Properties page, set the TTL% to 50%.

Question 22

Your proxy server supports 575 Web Proxy clients. What is the minimum recommended disk space you need to allocate for caching?

○ a. 155.5MB

○ b. 387.5MB

○ c. 287.5MB

○ d. 575MB

Question 23

A computer's IP address and computer name are combined to create a socket number.

○ a. True

○ b. False

Question 24

Which of the following are functions of a proxy server? [Check all correct answers]

❑ a. Decreases access time by caching content

❑ b. Protects a local network from unauthorized access via the Internet

❑ c. Decreases the amount of traffic on your local network

❑ d. Provides Internet services such as Web and FTP

Question 25

In a chained proxy environment, upstream and downstream proxy servers update each other automatically.

○ a. True

○ b. False

Question 26

Which of the following Internet connections provides two 64Kbps channels?

○ a. POTS

○ b. ISDN

○ c. Fractional T1

○ d. T1

Question 27

You administer a 200-client LAN. Your internal network uses NetBEUI only for communications; however, some clients have TCP/IP installed for RAS to remote clients. You want to install Microsoft Proxy Server and have all client computers connect to the Internet through the proxy server.

Required Result:

• All client computers must connect to the Internet using Microsoft Proxy Server.

Optional Desired Results:

• Client reconfiguration and administration should be kept to a minimum.

• Client computers will use the proxy server to publish internal Web pages.

Proposed Solution:

Install Microsoft Proxy Server and configure it to connect to the Internet using TCP/IP. Install TCP/IP and the WinSock Proxy client on all the client computers.

What results does the proposed solution produce?

○ a. The proposed solution produces the required result and produces both the optional desired results.

○ b. The proposed solution produces the required result but only one of the optional desired results.

○ c. The proposed solution produces the required result but neither of the optional desired results.

○ d. The proposed solution does not produce the required result.

Question 28

Which of the following types of protocols provides an interface to the user?

○ a. Transport

○ b. Network

○ c. Application

○ d. Routing

Question 29

Which service utilizes packet filtering to manage outbound access?

○ a. Web Proxy

○ b. WinSock Proxy

○ c. SOCKS Proxy

○ d. None of the above

Question 30

You have been successfully using Microsoft Proxy Server 1.0 on a Windows NT Server 4.0 machine that includes a Pentium Pro 233, 128MB of RAM, and a 4GB FAT hard drive. You are contemplating an upgrade to Microsoft Proxy Server 2.0. Which of the following should be considered before making the upgrade?

○ a. Upgrade the processor.

○ b. Add more disk space.

○ c. Add more memory.

○ d. Convert the FAT partition to NTFS.

○ e. Nothing; Proxy Server 2.0 will function optimally on the current system.

Question 31

What is the minimum bandwidth requirement for a network with 750 users with full Web access?

- ○ a. 787.5Kbps
- ○ b. 562.5Kbps
- ○ c. 7875Kbps
- ○ d. 5625Kbps

Question 32

Which of the following are used to define a packet filter? [Check all correct answers]

- ☑ a. Packet type   ☑ packet fragment
- ☑ b. Datagram
- ☐ c. IP address
- ☐ d. Domain name

Question 33

What is the function of the Control Channel in WinSock Proxy communication?

- ○ a. The Control Channel is used to provide connectivity between the WinSock Proxy service and the Web Proxy service.
- ○ b. The Control Channel is used as part of the gateway service for WinSock Proxy connections.
- ○ c. The Control Channel is used to manage the connection between the client and the server.
- ○ d. The Control Channel is used to monitor communication between the WinSock Proxy service and the Internet.

Question 34

Which of the following are examples of Network protocols? [Check all correct answers]

❏ a. Telnet

❏ b. ICMP

❏ c. SMTP

❏ d. IP

Question 35

Which of the following Registry entries are not shared by all the Proxy Server services? [Check all correct answers]

❏ a. Domain filtering keys

❏ b. Caching values

❏ c. Alerting keys

❏ d. Logging values

Question 36

Your multihomed Microsoft Proxy Server computer has four network interface cards. Two NICs connect to your LAN (IP addresses 223.197.18.1 and 223.197.19.1), one connects to your intranet LAN (223.197.20.2), and one connects to your ISP (206.99.204.187). Which of these addresses should not be included in your LAT?

○ a. 206.99.204.187

○ b. 223.197.18.1

○ c. 223.197.19.1

○ d. 223.197.20.2

Question 37

Which of the following is required to enable packet filtering on a proxy server?

○ a. Logging to the Event Viewer

○ b. An ISP that supports packet filtering

○ c. An external network interface

○ d. Installing the Packet Filter service in the Network applet

Question 38

Upon installation, Microsoft Proxy Server 2.0 automatically logs to which of the following?

○ a. Proxy Server 2.0 logs to a text file.

○ b. Proxy Server 2.0 logs to the Event Viewer.

○ c. Proxy Server 2.0 logs to an SQL or ODBC database.

○ d. Proxy Server 2.0 does not log upon installation.

Question 39

Which of the following answers is the correct binary representation of the number 199?

○ a. 11000111

○ b. 11001110

○ c. 00110100

○ d. 11001100

Question 40

Which of the following addresses should be included in the LAT for a proxy server? [Check all correct answers]

❏ a. The IP addresses of the proxy server's NICs that connect to your LAN

❏ b. The IP address of your default gateway at your ISP

❏ c. The IP addresses of the computers on your LAN

❏ d. The IP address of the primary Internet DNS server

Question 41

Which of the following steps would you use to limit the size of cached objects to 500K each?

○ a. From the WinSock Proxy Service Properties page, select the Caching tab, click the Advanced button, and then select the Limit Size Of Cached Objects checkbox and set the limit to 500K.

○ b. From the SOCKS Proxy Service Properties page, select the Caching tab, click the Advanced button, and then select the Limit Size Of Cached Objects checkbox and set the limit to 500K.

○ c. From the System Properties page, select the Performance tab. Under Virtual Memory, click the Change button. Select the Limit Size Of Cached Objects checkbox and set the limit to 500K.

○ d. From the Web Proxy Service Properties page, select the Caching tab, click the Advanced button, and then select the Limit Size Of Cached Objects checkbox and set the limit to 500K.

Question 42

Which of the following is the correct formula for calculating network capacity requirements?

- ○ a. Number of users x 1.4 x estimated growth = pipeline size
- ○ b. Number of users x bandwidth per user x 0.4 = pipeline size
- ○ c. Number of users x 0.75 x 1.4 = pipeline size
- ○ d. Number of users x bandwidth per user x 1.4 = pipeline size

Question 43

If you are planning to use Microsoft Proxy Server's WinSock Proxy service as a gateway between your NWLink network and the Internet, which of the following are required? [Check all correct answers]

- ❑ a. A second NIC configured to use NetBEUI
- ❑ b. A second NIC configured to use TCP/IP
- ❑ c. Microsoft Service Pack 3.0
- ❑ d. Microsoft Service Pack 2.0

Question 44

Why is CERN compliance important for Web browsers using Proxy Server?

- ○ a. CERN compliance provides support for PPTP and VPNs over the Internet.
- ○ b. CERN compliance enhances the security of Web transactions by utilizing SSL.
- ○ c. CERN compliance ensures that packets are filtered correctly.
- ○ d. CERN compliance provides non-Windows browsers the ability to utilize the Web Proxy service.

Question 45

Which of the following is the CIDR representation of a Class C subnet mask?

○ a. /12

○ b. /26

○ c. /24

○ d. /16

Question 46

Which of the following settings are not used to define a domain filter? [Check all correct answers]

❑ a. IP address

☑ b. NetBIOS computer name

❑ c. Host name

❑ d. Domain name

Question 47

You have 1,250 client desktops that will access the Internet via the proxy server. You would like to configure the proxy server to cache common URLs. What is the minimum recommended cache size needed?

○ a. 5MB per URL accessed

○ b. 500MB

○ c. 625MB

○ d. 725MB

Question 48

Using the class system, which of the following network numbers would be assigned by the InterNIC?

○ a. 127.199.0.0

○ b. 191.134.200.0

○ c. 10.119.0.0

○ d. 192.0.0.0

Question 49

Which of the following events can trigger proxy alerts?

○ a. A large number of packets from a single host

○ b. Storage volumes reaching capacity

○ c. Invalid name/password combinations

○ d. Frequency of accepted packets

Question 50

Which of the following statements is true concerning Performance Monitor?

○ a. You have to run the **diskperf -y** command before monitoring hard disk activity.

○ b. You have to run the **diskperf -start** command before monitoring hard disk activity.

○ c. You have to run the **diskmon -start** command before monitoring hard disk activity.

○ d. You have to run the **diskmon -y** command before monitoring hard disk activity.

Question 51

You have configured a new computer with the following information: IP address 192.168.100.99, subnet mask 255.255.255.192, gateway 199.168.100.66. After rebooting the computer, you successfully PING your own IP address. However, when you attempt to PING other computers on your local subnet or the gateway, you are unsuccessful. You double-check your address and it is correctly assigned. Which of the following is the most likely problem?

O a. Your DNS server setting is not configured.

O b. Your gateway address is incorrectly configured.

O c. You have a duplicate IP address.

O d. Your subnet mask is incorrectly configured.

Question 52

Which of the following agencies became integral in the evolution of the Internet by developing an HTTP proxy system?

O a. CERN

O b. IANA

O c. IEEE

O d. ARPA

Question 53

Permissions for all Proxy services can be granted on a protocol basis to users and groups.

O a. True

O b. False

Question 54

The WinSock Proxy service provides access for which of the following types of clients? [Check all correct answers]

❑ a. Macintosh clients running TCP/IP

❑ b. Windows 95 clients running IPX/SPX

❑ c. Unix clients running TCP/IP

❑ d. Windows NT Workstation clients running NWLink
       (IPX/SPX)

Question 55

Which of the following best fits this definition: "A distributed proxy server configuration that provides fault tolerance and better client response."

○ a. Proxy service

○ b. Proxy chain

○ c. Proxy array

○ d. Proxy cache

Question 56

Aside from using the IP address of the proxy server, which of the following identifiers can WinSock Proxy clients use to connect?

◉ a. Its NetBIOS computer name

○ b. Its gateway address

○ c. Its MAC address

○ d. Its NWLink name

Question 57

What function do keep-alive packets perform in ISAPI?

○ a. Keep-alive packets determine the amount of time an object remains in cache.

○ b. Keep-alive packets are used to retain a connection to a remote server so that subsequent requests do not go through the resolution process.

○ c. Keep-alive packets determine the length of time a packet is allowed to traverse the network.

○ d. Keep-alive packets are used to control the communication between a client and server.

Question 58

You have 2,000 client desktops. How would you configure your Microsoft Proxy Server computer?

○ a. One server for all 2,000 clients.

○ b. Two servers, manually configure half the clients to each.

○ c. Three servers, manually assign an equal number of clients to each.

○ d. Three servers in an array. Assign the clients to the array.

Question 59

Your proxy server will be supporting approximately 750 clients. What is the minimum hardware configuration for your proxy server?

○ a. Pentium 166, 32MB of RAM, 1GB to 2GB disk space for caching

○ b. Pentium 133, 32MB of RAM, 1GB to 2GB disk space for caching

○ c. Pentium 166, 64MB of RAM, 2GB to 4GB disk space for caching

○ d. Pentium 133, 64MB of RAM, 2GB to 4GB disk space for caching

Question 60

Which of the following Event Viewer source names includes information on cache events?

○ a. WebCacheEvent

◉ b. WebProxyCache

○ c. WinSockProxyCache

○ d. WebCache

Question 61

Which of the following statements best describes a chained proxy environment?

○ a. A hierarchical proxy client configuration that allows clients to connect to a proxy server through proxy clients

○ b. A hierarchical-structured multiple proxy server environment that provides better client response when accessing the Internet

○ c. A distributed, peer-to-peer-type multiple proxy server configuration that provides fault tolerance and better client response for the client when accessing the Internet

○ d. A proxy server configured to respond to requests from the Internet and forward the requests to an IIS server located on the internal network.

Question 62

Which of the following steps would you use to grant Web access to a particular local group?

○ a. Under the Security tab for the Web Proxy Server Properties window, click the HTTP Protocol button and type in the group name.

○ b. Open the Network Properties window, select the Protocol tab, and then select TCP/IP and add the local group to the access list.

○ c. Open the Web Proxy Service Properties dialog, select the Permissions tab, enable access control, and then add the group under the WWW protocol.

○ d. Open User Manager for Domains, select the local group, and add the WWW service to the group.

Question 63

Which of the following methods can you use to efficiently grant unlimited and unrestricted access to all protocols and ports for the WinSock Proxy service?

○ a. You cannot grant unlimited and unrestricted access via WinSock.

○ b. Add a user to the WinSock Administrators group.

○ c. Grant a user or group access to each protocol and port individually.

○ d. Assign unlimited access to a user or group.

Question 64

You want to evenly distribute clients across all array members on you local area network. You have decided to use the Microsoft DNS Server service to define all your proxy array members and provide back IP address resolution to the array in a round-robin fashion. How would you configure the DNS server?

○ a. Make an "A" type resource record for each array member and select the Enable Round Robin selection box under DNS Properties.

○ b. Make a CNAME resource record with the same name and the IP address of each array member.

○ c. Make a PROXYA resource record and add the IP address of each array member to the record.

○ d. Do nothing at all. Proxy server will automatically add resource records to the DNS server for you.

Question 65

Which type of proxy environment allows proxy servers to update each other regularly and provides fault tolerance?

○ a. Proxy array

○ b. Proxy chain

○ c. Proxy distribution

○ d. Proxy backup

Question 66

You have been asked to implement Microsoft Proxy Server 2.0 on your network. You want to configure the client Web browsers to utilize the proxy server. How can you automate this process?

○ a. In the Web Proxy Service Properties page in the Client Configuration applet, set the options so the client will automatically be configured when the client software is installed.

○ b. This process cannot be automated. You must configure each Web browser individually.

○ c. Do nothing at all. Client computers will automatically attempt to use the proxy server to connect to the Internet.

○ d. From the WinSock Proxy Service Properties page, select the Client Configuration button and set the options so that the client will automatically be configured during setup.

Question 67

While working on a member of your proxy server array, you receive the Synchronization Conflict message: Synchronizing Now or Cancel. What prompted this message?

○ a. It is time for a scheduled synchronization and the array member you are working on cannot participate.

○ b. You applied changes to one array member while another administrator applied changes to another array member.

○ c. Another administrator applied changes to another array member and the changes have not been synchronized to the member you are working on.

○ d. Multiple array members are undergoing changes and all members are out of synchronization.

Question 68

Which of the following provides the highest level of security for outbound traffic?

❍ a. Web Proxy service port control

❍ b. WinSock Proxy service port control

❍ c. Web Proxy service packet filtering

❍ d. WinSock Proxy service packet filtering

Answer Key

1. a	20. c	39. a	58. a
2. c	21. d	40. a, c	59. d
3. a, d	22. b	41. d	60. b
4. c, d	23. b	42. d	61. b
5. b	24. a, b	43. b, c	62. c
6. c	25. b	44. d	63. d
7. a	26. b	45. c	64. b
8. b	27. b	46. b, c	65. a
9. b, c	28. c	47. d	66. a
10. a	29. d	48. b	67. b
11. b	30. d	49. b	68. b
12. a	31. c	50. a	
13. a, c	32. a, b	51. d	
14. c	33. c	52. a	
15. a	34. b, d	53. b	
16. c	35. b	54. b, d	
17. b	36. a	55. c	
18. a	37. c	56. a	
19. a, b, c	38. a	57. b	

Question 1

The correct answer to this question is a, LOCALLAT.TXT. This file contains information specific to a client computer and is accessed in the event that the MSPLAT.TXT file does not contain the IP address information needed. The MSPLAT.TXT file is copied to the \Mspclnt directory on each client, but it's the same for all clients. Therefore, answer b is incorrect. The MSCLIENT.TXT and MSPCLLAT.TXT files are fictitious. Therefore, answers c and d are incorrect.

Question 2

Only NTFS drives can be used for caching information on your proxy server. Therefore, answer c is correct. Windows NT does not recognize FAT32 partitions. Therefore, answer a could not be correct. Windows NT Server 4 supports VFAT, but a VFAT partition cannot be used for caching. Therefore, answer b is incorrect. HPFS volumes are only supported by Windows NT 3.51 or older, which cannot run Proxy Server 2.0. Therefore, answer d is incorrect.

Question 3

The correct answers to this question are a and d. Reverse proxy and reverse hosting combine with IIS to create a secure Web publishing environment. The Proxy Server Web Proxy service is not included in secure Web publishing, but rather it provides access for internal Web clients to the Internet. Therefore, answer b is incorrect. Server proxy provides a method of shielding an internal server, such as an Exchange Server, from the Internet. Therefore, answer c is incorrect.

Question 4

The correct answers to this question are c and d. The Web Proxy security information and the WinSock Proxy service protocol information are shared among members of the array. Because the cache directory may be different for every member of the array, this information is not replicated. Therefore, answer a is incorrect. Packet filters, filter alerts, and logging information are also not replicated among members of an array. Therefore, answer b is incorrect.

Question 5

The WinSock Proxy service is the only service that is able to pass RealAudio. Therefore, answer b is correct.

Question 6

The correct answer to this question is c. You would need to create a local LAT file (LOCALLAT.TXT) on the computer that will be granted access to the network. If you edit the MSPLAT.TXT file on the computer that will be granted access, the server copy will overwrite it the next time it's refreshed. Therefore, answer d is incorrect. You cannot deny access to a network within an LAT; you can only grant access. Therefore, answers a and b are incorrect.

Question 7

The correct answer to this question is a. If another array member has been modified and the changes applied, the synchronization process starts. If you're making changes to your array member, a message will appear on the screen allowing you to accept the refresh from the other array member and lose your changes, or to overwrite the changes made on the other array member. Answer b is incorrect because the message would appear on the other array member's screen. Answer c is incorrect because a different message would appear on your screen. Answer d is incorrect because no changes have been applied, so the synchronization process would not have started.

Question 8

The proposed solution provides all the results except for ensuring that objects larger than 2MB are not cached, which is an optional desired result. Therefore, answer b is correct.

Question 9

The correct answers to this question are b and c. FTP uses port 20 for data transfer and port 21 for control. TCP port 25 is used for SMTP traffic. Therefore, answer a is incorrect. TCP port 23 is used for Telnet. Therefore, answer d is incorrect.

Question 10

A network that sees moderate network volume requires at least 32MB of RAM in the proxy server. Therefore, answer a is correct. Although 64MB, 128MB, or 1GB of RAM might be preferable, the question asked for the minimum. Therefore, answers b, c, and d are incorrect.

Question 11

The correct answer to this question is b. CARP was designed by Microsoft to manage caching for proxy servers. ICMP is the Internet Control Message Protocol and does not operate in the Proxy Server environment. Therefore, answer a is incorrect. RRAS is the Routing And Remote Access Service for Microsoft NT Server 4.0. Therefore, answer c is incorrect. HASH is the mathematical algorithm that helps determine where information is stored in a proxy server array. Therefore, answer d is incorrect.

Question 12

The correct answer to this question is a. VPNs are supported in conjunction with the Routing And Remote Access Service update for Windows NT Server 4.0. Although SSL and HTTPS are supported by Proxy Server, they are not functions of RRAS. Therefore, answers b and c are incorrect. Secure16 is a fictitious answer. Therefore, answer d is incorrect.

Question 13

The correct answers to this question are a and c. Connection-oriented communication and stream-oriented communication are one and the same, and are used by TCP. Point-to-point communication is not a term that is used to describe a protocol's communication method. Therefore, answer b is incorrect. UDP uses datagram-oriented communication. Therefore, answer d is incorrect.

Question 14

The correct answer to this question is c. Hashing is the mathematical algorithm used to determine which array member will provide the cache area for an Internet URL when retrieved. Hashing is not a protocol. Therefore, answers a and b are incorrect. DNS uses a round-robin method of distributing client workload to all members of a proxy array. Therefore, answer d is incorrect.

Question 15

Enabling port filtering is a method of controlling outbound access. Therefore, answer a is correct. Enabling packet filtering and installing Proxy Server in its own domain are two ways to control inbound access. Therefore, answers b and d are incorrect. Enabling IP forwarding does not have an effect on outbound traffic. Therefore, answer c is incorrect.

Question 16

Enabling active caching will let the proxy server request the information before it receives a request from the local clients, thus speeding up access for the clients. Therefore, answer c is correct. The other options will either decrease performance or have no effect on the speed at which requests are fulfilled. Therefore, answers a, b, and d are incorrect.

Question 17

The LAT, or local address table, contains the IP addresses for all computers on the local network. Therefore, answer b is correct. The term *limited access table* is fictitious. Therefore, answers a and d are incorrect. The LAT is not used to control access from the Internet. Therefore, answer c is incorrect.

Question 18

The correct answer to this question is a. Any event messages (including error messages) are logged in the Event Viewer. Once caching has stopped, running the Performance Monitor will not give you any useful information. Therefore, answer b is incorrect. Although restarting the Web Proxy service may help, it will give you no indication of where the problem lies. Therefore, answer c is incorrect. The Web Proxy service does not create or log information to a log file called WPS.LOG. Therefore, answer d is incorrect.

Question 19

Answers a, b, and c should all be asked during network capacity planning. However, desktop operating systems are not considerations for network capacity planning. Therefore, answer d is incorrect.

Question 20

The correct answer to this question is c. Enabling caching and updating the cache often will reduce the access time for the clients. Caching is not available for WinSock or SOCKS clients. Therefore, answers a and b are incorrect. There is no setting for Aggressive Caching in the Web Proxy Service Properties page. Therefore, answer d is incorrect.

Question 21

The correct answer to this question is d. By setting the TTL% to 50%, you are telling the server to attempt to retrieve new information from the Web site when 50% of the TTL has expired. This ensures that the information in cache is the most recent available. The SOCKS service and WinSock service do not use cached information. Therefore, answers a and c are incorrect. The Active Caching setting will not work in this situation. Therefore, answer b is incorrect.

Question 22

The minimum disk space requirements for caching are calculated as 0.5MB per Web Proxy client plus a 100MB base. Using this calculation, 575 x 0.5 = 287.5 and 287.5+100 = 387.5. Therefore, only answer b is correct.

Question 23

The correct answer to this question is b, False. A socket number is created by combining the computer's IP address with the TCP or UDP port being used, not a combination of the IP address and computer name.

Question 24

Answers a and b are correct. A proxy server provides the ability to decrease access time by caching content and to protect a local network from unauthorized access. A proxy server does not decrease the amount of traffic on your local network, rather it increases this traffic. Therefore, answer c is incorrect. Although Proxy Server utilizes the services of IIS, it does not provide the same services. Therefore, answer d is incorrect.

Question 25

The correct answer to this question is b, False. Upstream and downstream proxy servers do not update each other in a chained environment.

Question 26

Answer b is correct. ISDN provides up to 128Kbps on two 64Kbps channels. POTS has a maximum throughput of 56Kbps transmission. Therefore, answer a is incorrect. A fractional T1 is divided into 56Kbps channels, and a full T1 operates at 1.544Mbps. Therefore, answers c and d are incorrect.

Question 27

The correct answer is b; the proposed solution produces the required result but only one of the optional results. Although the proposed solution will provide connectivity to the Internet and allow the clients to publish internal Web pages, the reconfiguration and administration of the clients will be extensive when introducing TCP/IP for the first time.

Question 28

The correct answer to this question is c. Application protocols provide an interface to the user. Transport protocols ensure delivery between computers. Therefore, answer a is incorrect. Network protocols provide addressing and routing functions. Therefore, answer b is incorrect. Routing protocols, such as RIP, are a subset of Network protocols, but they do not provide addressing information. Therefore, answer d is incorrect.

Question 29

Answer d is correct. Packet filtering is a function of the Web Proxy service, but it controls inbound access, not outbound. Therefore, answers a, b, and c are incorrect.

Question 30

The correct answer to this question is d. NTFS is required for caching on Proxy Server 2.0 computers. Although adding a newer processor, more disk space, or more memory might be helpful, it is not required for this configuration. Therefore answers a, b, and c are incorrect. Although Proxy Server 2.0 will run on the current configuration, it will not run optimally. Therefore, answer e is incorrect.

Question 31

Seven hundred fifty users with full Web access require at least 7875Kbps, including room for growth. Therefore, answer c is correct. Answers a and b are incorrect because they are calculated for email only (0.75Kbps). Answer d is incorrect because it does not take into account room for growth.

Question 32

A packet filter can be established for a packet type, datagram, or packet fragment. Therefore, answers a and b are correct. An IP address and domain name can be used to create domain filters but not packet filters. Therefore, answers c and d are incorrect.

Question 33

The correct answer to this question is c. The WinSock Proxy Control Channel is used to manage the connection between the client and the server. Although the other answers may sound good, they are fictitious or do not apply to the WinSock Proxy service and are therefore incorrect.

Question 34

The correct answers to this question are b and d. ICMP and IP are both Network protocols. Telnet and SMTP are Application protocols. Therefore, answers a and c are incorrect.

Question 35

The correct answer to this question is b. Caching values apply only to the Web Proxy service. All Proxy Server services share domain filtering keys, alerting keys, and logging values. Therefore, answers a, c, and d are incorrect.

Question 36

The correct answer to this question is a. The address for the NIC that connects to your ISP should not be included in the LAT. Because answers b, c, and d are assigned to internal network cards, they should be included in the LAT. Therefore, they are incorrect.

Question 37

An external network interface is required to enable packet filtering. Therefore, answer c is correct. Although logging to the Event Viewer is convenient, it is not a requirement for packet filtering. Therefore, answer a is incorrect. Because packet filtering takes place on the proxy server, it does not require ISP intervention. Therefore, answer b is incorrect. There is no Packet Filter service. Therefore, answer d is incorrect.

Question 38

By default, Proxy Server logs to a text file. Therefore, the correct answer to this question is a. Logging to the Event Viewer or an SQL or ODBC database can be configured, but it is not enabled by default. Therefore, answers b and c are incorrect. Answer d is incorrect because logging is enabled upon installation.

Question 39

The correct answer to this question is a. Answer b is the binary representation of 206, answer c is the binary representation of 52, and answer d is the binary representation of 204. Therefore, answers a, c, and d are all incorrect.

Question 40

The correct answers to this question are a and c. The LAT for your proxy server should include the IP addresses of all NICs in the server that connect to your LAN, as well as the addresses of all computers on your LAN. The IP addresses of your ISP's gateway or the Internet's DNS server should not be included in your LAT. Therefore, answers b and d are incorrect.

Question 41

Because caching is a function of the Web Proxy Service, limiting the size of cached objects is performed through the Web Proxy Service Properties page. Therefore answer d is correct. Neither the WinSock service nor the SOCKS service support caching. Therefore, answers a and b are incorrect. Although the Virtual Memory setting is important to the operation of the computer, it has no bearing on cache. Therefore, answer c is incorrect.

Question 42

Answer d is correct; the number of users multiplied by the bandwidth per user multiplied by 1.4 (which allows for 40 percent growth) will give you the correct pipeline size for your network.

Question 43

The correct answers to this question are b and c. To use Proxy Server as an NWLink gateway, a second NIC must be installed that uses TCP/IP, and Service Pack 3.0 is required. A second NIC configured to use NetBEUI will not provide the connectivity necessary to communicate on the Internet. Therefore, answer a is incorrect. Microsoft Service Pack 2.0 does not contain the files necessary to run Proxy Server. Therefore, answer d is incorrect.

Question 44

The correct answer to this question is d. CERN-compliant browsers are required for non-Windows clients to utilize the services of the Web Proxy service.

Although each of the other answers are functions of Proxy Server, they are not part of the CERN specification.

Question 45

The correct answer to this question is c (/24). Answer d (/16) is the CIDR representation for a Class B mask, whereas answers a and b are truly classless masks.

Question 46

The NetBIOS computer name and host name cannot be used to define a domain filter. Therefore, answers b and c are correct. Domain filters can be defined by IP address or domain name. Therefore, answers a and d are incorrect.

Question 47

The correct answer to this question is d. Use the formula 100MB + 0.5MB per client desktop to come up with 725MB. There is no way to know the total number of URLs accessed, so the formula in answer a is not possible. Therefore, answer a is incorrect. 500MB is not sufficient for cache in this situation. Therefore, answer b is incorrect. 625MB takes into account 0.5MB per client desktop but does not include the 100MB base. Therefore, answer c is incorrect.

Question 48

The correct answer to this question is b; 191.134.200.0 is a Class C address (indicated by 191 in the first octet) and would be assigned by the InterNIC. Any address that begins with 127 is considered the loopback address. Therefore, answer a (127.199.0.0) is incorrect. Answer c is a private address (indicated by the 10 in the first octet) and would not be assigned by InterNIC. Therefore, answer c is incorrect. An IP address beginning with 192 is also a Class C address, but the InterNIC would assign the first three octets, not just one, as is the case in 192.0.0.0. Therefore, answer d is incorrect.

Question 49

Answers b is correct. A proxy alert can be triggered by storage volumes reaching capacity. A large number of packets from a single host, invalid name/password combinations, and the frequency of accepted packets, although they may be helpful, cannot trigger proxy alerts. Therefore, answers a, c, and d are incorrect.

Question 50

The correct answer to this question is a. By default, the disk counters are disabled, and you must enable them by running the **diskperf -y** command. The **diskperf** command does not have a -**start** option. Therefore, answer b is incorrect. There is no **diskmon** command. Therefore, answers c and d are incorrect.

Question 51

Answer d is correct. The most likely cause of this problem is a subnet mask that is different from the rest of the network. The DNS setting has no bearing on PINGs, which use IP addresses. Therefore, answer a is incorrect. If the gateway address is misconfigured, you'll not be able to communicate outside your local subnet, but you should still be able to PING addresses on your local subnet. Therefore, answer b is incorrect. If your computer was configured with a duplicate IP address, TCP/IP would generate an error and would not load, and you would not be able to PING your own address. Therefore, answer c is incorrect.

Question 52

The correct answer to this question is a. CERN was involved in developing the basis of HTTP and an HTTP proxy system. Each of the other answers are or were involved in the development of the Internet but were not responsible for HTTP proxy.

Question 53

This statement is false; only permissions for Web Proxy and WinSock Proxy can be granted on a protocol basis for users and groups. Therefore, answer b is correct.

Question 54

The correct answers to this question are b and d. The WinSock Proxy service provides access for Windows clients running TCP/IP and acts as a gateway for Windows clients running NWLink (IPX/SPX). Both Macintosh and Unix clients can utilize the services of Proxy Server; however, they do not use the WinSock Proxy service but rather the Web and SOCKS Proxy services. Therefore, answers a and c are incorrect.

Question 55

The correct answer to this question is c. A proxy array is a distributed proxying environment that provides fault tolerance. A Proxy service (such as Web or WinSock) provides access for an internal client to the Internet. Therefore, answer a is incorrect. A proxy chain is a hierarchical proxy structure, not a distributed structure. Therefore, answer b is incorrect. Proxy caching improves client response but does not provide fault tolerance. Therefore, answer d is incorrect.

Question 56

WinSock Proxy clients are able to connect to the proxy server by using its NetBIOS computer name. Therefore, answer a is correct. Clients are not able to connect using a server's gateway or MAC address. Therefore, answers b and c are incorrect. Computers are not assigned an NWLink name. Therefore, answer d is incorrect.

Question 57

The correct answer to this question is b. Keep-alive packets maintain a connection between the client and server so that subsequent requests do not have to each go through the full resolution and connection process. Keep-alive packets have no function in regard to cache entries. Therefore, answer a is incorrect. They also do not manage the length of time a packet traverses the network, nor do they control communication between a client and server. Therefore, answers c and d are incorrect.

Question 58

The correct answer to this question a. One proxy server can adequately support 2,000 client desktops. It may be a good idea to create multiple proxy servers, but it is not necessary. Therefore, answers b, c, and d are incorrect.

Question 59

The correct answer to this question is d. The minimum hardware requirements for a medium load server (300 to 2,000 clients) are a Pentium 133, 64MB of RAM, and 2 to 4GB disk space for caching. Answers a and b are incorrect because they do not have enough memory or disk space to adequately support 750 clients. Also, although the faster processor in answer c is a good idea, it's not a minimum requirement. Therefore, answer c is incorrect.

Question 60

The correct answer to this question is b. Any Web Proxy service event messages that deal with caching will by logged under the WebProxyCache source name. WebCacheEvent, WinSockProxyCache, and WebCache are not valid source names. Therefore, answers a, c, and d are incorrect.

Question 61

The correct answer to this question is b. In a chained proxy environment, client requests that cannot be fulfilled by the proxy server or array are forwarded to an upstream proxy server. Answer a is not a valid proxy configuration. Answer c is the definition of a proxy array. Answer d describes a proxy server that is configured to support reverse proxy. Therefore, answers a, c, and d are incorrect.

Question 62

The correct answer to this question is c. Access is granted to a particular group through the Permissions tab of the Web Proxy Service Properties dialog.

Although each of the other options may sound good, they are not possible in the Proxy Server 2.0 environment. Therefore, answers a, b, and d are incorrect.

Question 63

Unlimited access can be granted to a user or group through the Permissions tab of the WinSock Properties applet. Therefore, answer d is correct. As you've seen from the previous explanations, it is possible to grant unlimited and unrestricted access. Therefore, answer a is incorrect. There is no WinSock Administrators group. Therefore, answer b is incorrect. It may be possible to grant access to each protocol and port individually, but it's not the most efficient way to provide access. Therefore, answer c is incorrect.

Question 64

The correct answer to this question is b. A CNAME record is an alias record. You make a CNAME resource record for each array member with the IP address of each but use the same alias name. Answer a is incorrect because a CNAME resource record is created, not an A resource record. Answer c is incorrect because there is no PROXYA-type resource record defined in DNS. Answer d is incorrect because the proxy servers do not attempt to contact the DNS server.

Question 65

The correct answer to this question is a. In a proxy array, all proxy members update each other's configuration information, and clients can access any available proxy server array member. If a server fails, the other members of the array are able to service client requests, thus providing fault tolerance. In a proxy chain, members do not update each other. Therefore, answer b is incorrect. Answers c and d are fictitious and are therefore incorrect.

Question 66

The correct answer to this question is a. The client's Web browser can be configured automatically by utilizing the options in the Client Configuration applet of the Web Proxy Service Properties page. As mentioned, this process can be automated. Therefore, answer b is incorrect. Clients must be configured to use the proxy server. Therefore, answer c is incorrect. The WinSock Proxy Service Properties page cannot be used to configure client Web browsers. Therefore answer d is incorrect.

Question 67

The correct answer to this question is b. If you apply changes to an array member and another administrator has also applied changes to an array member, a synchronization conflict occurs. The other answers will produce different error messages and are therefore incorrect.

Question 68

The correct answer to this question is b. The WinSock Proxy service port control function provides the highest level of security for outbound traffic. The Web Proxy Service does not support port control. Therefore, answer a is incorrect. Packet filtering is a function of the Web Proxy service, which controls inbound access. Therefore, answers c and d are incorrect.

Glossary

AATP (Authorized Academic Training Program)—A program that authorizes accredited academic institutions of higher learning to offer Microsoft Certified Professional testing and training to their students. The institutions are also allowed to use the Microsoft Education course materials and Microsoft Certified Trainers.

ARP (Address Resolution Protocol)—A Network layer protocol that associates a logical (IP) address to a physical (MAC) address.

array—A group of proxy servers that are linked and use peer-to-peer communication.

assessment exam—Similar to the certification exam in layout and content, but for practice only. This type of exam gives you the opportunity to answer questions at your own pace. It also uses the same tools as the certification exam.

ATEC (Authorized Technical Education Center)—The location where you can take a Microsoft Official Curriculum course taught by Microsoft Certified Trainers.

Auto Dial—An on-demand dial-out feature of Microsoft Proxy Server that works in conjunction with the Windows NT Remote Access Service (RAS) to schedule dial-out connection times to the Internet.

bandwidth—The range of frequencies that a communications medium can carry. For baseband networking media, the bandwidth also indicates the theoretical maximum amount of data that the medium can transfer; for broadband networking media, the bandwidth is measured by the variations that any single carrier frequency can carry, less the analog-to-digital conversion overhead.

BDC (Backup Domain Controller)—A backup server that protects the integrity and availability of the SAM database. BDCs are not able to make changes or modifications, but they can use the database to authenticate users.

beta exam—A trial exam that is given to participants at a Sylvan Prometric Testing Center before the development of the Microsoft Certified Professional certification exam is finalized. The final exam questions are selected based on the results of the beta exam. For example, if all beta exam participants all get an answer correct or wrong, that question generally will not appear in the final version.

cache—A temporary storage area that holds current information and is able to provide that information faster than other methods. In the case of the Web Proxy server, cache is local hard drive space on the Proxy Server computer that stores files received from a Web server.

caching—The process of temporarily maintaining a local copy of a resource to speed up requests.

capacity analysis—The process of examining the amount of data that can be transmitted over a network.

CARP (Cache Array Routing Protocol)—An integral part of the multiple proxy server capability in MS Proxy Server. It replaced the Internet Cache Protocol (ICP) and was designed by Microsoft.

cascading proxying—See *hierarchical proxying*.

CIDR (Classless Inter-Domain Routing)—An IP addressing scheme that removes the class boundaries for subnet masks and introduces a new system for determining the network and host ID of an address. It is pronounced *cider*.

client configuration script—A script downloaded from the proxy server each time the browser is opened. It is used to improve browser performance and update configuration parameters.

counter—In Performance Monitor, a single collection point of information for a system resource. An example of a counter would be DNS Cache Hits under the Web Proxy Server Cache object.

cut score—On the Microsoft Certified Professional exam, the lowest score a person can receive and still pass.

database—A collection of information arranged and stored so that data can be accessed quickly and accurately.

distributed proxying—When multiple Proxy Server computers are connected in a logical peer-to-peer fashion to form an array.

domain filter—A utility used to grant or deny access to Internet domain sites. It can include WWW, FTP, and Gopher sites.

dotted-decimal format—A way of representing an IP address as four groups of numbers, called *octets*, each separated by a dot (.).

downstream proxy server—The lower Proxy Server computer in a communication path.

event log—An option in the Event Viewer in the Administrative Tools group that lets you view all the events that have taken place on a particular computer.

Exam Preparation Guides—Guides that provide information specific to the material covered on Microsoft Certified Professional exams to help students prepare for the exam.

Exam Study Guide—Short for *Microsoft Certified Professional Program Exam Study Guide*. It contains information about the topics covered on more than one of the Microsoft Certified Professional exams.

firewall—A piece of equipment used to secure an Internet connection.

FTP (File Transfer Protocol)—An Application layer protocol used for file transfer, file manipulation, and directory manipulation.

Gopher—The protocol used to host the term-only information service of Gopher.

hashing—The technique the Cache Array Routing Protocol (CARP) uses to determine the location of stored objects in distributed proxying. Hashing is performed on all available array members and on the URL the client requests.

hierarchical proxying—When individual Proxy Server computers or arrays are "chained" together rather than being connected in a peer-to-peer fashion, like in distributed proxying. Also referred to as *proxy chaining* and *cascading proxying*.

HTTP (Hypertext Transfer Protocol)—The World Wide Web protocol that allows for the transfer of HTML documents over the Internet or intranets.

IANA (Internet Assigned Numbers Authority)—The governing body responsible for maintaining the list of well-known ports, among other things.

ICMP (Internet Control Message Protocol)—A Network layer protocol used to send control messages. The PING utility uses ICMP to request a response from a remote host. ICMP provides information such as whether the response was received and how long it took to make the trip.

IIS (Internet Information Server)—A Web server software developed by Microsoft. It is included and implemented with Windows NT Server.

inbound access—Network traffic from the Internet destined for a local network.

instance—In Performance Monitor, multiple units of an object. For example, the PhysicalDisk object might have multiple instances if more than one hard disk is installed.

Internet—The collection of TCP/IP-based networks around the world. Information on nearly every subject is available in some form somewhere on the Internet.

InterNIC (Internet Network Information Center)—The organization responsible for allocating and assigning IP addresses to those who want to connect their networks with the Internet.

intranet—An internal, private network that uses the same protocols and standards as the Internet.

IP (Internet Protocol)—A Network layer protocol that provides source and destination addressing and routing.

IP address—Four sets of numbers, separated by decimal points, that represent the numeric address of a computer attached to a TCP/IP network, such as the Internet.

IP address class—A system developed to delineate which bits of the IP address represent the network ID and which bits represent the host ID for a particular computer. The class of an IP address is defined by the value of the first octet of the address.

IPX/SPX (Internet Packet Exchange/Sequenced Packet Exchange)—Novell's NetWare protocol, reinvented by Microsoft and implemented in Windows NT under the name *NWLink*. It's fully compatible with Novell's version and, in many cases, is a better implementation than the original.

IPX-to-IP gateway—A gateway that enables the use of Internet information services served via Proxy Server 2.0 to be accessed by clients on an IPX network.

ISDN (Integrated Services Digital Network)—A form of digital communication that has a bandwidth of 128Kbps.

ISP (Internet Service Provider)—A service company that sells network access to the Internet. ISPs purchase bandwidth in bulk and in turn resell it in smaller packages.

job function expert—A person with extensive knowledge about a particular job function and the software products/technologies related to that job.

Typically, a job function expert is currently performing the job, has recently performed the job, or is training people to do this job.

keep-alive packets—Allow TCP connections to remain intact after the server has responded to a request.

LAN (local area network)—A network that is confined to a single building or geographic area and comprised of servers, workstations, peripheral devices, a network operating system, and a communications link.

LAT (local address table)—The table of all internal IP address pairs on the internal network where Microsoft Proxy Server is installed. This list is used to control access between clients on the internal network and remote IP addresses on external IP networks (or the Internet).

loopback address—An IP address with a first octet of 127. A loopback address cannot be used as the address for a host on a network. It's used to test the TCP/IP protocol stack within a computer without sending information out onto the network.

MCP (Microsoft Certified Professional)—An individual who has taken and passed at least one certification exam and has earned one or more of the following certifications: Microsoft Certified Trainer, Microsoft Certified Solution Developer, Microsoft Certified Systems Engineer, or Microsoft Certified Product Specialist.

MCPS (Microsoft Certified Product Specialist)—An individual who has passed at least one of the Microsoft operating system exams.

MCSD (Microsoft Certified Solution Developer)—An individual who is qualified to create and develop solutions for businesses using the Microsoft development tools, technologies, and platforms.

MCSE (Microsoft Certified Systems Engineer)—An individual who is an expert on Windows NT and the Microsoft BackOffice integrated family of server software. This individual also can plan, implement, maintain, and support information systems associated with these products.

MCT (Microsoft Certified Trainer)—An individual who is qualified by Microsoft to teach Microsoft Education courses at sites authorized by Microsoft.

MIB (Management Information Base)—A set of manageable objects representing various types of information about a network device that an SNMP management tool can request.

Microsoft Certification Exam—A test created by Microsoft to verify a test-taker's mastery of a software product, technology, or computing topic.

Microsoft Certified Professional Certification Update—A newsletter for Microsoft Certified Professional candidates and Microsoft Certified Professionals.

Microsoft NetShow—A streaming multimedia architecture and toolset developed by Microsoft.

Microsoft official curriculum—Microsoft education courses that support the certification exam process and are created by the Microsoft product groups.

Microsoft Proxy Server 2.0—Acts as an IPX-to-IP gateway for LAN clients, as a firewall to protect the internal network from the external network, and as a cache area for Internet objects, which allows faster response time when a client requests an Internet object, such as a URL.

Microsoft Roadmap to Education and Certification—An application, based on Microsoft Windows, that takes you through the process of deciding what your certification goals are and informs you of the best way to achieve them.

Microsoft Sales Fax Service—A service through which you can obtain Exam Preparation Guides, fact sheets, and additional information about the Microsoft Certified Professional Program.

Microsoft Solution Provider—An organization, not directly related to Microsoft, that provides integration, consulting, technical support, and other services related to Microsoft products.

Microsoft TechNet Technical Information Network (TechNet)—A service provided by Microsoft that provides helpful information via a monthly CD-ROM. TechNet is the primary source of technical information for people who support and/or educate end users, create automated solutions, or administer networks and/or databases.

MOLI (Microsoft Online Institute)—An organization that makes training materials, online forums and user groups, and online classes available.

MRI (multiple-rating item)—An item that gives you a task and a proposed solution. Every time the task is set, an alternate solution is given and the candidate must choose the answer that gives the best results produced by one solution.

MSDN (Microsoft Developer Network)—The official source for Software Development Kits (SDKs), Device Driver Kits (DDKs), operating systems, and programming information associated with creating applications for Microsoft Windows and Windows NT.

multihomed server—A computer with two or more network interfaces connected to different networks.

NDA (nondisclosure agreement)—A legal agreement signed both by Microsoft and by a vendor or client, rendering certain rights and limitations.

needs analysis—The process of determining your company's network needs by making a list of services and features required to improve or expand its current capabilities.

network—A collection of server and client computers that communicate over a wire-based media for the purposes of sharing resources.

object—In the Performance Monitor, a system resource, such as the Web Proxy Cache object that groups counters together.

ODBC (Open Database Connectivity)—A standard API (Application Programming Interface) used to construct platform/application-independent databases.

OS (operating system)—A software program that controls the operations on a computer system.

OSI (Open Systems Interconnection) Reference Model—An international standard set by the ISO (International Standards Organization) that defines how networking protocols operate.

outbound access—Network traffic generated on the local network destined for the Internet.

packet filter—An Internet Service Manager (ISM) option that controls inbound access to a network on a packet level. By utilizing this option, users can accept or deny traffic based on packet types, datagrams, or packet fragments.

passive caching—The basic mode of caching used by Proxy Server.

permissions—A level of access assigned to files or folders. Permissions determine who has access rights to those files or folders.

port—Used to name the ends of logical connections that carry on long-term conversations.

PPTP (Point-to-Point Tunneling Protocol)—A protocol that enables "tunneling" of IPX, NetBEUI, or TCP/IP inside PPP packets in such a way as to establish a secure link between a client and a server over the Internet.

proxy array—A distributed, peer-to-peer-type multiple proxy server configuration that provides fault tolerance and better client response for the client when accessing the Internet.

proxy chaining—See *hierarchical proxying*.

proxy route—The configuration of chained proxy servers used to determine a path through the proxy server chain to the Internet.

proxy server—A software product that acts as a moderator or go-between for a client and a remote host. Most proxy servers also offer content caching and firewall capabilities.

proxy server arrays—A group of Proxy Server computers configured and administered as a single entity with a large cache. Arrays provide scalability and ease of administration.

RealAudio—A multimedia tool, protocol, and enhancement that streams audio (and video) over TCP/IP networks.

Registry—A database that stores all the configuration information for Windows NT.

Resource Kit—The additional documentation and software utilities distributed by Microsoft to provide information and instruction on the proper operation and modification of its software products.

reverse hosting—A feature of Proxy Server that is a companion to the reverse proxy feature in that it enables several distinct Web servers hosted inside your network to be integrated by Proxy Server into what looks like a single large Web site to all external viewers. This method of Web publishing maintains tight security, isolates the Web servers from the Internet, and offers you greater flexibility in design, layout, and navigation.

reverse proxy—A feature of Proxy Server that enables you to setup a World Wide Web publishing server within your network behind the proxy server and still be able to offer its contents to the external world of the Internet.

RIP (Routing Information Protocol)—Used to distribute route information throughout a network. RIP is a Network layer protocol that uses distance-vector routing algorithms to identify the best path through an internetwork.

security—The protection of data by restricting access to only authorized users.

server proxying—A feature of Proxy Server that "listens" for or identifies inbound traffic bound for specific information service servers within the internal network and then forwards those packets to those servers.

Service Pack—A patch or fix distributed by Microsoft after the final release of a product to repair errors, bugs, and security breaches.

site filtering—A security feature that prevents internal users from accessing specified sites by filtering responses from that site or preventing requests from being processed. Site filtering is a form of user access control.

site restriction—The specifying of an IP address, domain name, or URL that is restricted. Also known as *site filtering*.

SMTP (Simple Mail Transport Protocol)—Another upper-layer protocol. SMTP is used by messaging programs such as email.

SNMP (Simple Network Management Protocol)—Used to manage network devices. It can be used to configure devices, such as bridges, repeaters, and gateways, as well as monitor network events using MIBs and SNMP managers.

socket—A communication channel made up of two pieces of information—an address and a port.

SOCKS Proxy—One of the components of Proxy Server. SOCKS Proxy is a cross-platform network service that creates a secured communications link between a client and a server. SOCKS Proxy supports SOCKS 4.3a and offers non-Windows or non-WinSock applications access to Internet services.

SQL Server—A Microsoft product that supports a network-enabled relational database system.

subnet—A portion or segment of a network.

subnet mask—A 32-bit address that indicates how many bits in an address are being used for the network ID.

TCP (Transmission Control Protocol)—A connection-oriented Transport layer protocol that accepts messages of any length from the upper layers and provides transportation to another computer. TCP is responsible for packet fragmentation and reassembly, as well as sequencing.

TCP/IP (Transmission Control Protocol/Internet Protocol)—The most commonly used network protocol and the central protocol of the Internet.

Telnet—A very useful remote terminal emulation application that has its own protocol for transport (defined in RFC 854).

TTL (Time To Live)—The number of seconds a packet is allowed to traverse the network.

UDP (User Datagram Protocol)—A protocol that provides connectionless Transport layer functions for the TCP/IP suite. UDP is the counterpart to TCP.

Unix—An interactive time-sharing operating system developed in 1969 by a hacker to play games. This system developed into the most widely used industrial-strength computer operating system in the world, and it ultimately supported the birth of the Internet.

upstream proxy server—The Proxy Server computer, or array, that is above other proxy servers in the communications path.

URL (Universal Resource Locator)—The addressing scheme used to identify resources on the Internet.

user access control—When a caching, or proxy, server is used to prevent resource access.

VDOLive—A streaming audio and video protocol and tool for TCP/IP networks.

VPN (virtual private network)—A WAN, provided by a common communications carrier, that works like a private network; however, the backbone of the network is shared with all the customers in a public network.

WAN (wide area network)—A network that spans geographically distant segments. Often the distance of two miles or more is used to define a WAN; however, Microsoft equates any RAS connection as establishing a WAN.

Web Proxy—One of the components of Proxy Server. Web Proxy supports those protocols and communication mechanisms typically associated with Web documents, access, and interaction.

Web Proxy service—The service that enables Microsoft Proxy Server to function as a proxy host.

well-known ports—Those ports below 1023 that are assigned to specific TCP/IP protocols and functions.

WinSock—A mechanism for interprocess communication.

WinSock Proxy—One of the components of Proxy Server. WinSock Proxy supports client applications designed around the Windows Sockets API. This includes utilities and services such as Telnet and RealAudio.

WinSock Proxy service—A Microsoft Proxy Server API service that allows Windows Sockets–compatible applications to be redirected and remotely executed via intranets and remote computers.

Index

Bold page numbers indicate
sample exam questions.

A

AATP (Authorized Academic Training
  Program), 255
Access, restricting. *See also* Security.
  datagrams, 82–83
  domains, 82–85
  email, 85–86
  FTP, 83, 107, 129–130
  Gopher, 83, 107
  groups, 83, **237**
  IMC, 85–86
  Internet service control, 83
  Internet services, 83
  IP addresses, 83–85
  IP forwarding, 81–82
  LAT, 81–82
  packet filtering, 82–83
  port numbers, 85
  protocols, 83–84, 107–108, 112–113, 129–130
  Secure services, 83, 107
  server proxies, 85–86
  subnets, 83–85
  unlimited access, 113
  users, 83, **215**
  Web services, 83, 107
Access, unlimited, 113, **237**
Access control, defined, 14
Active caching, 25, 108–109, 120,
  124–125, 217, 220
Addressing and routing functions, 65, **73**
Addressing protocols, 65
Administration. *See* ISM (Internet
  Service Manager).
Administrative privileges, 38
Administrative tools, 17, 40
Advanced button, ISM, 120
Alert events, source names, 88
Alerting keys, 179, **188**
Alerts, 86–88, **100, 232**
Alias records, 159
Ambiguous questions, certification exams, 211
Application Event log, 121
Application protocols, 65, **74**
Architecture
  SOCKS Proxy service, 28–29
  Web Proxy service, 21–29

WinSock Proxy service, 25–28
ARP (Address Resolution Protocol), 65, 255
ARPA (Advanced Research Projects Agency), 64
ARPANet (Advanced Research Projects Agency
  Network), 64
Array button, ISM, 107
Array Configuration Conflict message, 162
Array members, defined, 154
Arrays, **234, 238**
  Array Configuration Conflict message, 162
  cache, 154
  Configuration Changed message, 162
  configuration information, sharing,
    154–156, **166**
  conflicts, 156, 162
  creating, 107
  defined, 154, 255
  distributed proxying, 154–156
  error messages, 161–163
  event messages, 181
  modifying members, 156, 162, **168–169, 216**
  Refresh or Overwrite message, 156, **169**
  Registry keys, 179
  replication, 156, **166**
  routing options, setting, 109
  sharing information, 154–156, **166**
  synchronization, 154–156
  Synchronize Now or Cancel message, 156, **168**
  upstream proxy server, 264
  upstream routing, 109, 158
  when to use, 144, **150**
Assessment exam, 255. *See also* Practice exams.
ATEC (Authorized Technical Education
  Center), 255
Audit trail. *See* Logging.
Auto Dial, 46–50, 140, 255
Auto Dial button, ISM, 107

B

Backing up server configuration, 143–144
Backup file, specifying, 107
Backup route keys, 179
Bandwidth, **226**
  defined, 255
  formula, 201
  options, ISP, 200
BDC (Backup Domain Controller), 256
Best practices, multiple proxy servers, 161
Beta exam, 256

Binary data types, 178
Binary representations, 67–68, **74, 228**
Bind operation, 29
Bit patterns, IP addresses, 67–68
Blank answers, 7
Business background, ISP, 199
Bytes, IP addresses, 67–68

C

Cache, **33, 55–56**
  active, 25, 108–109, 120, **124–125, 217, 220**
  and arrays, 154
  bypassing, 25
  CARP, 17
  configuring, 41–42, 107–109, **124, 127–128,** 129
  counters, 116
  defined, 14, 23–25, 256
  disabling, 107
  disk space requirements, 38, 42, **56**
  and distributed proxying, 154
  enabling, 107, **217**
  error messages, list of, 121–122
  event messages, 121–122, 180–181
  expiration policy, 120, **125–126, 217**
  and FAT partitions, 142, **149, 225**
  filtering, 120
  force updates without client request, 108–109, **125**
  installing, 41–42
  Internet objects, 142–143
  local disk requirement, 42
  location, changing, 120
  monitoring, 118–120
  multiple proxy servers, 17
  new disk, adding, 42, 129
  NTFS requirement, 38
  partitions, 41, 120, 129, **214**
  passive, 24, 109, 261
  performance, 17, 107–109, 118–120, 130, **220–222**
  Registry values, 182
  server configuration, 142–143
  size, **148**
    adjusting, 120
    formula, 144
    objects, limiting, 119–120, **125–128**
    recommended, 118, **231**
  source names, 121–122, 180, **236**
  TechNet topics, 131
  TTL, 119–120, **125–126,** 130, **217, 222**
  tuning, 118–120
  update frequency, 109
  upgrading from Proxy Server 1.0, 142, **149**
  WebProxyCache source name, 121–122
Cache Size button, ISM, 120, 129
Caching tab, Web Proxy service, 107–109
Caching value Registry entries, **227**
Capacity analysis, 192–193, 256
Capacity planning, **221**

CARP (Cache Array Routing Protocol), 17, 158–159, **170, 218,** 256
Cascaded chaining, defined, 157
Cascading proxying, defined, 256
CERN (European Laboratory for Particle Physics), 22, **31, 233**
Certification exams
  Exam Preparation Guides, 8, 257
  Exam Study Guides, 257
  Microsoft Training And Certification Web site, 8–9
  preparation strategy, 212–213
  strategies, 5–8, 213
  Sylvan Prometric Testing Centers, 2–3
  Web sites of interest, 8–9
Chained arrays, troubleshooting
  event messages, 181
  Registry keys, 179
  source names, 181
Chained proxying, 156–158, **164, 166, 223, 236.** *See also* Arrays.
CIDR (Classless InterDomain Routing), 71, **75, 231,** 256
Class A IP addresses, 68–69
Class B IP addresses, 68–69, **75**
Class C IP addresses, 68–69, **231**
Classes, IP addresses, 68–69, **76, 232**
Client Configuration button, ISM, 107
Client share, configuring, 107, **126**
Clients, **126, 239**
  configuration file, editing, 137–138
  configuration script, 256
  configuring, 44–46, 52–54, 107, 135–140
  default, 40
  defined, 21–22, 26–27
  installing, 39–41, 44–46
  IPX/SPX, 27, 52–53
  LAT, customizing, 139
  load balancing, 159–160, **238**
  LOCALLAT.TXT file, creating, 139
  logging, 93
  memory requirements, **56**
  MSPCLNT.INI, editing, 137–138
  MSPLAT.TXT file, changing, 139
  multiple proxy servers, 159–160, **165, 170, 238**
  parameters, changing, 135–137
  scripts, 137
  system changes, 53–54
  Web Proxy, 21–22, 139
  WinSock Proxy, 26–27, 44, 53–54, **57–58,** 139–140
CNAMEs (canonical names), 159, **238**
Comma delimited format, logs, 91
Communication concerns, ISP, 198
Compatibility, ISP, 199
Components
  adding, 50
  installing, 39–41
  uninstalling, 50
Computer name formats, 44, **57–58**
Configuration, recommended, 118

Configuration area, ISM, 107
Configuration Changed message, 162
Configuration file, editing, 137–138
Configuration information, sharing, **165–166**
    distributed proxying, 154–156
    hierarchical proxying, 157
Configuration parameters, changing, 135–137
Configuration tips, Proxy Server, 118
Configuring. *See also* Clients; Installation.
    alerts, 86–88
    Auto Dial, 46–50, 140
    cache, 107–109, **124, 127–128**, 129
    clients, 44–46, 52–54, 107, **126**, 135–140, **239**
    LAT, 42–44, 51, **57–59**
    multiple protocols, 52–53
    TechNet topics, 61
Conflicts, arrays, 156, 162
Connection requests, 28–29
Connectionless communication, 26–28, 66, 72, **76**
Connection-oriented communication, 26–27,
    66, 72, **219**
Connections
    choosing communication links, 200–202, **224**
    concerns, 194
    displaying, 106
    logging, 93–94
    managing, 27–28
Control Channel, 27–28, **32, 226**
Counters, 115–117, 185–186, 256
Current sessions, displaying, 106
Current Sessions button, ISM, 106
Cut score, defined, 256

D

Daily logs, 146
Data items, in logs, 89–90
Data strings, 178
Data types, list of, 178
Database, defined, 256
Datagram-oriented communication, 26, **30**
Datagrams, as access controls, 82–83
Decimal representations, IP
    addresses, 67–68
Dedicated services, 202
Default file format, logs, 145
Default file names, logs, 145–146
*Designing and Implementing Microsoft Proxy
    Server*, 102, 207
Dial on demand, 107, 140
Digital communication links, 201–202
Disk counters, 186, **189**
Disk full alerts, 87
Disk space
    recommended, 118, 144, 202–203, **223**
    required, 38, 41–42, **56**
diskperf command, 186, **189, 232**
Distributed caching, 17, **33**
Distributed proxying, 154–156, **234**, 256. *See
    also* Arrays.
DNS load balancing, 159–160, **165, 170, 238**
Documentation, installing, 40, 46

Domain filtering keys, 178
Domain filters, 82–85, **99–100**, 107, **231**, 257
Domain separation, 82, **99**
Dotted-decimal format, 67, 257
Downstream proxy servers, 157, 257
Downtime, ISP, 199
DUN (Dial-Up Networking), 46–50
DWORD entries, 178
Dynamic packet filtering, 16, 83

E

Editing Registry entries, 176–178
Email
    access, restricting, 85–86
    alerts, 87–88
Email alert keys, 179
Email-only installation, planning, 201
Encryption, 86
Error logging. *See* Logging.
Error messages
    cache, 121–122
    multiple proxy servers, 162–163
    SOCKS Proxy service, 122–123
    Web Proxy service, 121
    WinSock Proxy service, 122
Event log, defined, 257
Event messages, **221**
    SOCKS Proxy service, 184
    Web Proxy service, 179–181
    WinSock Proxy service, 182–184
Event Viewer, 121, 174–175, **221**
Events. *See* Alerts.
Exams. *See* Certification exams.
Expandable string entries, 178
Expiration policy, 120, **125–126, 217**
Extended characters in logs, 90
External clients, Internet publishing, 96–97. *See
    also* Security.

F

FAT partitions, and cache, 142, **149, 225**
Fault tolerance, 154, 157, **165, 238**
56Kbps connections, 201
File formats, logs, 91
File names, logs, 91, 145–146
File transfer protocols, 65
Files, restoring, 50–51
Filters, **99–101, 225–226, 228, 231**
    cache, 120
    configuring, 107
    domain, 82–85, 257
    ISAPI, 22–23
    logging, 88, 95–96
    packet, 16, 82–83, 95–96, 261
    ports, 72
    site, 14, 262
Firewall, defined, 14, 257
Flow control, 65
404 File Not Found error, 10
FTP (File Transfer Protocol)
    access control, 83, 107, 129–130

defined, 65, 257
support, 18
well-known ports, 72, **218**

G

General information, logging, 95
Geographic location, ISP, 198
Gopher, 83, 107, 257
Groups, 83, 107, **237**

H

Hardware
    planning, 202–203
    recommendations, **235**
    requirements, 21
Hashing, 158–159, **167, 219**, 257
Help, where to get, 174–176
Hierarchical proxying, 156–158, 257. *See also*
    Arrays.
Host addresses, 68–69
HTTP (Hypertext Transfer Protocol), **31, 233**
    CERN, 22
    defined, 65, 257
    development, 22
    requests, security, 96–97
    support, 18
    well-known port, 72
Hybrid product, 15, **30**

I

IANA (Internet Assigned Numbers Authority),
    72, 257
ICMP (Internet Control Message Protocol),
    65, 257
ICP (Internet Cache Protocol), 158, **170, 218**
IIS (Internet Information Server). *See also*
    Internet publishing; Reverse proxies.
    defined, 257
    IIS 3.0 requirement, 38
IMC (Internet Mail Connector), 85–86
Inbound access, restricting, **99**
    datagrams, 82–83
    defined, 80–81, 258
    domains, 82
    IP forwarding, 81–82
    LAT, 81–82
    packet filtering, 82–83
Installation, **55–60**
    administrative privileges, 38
    administrative tools, 40
    Auto Dial, 46–50
    cache, 41–42
    clients, 39–41, 44–46, 53–54
    components, 39–41, 50
    computer name formats, 44
    disk space requirements, 38, 41–42, **56**
    documentation, 40, 46
    DUN, 46–50
    files, restoring, 50–51
    IIS 3.0 requirement, 38

Internet connection
    automatic, 46–50
    direct, 54
    IPX/SPX, forcing, 52–53
    LAT, 43–44, 51, **57–59**
    MSPfolder, 53
    multiple protocols, 52–53
    NIC, 38, 43, **55**
    NT Server 4 requirement, 38
    NTFS requirement, 38
    NWLink, 38, 52–53
    options, selecting, 40
    preparation, 38
    protocols
        multiple, 52–53
        requirements, 38
    Proxy Server 2.0
        installing, 39–46
        uninstalling, 51
    RAS, 46–50
    requirements, 38, **56–57**
    SAP agent, 41
    Service Pack 3, 38
    system changes
        client, 53–54
        server, 50
    TCP/IP, 38, 52–53
    TechNet topics, 61
    uninstalling
        components, 50
        Proxy Server, 51
        WinSock Proxy client, 53
Instance, defined, 258
Internet, defined, 258
Internet access, **148–150**. *See also* Access;
    restricting; Security.
    about, 134
    Auto Dial, 140
    backing up configuration, 143–144
    cache, 142–144
    client configuration, 135–140
    configuration file, editing, 137–138
    dial on demand, 140
    disk space, recommended, 144
    LAT, 139–142, 147
    LOCALLAT.TXT file, creating, 139
    logging, 145–146
    MSPCLNT.INI, editing, 137–138
    MSPDIAG.EXE, 146–147
    MSPLAT.TXT file, changing, 139–142
    parameters, changing, 135–137
    partial restore, 143–144
    performance, 144
    planning, 193–194
    processor speed, recommended, 144
    RAM, recommended, 144
    reasons to use, 193–194
    recommended configuration, 144
    restoring configuration, 143–144
    scripts, 137
    server configuration, 140–144

TechNet topics, 151
troubleshooting, 146–147
tuning, 144
upgrade from Proxy Server 1.0, 143
Internet connection, **224**
automatic, 46–50
direct, 54
planning, 200–202
Internet information service availability, ISP, 198
Internet publishing, 96–97, **98**, 110–111, **128**, **214**
Internet service control, 83
Internetwork, defined, 68
InterNIC (Internet Network Information Center), 68, **73**, **76**, **232**, 258
Interprocess communication, 25–26
Intranet, defined, 258
IP addresses
as access controls, 83–85
adding to LAT, 140–142
assigning, 68, **73**
binary representations, 67
classes, 68–69, **76**, 258
defined, 258
dotted-decimal format, 67
host IDs, 68–69
logical, 67
network IDs, **75**
assigning, 68–69
identifying, 69–71
physical, 66–67
private, 68
reserved, 68
subnet masks, 69–72
valid, 67–68, **75–76**
IP forwarding, as access control, 81–82
IP (Internet Protocol), 66, 258
IPX/SPX (Internet Packet Exchange/ Sequenced Packet Exchange)
defined, 258
forcing, 52–53
network IDs, 68
support, 18, 25–27, **31**
IPX-to-IP gateway, 258
IRC support, 111
ISAPI application interface, 22–23
ISAPI extensions (encryption), 86
ISAPI filter interface, 22–23
ISDN (Integrated Services Digital Network), **224**
defined, 258
planning, 201
ISM (Internet Service Manager)
Advanced button, 120
alerts, 86–88
Array button, 107
Auto Dial button, 107
Cache Size button, 120, 129
Caching tab, Web Proxy service, 107–109
Client Configuration button, 107
Configuration area, 107
Current Sessions button, 106
Local Address Table button, 107

Logging tab, 110, 121
opening, 104–105
packet filtering, 82
Permissions tab
SOCKS Proxy service, 114
Web Proxy service, 107–108
WinSock Proxy service, 112
Plug-Ins button, 107
Properties menu options, 105
Properties Page
SOCKS Proxy service, 113
Web Proxy service, 106
WinSock Proxy service, 112
Protocols tab, WinSock Proxy service, 112–113
Publishing tab, Web Proxy service, 110, 160
Routing tab, Web Proxy service, 109, 158
Security button, 107
Server Backup button, 107
Server Restore button, 107
Service tab, 106–107
Shared Services area, 107
SOCKS Proxy service, managing, 113–114
viewing options, 105
Web Proxy service, managing, 106–111
WinSock Proxy service, managing, 111–113
ISPs (Internet Service Providers), 195–200, 258

J

Job function expert, 258–259

K

Keep-alive packets, 23, **33–34**, **235**, 259
Knowledge Base topics
planning, 207
security information, 102
troubleshooting, 175

L

LAN (local area network), 259
LAT (local address table), **57–59**, **220**, **227**
as access control, 81–82
adding entries, 44, 140–142
configuring, 51
creating, 43–44
customizing, 51, 139–142
defined, 28, 259
external file names, 147, **148**
LOCALLAT.TXT file, 51
modifying, 107
directory, 51
MSPLAT.TXT file, 51
NICs, 43
private addresses, 43
viewing, 107
Load balancing, 157, 159–160, **165**, **170**, **238**
Local Address Table button, ISM, 107
Local copies of resources, 14

Local disk requirement, cache, 42
Local information, logging, 95
LOCALLAT.TXT file, 139, **214–215**
Logging. *See also* Event messages; Troubleshooting.
  comma delimited format, 91
  configuring, 88–89
  daily logs, 146
  data items, list of, 89–90
  default file format, 91, **98**, 145, **228**
  default file names, 110, 113–114, 145–146
  enabling, 89
  extended characters, 90
  file names, 91, 145–146
  format, 89
  Internet access, 145–146
  modes, 145
  monthly logs, 146
  to network share, 179
  packet filter information, 95–96
  packet log, 145
  regular format, 89
  to remote drive, not recommended, 145
  security filter log, 88
  service information, 92–94
  service logs, 145
  setting options, 110, 121
  source names, list of, 145
  to SQL/ODBC database, 91–92
  storing logs, 89
  TechNet topics, 131
  to text files, 91
  verbose format, 89
  weekly logs, 146
  Windows NT System Event log, 145
Logging tab, ISM, 110, 121
Logging value keys, 179, **188**
Logical addresses, 67
Logical connections, naming, 72
Loopback address, 259

M

MAC (Media Access Control) address, 66
Memory. *See also* Disk space.
  monitoring, 115–118
  recommendations, 202–203
  tuning, 115–118
MIB (Management Information Base),
  115–117, 259
MIB values, 182, 184
Microsoft certification exams, 259. *See also*
  Certification exams.
Microsoft Certified Professional certification
  update, 260
Microsoft Event Viewer. *See* Event Viewer.
Microsoft NetShow, 18, 111, 260
Microsoft Performance Monitor. *See* Perfor-
  mance Monitor.
Microsoft Proxy Server. *See* Proxy Server.
Microsoft TechNet, 260. *See also* TechNet topics.
Microsoft Training And Certification Web site, 8–9
Modes, logging, 145
MOLI (Microsoft Online Institute), 260

Monitoring
  cache, 118–120
  memory, 115–118
Monthly logs, 146
MRI (multiple-rating item), 260
MSDN (Microsoft Developer
  Network), 260
MSPfolder, 53
MSPCLNT.INI, editing, 137–138
MSPDIAG.EXE, 146–147, 175
MSPLAT.TXT file, changing
  client configuration, 139
  server configuration, 140–142
Multihomed servers, 15, 260
Multiple protocols, 52–53
Multiple proxy servers, **164–171**
  best practices, 161
  caching, 17
  clients, 159–160
  distributed proxying, 154–156
  error messages, 162–163
  hashing, 158–159
  hierarchical proxying, 156–158
  load balancing, 159–160
  reverse hosting, 160
  troubleshooting, 161–163
Multiple requests to same site, 23, **33–34**
Multipoint communication support, 26

N

Name formats, 44
Needs analysis, 193, 261
NetBIOS Name Service well-known port, 72
NetBUI support, 25–26
NetShow, 18, 111, 260
Network, defined, 261
Network addresses
  assigning, 68–69, **76**, **232**
  identifying, 69–71, **75**
Network capacity analysis, 192–193
Network capacity planning, **221**
Network protocols, 65, **227**
NICs (network interface cards), **55**
  adding to LAT, 43
  installation requirement, 38
  MAC address, 66
NT Server 4 requirement, 38
NTFS requirement, 38
NWLink, 38, 52–53

O

Object, defined, 261
Object information, logging, 94
Octets, 69
ODBC (Open Database Connectivity), 261
OIDs (object identifiers)
  Web Proxy service, 117
  WinSock Proxy service, 117
OS (operating system), 261
OSI (Open Systems Interconnection), 261
Outbound access, restricting, **220**, **225**, **240**

defined, 80–81, 261
domains, 83–85
email, 85–86
FTP Read, 83
Gopher, 83
groups, 83
IMC, 85–86
Internet service control, 83
Internet services, 83
IP addresses, 83–85
port numbers, 85
Secure services, 83
server proxies, 85–86
subnets, 83–85
users, 83
Web services, 83

P

PAC (Proxy Auto-Config) file, 158
Packet filtering keys, 178, **188**
Packet filters, **99–101, 225–226, 228**
    as access controls, 82–83
    configuring, 107
    defined, 261
    dynamic, 16
    logging, 95–96
Packet log, 145
Packets. *See also* IP addresses.
    IP network IDs, 68–71
    IPX/SPX network IDs, 68
    network IDs, 68–71
Partial restore, 107, 143–144
Partitions, cache, 41, 120, 129, 142, **149, 214, 225**
Passive caching, 24, 109, 261
Peak times, ISP, 200
Peer-to-peer (distributed) proxying, 154–156.
    See also Arrays.
Performance. *See also* Cache.
    cache, 107–109, 118–120, 130
    configuration tips, 118
    Internet access, 144
    memory, 115–118
    Microsoft Proxy Server 2.0, 17
    RAM, adding to Proxy Server, 118
    TechNet topics, 131
    troubleshooting, 185–186
    tuning, 115–118
Performance Monitor, 115–117, 185–186,
    189, 232
Permissions. *See also* Security.
    defined, 261
    SOCKS Proxy service, 114
    Web Proxy service, 107–108
    WinSock Proxy service, 112
Permissions tab, ISM
    SOCKS Proxy service, 114
    Web Proxy service, 107–108
    WinSock Proxy service, 112
Physical addresses, 66–67
PING failure, **233**
Pipeline, choosing, 200–202
Planning, **204–206**

bandwidth needs (formula), 201
capacity analysis, 192–193
connectivity
    choosing, 200–202
    concerns, 194
dedicated service, 202
digital communication links, 201–202
disk storage recommendations, 202–203
email only installation, 201
56Kbps, 201
hardware needs, 202–203
Internet access, reasons to use, 193–194
Internet connection, choosing, 200–202
ISDN, 201
ISP concerns, 195–200
memory recommendations, 202–203
needs analysis, 193
network capacity analysis, 192–193
pipeline, choosing, 200–202
POTS, 201
processor speed recommendations, 202–203
RAM recommendations, 202–203
security, 195
site analysis, 192–195
T1, 201
VPNs, 199
Plug-ins, installing, 107
Plug-Ins button, ISM, 107
Port access control, **220, 240**
Port number, Control Channel, 28
Ports
    as access controls, 85, **101**
    assigning, 72
    defined, 261
    filtering, 72
    well-known, list of, 72
POTS (plain old telephone service), 201
PPTP (Point-to-Point Tunneling Protocol),
    86, 261
Practice exams, 7–9, 11, **214–240**
Preparation guides, exam, 8
Preparation strategy, exam, 212–213
Private internal networks, 139, **149**
Private IP addresses, 68
Processor speed, recommended, 118, 144, 202–203
Properties menu, ISM, 105
Properties Page, ISM
    SOCKS Proxy service, 113
    Web Proxy service, 106
    WinSock Proxy service, 112
Protocol violation events, 87
Protocols, **73–76**. *See also* IP addresses.
    access, restricting, 107–108, 112–113, 129–130
    Application, **225**
    installation requirements, 38
    multiple, configuring, 52–53
    Network, **227**
    outbound access, restricting, 83–84, **101**
    publications, 77
    restricting access, **233**
    TCP/IP, 65–66

TechNet topics, 77
types of, 65–66
Protocols tab, WinSock Proxy service, 112–113
Proxy array keys, 179
Proxy arrays, **215**, **234**, **238**, 261
Proxy caching. *See* Cache.
Proxy chaining, 157, 261. *See also* Arrays.
Proxy route, 262
Proxy Server 1.0, **31**
    cache, 142, **225**
    FAT partition, 142
    missing features, 16
    server configuration file, 143
Proxy Server 2.0
    administration, 17
    advantages, 19–20
    architecture
        SOCKS Proxy service, 28–29
        Web Proxy service, 21–25
        WinSock Proxy service, 25–28
    CARP, 17
    configuration tips, 118
    defined, 260
    error logging, 121–123
    features, 17–19
    hardware requirements, 21
    hybrid product, 15, **30**
    installing, 39–46
    and intranets, 29
    ISM, 104–114
    monitoring
        cache, 118–121
        memory, 115–118
        Performance Monitor, 114–115
    versus Netscape Server 2.5, 19–20
    new features, 18–19
    versus Novell Border Manager, 19–20
    performance, 17
    Performance Monitor, 114–115
    proxy server, defined, 14–15
    proxy services, defined, 18
    recommended configuration, 118
    removing, 51
    Routing and Remote Access, 16, **32**
    security, 16–17
    software requirements, 20–21
    tuning
        cache, 118–121
        memory, 115–118
    uninstalling, 51
    versus version 1.0, 16, 18–19, **31**
    VPN support, 16
Proxy server arrays, 154, 158, **164–165**, 262. *See also* Arrays.
Proxy server functions, **223**
Proxy Server home page, 176
Proxy Server online documentation, 176
Proxy server routes, 158
Proxy servers
    defined, 14–15, 262
    multiple, 154

Proxy services, defined, 18
Publishing tab, Web Proxy service, 110, 160
Publishing values, Web Proxy service, 182

R

RAM
    adding to Proxy Server, 118
    recommended, 118, 144, 202–203, **218**
RAS (Remote Access Service), 46–50
Readnews well-known port, 72
RealAudio, 18, 111, **127**, **215**, 262
Recommended configuration, 118, 144
Redirecting requests, 28
Refresh or Overwrite message, 156, **169**, **216**
REGEDIT.EXE, 176–177
REGEDT32.EXE, 176–177
Registry, defined, 176, **188**, **227**, 262
Registry, troubleshooting. *See also* Troubleshooting.
    alerting keys, 179, **188**
    array keys, 179
    backup route keys, 179
    binary data types, 178
    cache values, Web Proxy service, 182
    chained array keys, 179
    data strings, 178
    data types, list of, 178
    domain filtering keys, 178
    DWORD entries, 178
    editing, 176–178
    email alert keys, 179
    expandable string entries, 178
    logging value keys, 179, **188**
    MIB values
        Web Proxy service, 182
        WinSock proxy service, 184
    packet filtering keys, 178, **188**
    proxy array keys, 179
    publishing values, Web Proxy service, 182
    reverse proxy values, Web Proxy service, 182
    route keys, 179
    service keys
        SOCKS Proxy service, 185
        Web Proxy service, 181–182
        WinSock Proxy service, 184
    SOCKS Proxy service, 178–179, 185
    subtrees, defined, 176
    value classes, list of, 178
    value entries, format, 178
    Web Proxy service, 178–179, 181–182
    WinSock Proxy service, 178–179, 184
Regular format logs, 89
Rejected packet alerts, 87
Remote connectivity, ISP, 199
Remote information, logging, 95
Remote logging, not recommended, 145
Remote users, restricting access. *See* Access, restricting; Security.
Replication, arrays, 156, **166**, **215**
Requests, **33–34**
    multiple to same site, 23
    redirecting, 28

validating, 22–23
Reserved IP addresses, 68
Resource Kit, 262
Resource object information, logging, 94
Resources
  access control, 14
  local copies, 14
Restoring from backup, 107, 143–144
Reverse hosting, 97, 110–111, 160, 262
Reverse proxies, 96–97, 110–111, 182, 262
RIP (Routing Information Protocol), 66, 262
Round-robin fashion, 159, **238**
Route keys, 179
Routing and Remote Access, 16, **32**
Routing options
  arrays, 109
  proxy servers, 158
Routing protocols, 65
Routing tab, Web Proxy service, 109, 158
RRAS, **219**

S

SAP agent, 41
Scripts, client configuration, 137
Search tools, 10
Secure services, restricting access, 83, 107
Secure Web publishing, 96–97, **98**, **214**
Security, **98–101**, **240**. *See also* Access,
  restricting.
  alerts, 86–88
  Auto Dial, 47–48
  defined, 262
  encryption, 86
  events. *See* Alerts.
  external clients, 96–97
  features, 16–17
  HTTP requests, 96–97
  inbound access, restricting, 80–83, **99**
  Internet publishing, 96–97
  ISAPI extensions (encryption), 86
  ISM (Internet Services Manager), 82
  Knowledge Base, 102
  logging, 88–96
  outbound access, restricting, 80–81, 83–86
  planning, 195
  RAS settings, 47–48
  reverse hosting, 97
  reverse proxy, 96–97
  secure Web publishing, 96–97
  source names (alert events), 88
  TechNet topics, 102
  Web publishing, 96–97
  Windows NT System log, 88
Security button, ISM, 107
Security filter log, 88
Server arrays. *See* Arrays.
Server Backup button, ISM, 107
Server configuration, **235**
  Auto Dial, 140
  backing up configuration, 143–144
  caching Internet objects, 142–143

dial on demand, 140
LAT, customizing, 140–142
MSPLAT.TXT file, changing, 140–142
partial restore, 143–144
restoring configuration, 143–144
upgrade from Proxy Server 1.0, 142–143
Server information, logging, 92–93
Server proxies, as access controls, 85–86
Server proxying, defined, 262
Server Restore button, ISM, 107
Service counters, 117
Service information, logging, 92–94
Service keys
  SOCKS Proxy service, 185
  Web Proxy service, 181
  WinSock Proxy service, 184
Service logs, 145
Service Pack, defined, 262
Service Pack 3 requirement, 38
Service tab, ISM, 106–107
Services, configuring, 106–107
Shared Services area, ISM, 107
Sharing information, 154–157, **166**
Site analysis, 192–195
Site filtering, 14, 262
Site restriction, 263
SMTP (Simple Mail Transport Protocol)
  alerts, 87–88
  defined, 66, 263
  well-known port, 72
SNMP (Simple Network Management
  Protocol)
  defined, 66, 263
  monitoring, 115–118
  well-known port, 72
Socket numbers, **223**
Sockets, 26, **33**, 263
SOCKS 4.3a support, 18
SOCKS Proxy service
  alerts, configuring, 86–88
  architecture, 28–29
  arrays, creating, 107
  backup file, specifying, 107
  client share, configuring, 107
  clients, configuring, 107
  connection information, displaying, 106
  counters, 117
  current sessions, displaying, 106
  defined, 263
  dial on demand, 107
  domain filters, configuring, 107
  error messages, list of, 122–123
  event messages, 184
  filters, configuring, 107
  group permissions, setting, 107
  Internet logging, 145–146
  ISM, 113–114
  LAT, 107
  logging, 88–96
    default file name, 114
    setting options, 110, 121

multiple proxy servers, 159–160
packet filters, configuring, 107
partial restores, 107
permissions, setting, 114
plug-ins, installing, 107
Properties Page, accessing, 113
protocols supported, 18
Registry keys, 178–179, 185
restoring from backup file, 107
services, configuring, 106–107
source names, 122–123, 184
UDP support, 18
user permissions, setting, 107
users, displaying, 106
SocksProxy source name, 122–123
SocksProxyLog source name, 122–123
Software requirements, 20–21
Source names
    alert events, 88
    array event messages, 181
    cache, 180, **236**
    chain event messages, 181
    list of, 145
    SOCKS Proxy service, 122–123, 184
    Web Proxy service, 121, 180–181
    WinSock Proxy service, 122, 183–184
SQL Server, 263
SQL/ODBC database, logging to, 91–92
SSL (Secure Sockets Layer), 86
Static packet filtering, 83
Storage. *See* Disk space.
Storing logs, 89
Strategies, certification exams, 213
Stream-oriented communication, 26, **219**
Subnet masks, 69–71, **75**, 83–85, **231, 233**, 263
Subtrees, defined, 176
Synchronization, arrays, 154–156
Synchronize Now or Cancel message, 156, **168, 239**
System changes after installation
    client, 53–54
    server, 50
System configuration, recommended, 118
System Event log, 121
System log, 88, 121

T

T1 communication links, 201
TCP (Transmission Control Protocol), 26, 66,
    219, 263
TCP/IP Illustrated, Volume 1, 77
TCP/IP (Transmission Control Protocol/
    Internet Protocol)
    defined, 263
    history of, 64
    installation, 52–53
    protocols, 65–66
    support, 18
    well-known ports, 72
TechNet topics
    caching, 131
    configuration, 61

installation, 61
Internet access, 151
Internet Explorer, 131
logging, 131
performance, 131
planning, 207
protocols, 77
security, 102
troubleshooting, 175
tuning, 131
Technical support, ISP, 197–198
Telnet, 18, 66, 72, 263
Tests. *See* Certification exams.
Text files, logging to, 91. *See also* Logging.
Time-remaining display, 3
Traffic, filtering. *See* Access, restricting; Security.
Transport protocols, 65
Troubleshooting, **187–189**. *See also* Registry.
    about, 174
    alerting keys, 179, **188**
    arrays, 161–163, 179, 181
    backup route keys, 179
    binary data types, 178
    cache, 180–182
    chained arrays, 179, 181
    counters, Performance Monitor, 185–186
    data strings, 178
    data types, list of, 178
    disk counters, 186, **189**
    diskperf command, 186, **189**
    domain filtering keys, 178
    DWORD entries, 178
    editing Registry entries, 176–178
    email alert keys, 179
    event messages
        SOCKS Proxy service, 184
        Web Proxy service, 179–181
        WinSock Proxy service, 182–184
    Event Viewer, 174–175
    expandable string entries, 178
    help, where to get, 174–176
    Internet access, 146–147
    Knowledge Base, 175
    logging value keys, 179, **188**
    MIB values
        Web Proxy service, 182
        WinSock proxy service, 184
    MSPDIAG.EXE, 175
    multiple Proxy Servers, 161–163
    packet filtering keys, 178, **188**
    performance, 185–186
    Performance Monitor, 185–186, **189**
    proxy array keys, 179
    Proxy Server home page, 176
    Proxy Server online documentation, 176
    publishing values, Web Proxy service, 182
    REGEDIT.EXE, 176–177
    REGEDT32.EXE, 176–177
    reverse proxy values, 182
    route keys, 179
    service keys

SOCKS Proxy service, 185
Web Proxy service, 181
WinSock Proxy service, 184
source names
array event messages, 181
cache event messages, 180
chain event messages, 181
SOCKS Proxy service event messages, 184
Web Proxy service event messages, 180–181
WinSock Proxy service event messages, 183–184
subtrees, defined, 176
TechNet, 175
value classes, list of, 178
value entries, format, 178
TTL (time to live), 24, 119–120, **125–126**, 130, 263
Tuning
cache, 118–120
Internet access, 144
memory, 115–118
performance, 115–118
TechNet topics, 131

U

UDP (User Datagram Protocol), **30, 76**
Control Channel, 27–28
defined, 66, 263
ports, 72
SOCKS Proxy service, 18
WinSock Proxy service, 26
Uninstalling
components, 50
Proxy Server, 51
WinSock Proxy client, 53
Unix, defined, 263
Unlimited access, **99**, 113, **237**
Update frequency, cache, 109
Upgrade from Proxy Server 1.0
cache, 142, **225**
server configuration, 143
Upstream proxy server, 264
Upstream routing, 109, 158
URLs (Universal Resource Locators), 264
changed on Web, 10
hashing, 158–159, **167**
User access, restricting. *See* Access, restricting; Security.
User access control, 14, 107
User interface functions, 65, **225**
User permissions, 107
Users, displaying, 106

V

Validating requests, 22–23
Value classes, 178
Value entries, 178
VDOLive, 18, 264

Verbose format logs, 89
Viewing options, ISM, 105
Virtual connections, 28
VPNs (virtual private networks), 16, **32**, 199, **219**, 264

W

WAN (wide area network), 16, 264
Web access, restricting. *See* Access, restricting; Security.
Web browsers. *See* Clients; Internet access; Web Proxy service.
Web caching. *See* Cache.
Web pages. *See* Cache; Internet publishing.
Web Proxy cache. *See* Cache.
Web Proxy service. *See also* Cache; Clients.
alerts, configuring, 86–88
architecture, 21–29
arrays
creating, 107
routing through, 109
backup file, specifying, 107
CERN-compliant, 22
client configuration, 107, 135–140
client share, configuring, 107
connection information, displaying, 106
counters, 116–117
current sessions, displaying, 106
defined, 18, 264
dial on demand, 107
domain filters, configuring, 107
error messages, list of, 121
event messages, 179–181
filters, configuring, 107
group permissions, setting, 107
Internet access, 139
Internet publishing, 96–97, 110–111
ISAPI, 22–23
ISM, 106–111
LAT, 107
logging, 88–96
default file name, 110
Internet, 145–146
setting options, 110, 121
MIB file, 117
multiple proxy servers, 159–160
OIDs, 117
outbound access, restricting, 83–86
packet filtering, 82–83, 107
partial restores, 107
permissions, setting, 107–108
plug-ins, installing, 107
Registry keys, 178–179, 181–182
restoring from backup file, 107
reverse hosting, 97, 110–111
reverse proxies, 96–97, 110–111
routing options, 109, 158
secure Web publishing, 96–97
services, configuring, 106–107
SNMP monitoring, 115–118

source names, 121, 180–181
upstream routing, 109
user permissions, setting, 107
users, displaying, 106
Web publishing, 96–97
versus WinSock Proxy Services, 26–27
W3P.MIB file, 117
Web publishing, 96–97
Web services, access control, 107
WebProxyCache source name, 121–122
WebProxyLog source name, 121
WebProxyServer source name, 121
Weekly logs, 146
Well-known ports, 72, **73**, 77, **218**, 264
Windows NT Registry. *See* Registry.
Windows NT System Event log, 145
Windows NT System log, 88, 121
Windows Sockets API support, 18
WINS service, load balancing, 159–160, **165**
WinSock, 264
WinSock Control Channel. *See* Control
    Channel.
WinSock Proxy service, **31–32, 234**. *See also*
    Clients.
    alerts, configuring, 86–88
    architecture, 25–28
    arrays, creating, 107
    backup file, specifying, 107
    client share, configuring, 107
    computer names, 44, **57–58**
    connecting to, 111–112
    connection information, displaying, 106
    Control Channel, 27–28
    counters, 117
    current sessions, displaying, 106
    defined, 18, 264
    dial on demand, 107
    disabling, 54
    domain filters, configuring, 107
    enabling, 54
    error messages, list of, 122
    event messages, 182–184
    filters, configuring, 107
    group permissions, setting, 107
    Internet access, 139–140

IPX/SPX support, 18, 25–27
ISM, 111–113
LAT, 107
logging, 88–96
    default file name, 113
    Internet, 145–146
    setting options, 110, 121
mail service, restricting access, 85–86
MIB file, 117
multiple proxy servers, 159–160
naming methods, 44, **57–58**
OIDs, 117
outbound access, restricting, 85
packet filters, configuring, 107
partial restores, 107
permissions, setting, 112
plug-ins, installing, 107
ports, restricting access, 85
Properties Page, accessing, 112
protocols, restricting access, 112–113
Registry keys, 178–179, 184
restoring from backup file, 107
services, configuring, 106–107
SNMP monitoring, 115–118
source names, 122, 183–184
UDP support, 26
uninstalling, 53
unlimited access, 113
user permissions, setting, 107
users, displaying, 106
versus Web Proxy Service, 26–27
WSP.MIB file, 117
WinSockProxy source name, 122
WinSockProxyLog source name, 122
Wolfe, David, 102, 207
W3P.MIB file, Web Proxy service, 117
WSP.MIB file, WinSock Proxy service, 117
WWW services, access control, 107